ADVANCEMENT OF INDIA
Attainments and Alternatives

Advancement of India

Attainments and Alternatives

Edited by:
R. Venkata Ravi
V. Narayana Reddy
D. Sunder Raj

KANISHKA PUBLISHERS, DISTRIBUTORS
NEW DELHI-110 002

KANISHKA PUBLISHERS, DISTRIBUTORS
4697/5-21 A, Ansari Road, Daryaganj
New Delhi-110 002
Phones : 2327 0497, 2328 8285
Fax : 011-2328 8285
E-mail: kanishka_publishing@yahoo.co.in

First Published 2010

ISBN 978-81-8457-184-4

PRINTED IN INDIA

Published by Madan Sachdeva for Kanishka Publishers, Distributors, 4697/5-21A, Ansari Road, Daryaganj, New Delhi-110 002, Typeset by Sunshine Graphics, Delhi, and Printed at Rajdhani Printers, Delhi.

Acknowledgements

Development is a subject matter, which continuously attracts interest of the academics, development professionals, administrators, non-governmental organizations and also donors. In our country, during the last five decades efforts have been made to improve the people through various strategies and development programmes. The experiments made also include shift in the approach, design of intervention and organizational framework to initiate the process of sustainable development and welfare activities in the society. Over a period of five decades, we have experimented and also learned in the field that enlightened us on many issues and concern. We have realized that, unless the capacity of the people is enhanced, they cannot absorb the development and its impact. In this process people are need to be enabled to have access and effective participation in development as well in welfare activities. Hence, the focus of the Government and Non-Government efforts shifted towards the capacity building of people for sustainable development. Empowerment is a process focused on the capacity building of the people to initiate, sustain and own the developmental benefits. In this process, people are enabled to have access, participate and control decision of various aspects/activities of welfare as well as in development programmes. The process of empowerment includes economic, political, social and psychological aspects of human life.

The present volume is a documentation of perspectives, reviews, findings of the studies related to the Experience in Development of our country. The book has five major sections, each one presenting papers related to Literacy and Education, Rural Development, Employment and Social Security, Environment Management and Women Empowerment. The academics, social scientists, social workers and development consultants have contributed the papers, which has narrated our developmental experience. We presume that the volume would be valuable reference material for those who have concern for the development of our society.

Many have played their role and contributed significantly to shape this volume to its present stage, we sincerely owe our regards to all of them. Especially, we record our gratitude to all the authors who have taken pains to respond to our request and contributed papers to this volume.

We are thankful to the Council for Social Development, Hyderabad for providing us the necessary infrastructure facilities to take up the major part of work on this book. Especially we are grateful to Dr. K.S. Bhat, Regional Director, Council for Social Development, Hyderabad for his inspiration and support in many ways for successful completion of this volume.

We are thankful to Prof. C.R. Visweswara Rao, Vice Chancellor, Vikarama Simhapuri University, Nellore for support and encouragement while working to bring out this volume.

We have always gained through Dr. S. Vijaya Kumar by his guidance and constant inspiration that formed the very basis for this venture; we are indebted to him forever.

We are thankful to Ms. K. Mahalakshmi for her usual commitment and efficiency with which she has handled the manuscripts and provided spontaneous assistance during our efforts to bring out this volume. We are also thankful to Shri P. Kumar and Y.S.S. Prasad who has provided help whenever we required computer assistance in connection with this project.

We are very grateful to Shri Madan Sachdeva of Kanishka Publishers and Distributors, New Delhi for making our dream as reality — that is publication of this book in a nice way. We thank all those who have helped and contributed directly and indirectly in our venture.

R. Venkata Ravi
V. Narayana Reddy
D. Sunder Raj

Contents

PART-2
RURAL DEVELOPMENT AND EXTENSION

PART-3
EMPLOYMENT AND SOCIAL SECURITY

PART-4
ENVIRONMENTAL MANAGEMENT

List of Contributors

Adinarayana Reddy. P., Professor, Centre for Adult and Continuing Education, Sri Venkateswara University, Tirupathi.

Aparajita Chattopadhyay, Lecturer, International Institute for Population Sciences, Deonar, Mumbai.

Bindu Ramachandran, Lecturer, Department of Anthropology, Kannur University, Kerala.

Chakraborty. M., National Informatics Centre Training Unit, Lal Bahadur Shastri National Academy of Administration, and Mussoorie, Dehradun, U.P.

Gunavathy. J.S., Lecturer, Madras School of Social Work, Chennai.

Gupta. S.P., Department of Sociology, Jai Narain Vyas University, Jodhpur.

Martina R. Noroha, 102, Divya Jyot Apartments, City Light Road, Opp. Maheswari Bhavan, Surat.

Narayana Reddy. V., Professor of Anthropology, Sri Venkateswara University, Tirupathi. He is currently Registrar of Vikarama Simhapuri University, Nellore.

P.N. Pandey, Visiting Faculty, MA-DS Programme, Institute of Development Studies, Lucknow University.

Pankaj Agrawal, Research Scholar, Department of Anthropology, University of Rajasthan, Jaipur.

Prakash Rao. M.V.S.S., Department of Adult and Continuing Education, Andhra University, Visakhapatnam.

Pulla Rao. D., Associate Professor, Department of Cooperation and Applied Economics, Andhra University, Visakhapatnam.

Reddappa. L., Senior Assistant Professor, Council for Social Development, Rajendranagar, Hyderabad.

Reddeppa Reddy M.C., Professor, Centre for Adult and Continuing Education, Sri Venkateswara University, Tirupathi.

Roy. T.K., Director, International Institute for Population Sciences, Deonar, Mumbai.

Satya Narayana Reddy. K., Associate Professor, Sri Krishnadevaraya University, Anantapur, Andhra Pradesh.

Satyanarayana Rao. P.P., Associate Professor, Department of Adult and Continuing Education, Andhra University, Visakhapatnam.

Seema Agrawal, Asst. Professor, Department of Anthropology, University of Rajasthan, Jaipur.

Singh, Awadhesh Kumar, Faculty, MMEM Programme, Institute of Management Sciences, Lucknow University.

Singh. U.B., Professor and Head, Department of Public Administration , Mizoram Central University, Aizwal, Mizoram.

Subbiah. A., Reader, Post-Graduate and Research Department of Commerce, Sri S.R.N.M. College, Sattur, Virudhunagar District, Tamil Nadu.

Sunder Raj. D., Research Associate, Council for Social Development, Rajendranagar, Hyderabad.

Surapa Raju. S., Assistant Professor, Council for Social Development, Rajendranagar, Hyderabad.

Surendra. G., Research Associate, Research Unit, Catalyst Management Services, Bangalore.

Talwar Sabanna, Faculty, Department of Economics, Karnataka University, KRC PG Centre, Belgaum, Karnataka.

Thaigarajan. B.P., Joint Director (M&E), Population Foundation of India, New Delhi.

Thulsai Naik. K., Associate Professor, Department of Economics, S.K. University, Anantapur.

Uma Devi. D., Centre for Adult and Continuing Education, Sri Venkateswara University, Tirupathi.

Usha Rani. M., Research Scholar, Department of Economics, S.K. University, Anantapur.

Vasudeva Rao. B.S. Professor, Department of Adult and Continuing Education, Andhra University, Visakhapatnam.

Venkata Narayana Reddy. S., Research Scholar, Department of Economics, S.K. University, Anantapur.

Venkata Ramana Reddy. P., Research Scholar, Department of Economics, Sri Krishnadevaraya University, Anantapur.

Venkata Ravi. R., Associate Professor [RBI Chair], Council for Social Development, Rajendranagar, Hyderabad.

Venkataramana. M., Faculty Member, Council for Social Development, Rajendranagar, Hyderabad.

Viswanath Gupta. P., Research Scholar, Department of Adult and Continuing Education, Andhra University, Visakhapatnam.

Sustainable Development: The Indian Experience

R. Venkata Ravi and V. Narayana Reddy

In recent decades, India has significantly improved the well-being of its people. Since the 1970s, India's economic growth rate has risen, poverty has declined to large extent and social indicators have also improved. Significant level achievements have led to improvement of the standard living that has reflected in the indicators like increased life expectancy and dramatic reduction in infant mortality. During 1950s, planned efforts for development were started nearly half of population was living in poverty. But constant efforts through various line of attack have resulted in reduction of poverty and its incidence during the 1970s. Culmination of various sustained development interventions in the form of programmed initiatives and change in the development policies have led to not only in poverty reduction, but also advancement in many key aspects like, literacy and enrollment of children in the primary schools. India today has 108 million children aged 6 to 10 attending primary school, making it the world's second largest education system after China.[1] Development trends in India demonstrate, achievements made during the last five decades in a challenging environment.

Despite of our efforts to implement various poverty reduction strategies, still Poverty reduction remains one of the significant challenges. Influence of non-economic factors such as health and education, on poverty situation is also a significantly current challenge for development. Though noteworthy development attained in the field of education, still large number of illiterates are found in the country. Illiteracy and school drop out, are continue to be major problems relating to the development of Women and Child and also remains as big challenge in the area of social development.

In the context of sustainable development, India has a three pronged strategy for poverty eradication: economic growth and overall development; human development with emphasis on health, education and minimum needs, including protection of human rights and raising the social status of the weak and the poor; and directly targeted programmes for poverty alleviation through employment generation, training, and building up the poor's asset endowment.

In this line, many measures are implemented by the National Level Government and also State Governments. These strategic measures for the development have been strengthened and supplemented by the efforts of the international organizations like World Bank. The Government of India has also launched various national level programmes to attend the needs of women, children, aged; also taken initiatives for employment generation, providing basic amenities and enhancing accessibility to the available opportunities for socio-economic upliftment and infrastructure development.[2]

The Agricultural Development Strategy was revised in 1999, as the national strategy on Sustainable Agriculture and Rural Development (SARD). The Strategy is essentially based on the policy on food security and alleviation of hunger. A regionally differentiated strategy, based on agro climatic regional planning based on local conditions, has been adopted to realize the existing potentials for growth in every region of the country. This has been focused to correct the regional imbalances in development by giving priority to the available resource endowment in all the regions. The thrust will be on ecological, sustainable use of basic resources such as land, water, and vegetation; in such a way that it serves the objectives of accelerated growth, employment and alleviation of hunger.[3] Efforts are on to promote the environment friendly farming that can also directly save the earth and produce healthy food for consumption. As result the focus has shifted towards organic farming and reduce the indiscriminate use of chemical inputs in the farming sector. In the development process, environmental concerns have taken front seat to drive towards sustainability.

Rural poverty largely exists among the landless and marginal farmers. Access to land, therefore, remains one of the key challenges in implementation of poverty reduction strategy in rural areas. In this context rural non-farm employment and self-employment has been considered as a major source of livelihood in rural areas. To make self-employment programmes more effective, strategy has been shifted from an individual approach to a group or cluster approach. It could facilitate flow of more investment to ensure project viability and sustainability. In addition, this approach would also include skills development of the poor through an inbuilt training component, upgrading of technology, establishment of forward and backward linkages, availability of appropriate infrastructure, and market tie-ups. Likewise, in each and every development experiments made in India have given birth to new challenges and risk that has compelled the planners and policymakers to look for new methods and approaches for sustaining the development initiatives. This has helped to fine tune process and minimum risk while attempting to optimize benefits.

In the recent years, the concept of development has been looked up with re-orientation in recent years, to mean more than just economic growth. Development has been considered as the appreciative approach towards use of existing potentialities of human being, satisfaction of basic needs, and improvement in quality of life.[4] Essential components for quality of life, includes minimum education, better place to dwell, access to health services, adequate infrastructure facilities and provision of such vital inputs have become a significant developmental strategy. Approach in judging the nature and level of development, need to focus on status and achievement in these aspects as basic criteria.

Improvement of infrastructure facilities has been considered as a critical area for development process as that can influence the socio-economic activities. Seven essential services have been recognized as priority areas that need policies and programmes be given a thrust under different Plans. The services included are safe drinking water, availability of primary health service facilities, universal primary education, provision of public housing assistance to all shelter less poor families, nutritional support to children, road links to all villages and habitations, and public distribution system targeted to the poor.

In the larger framework of economic reforms and decentralization many measures have been initiated in India. It includes Institutional reforms for effective people participation, chiefly, in the local self-government and through various Stakeholder

Associations. The Panchayat Raj Institutions (PRIs) has been revitalized to function as effective institutions of local self-governance and they are empowered to prepare plans for economic development and social justice and implement them. The PRIs are considered as the umbrellas for the integration of sectoral programmes with poverty alleviation and rural development programmes. Stress is being laid on organizing SHGs to institutionalize people's participation to improve household production systems (cattle rearing, mushroom cultivation, sericulture, bee-keeping etc.) and have sustainable livelihood at grassroots level.

As part of the administrative decentralization, beneficiaries (users) are organized at grassroots level as Community Based Organizations [CBOs] that can empower poor communities and other marginalized groups to drive their own development.[5] It is considered as viable strategy for strengthening the people organization with appropriate Stakeholders' forum and as one of the key elements in the Institutional reforms for decentralized sustainable development. In the decentralization efforts, Institutional strengthening of panchayats is also a crucial strategy at the micro-level, in addition to the promotion of Community Based Organizations[6] (CBOs) and their capacity building for sustainable rural development. Over a period of last five decades, the NGOs in India has gradually shifted their focus in their operations and have become one of the major stakeholders at the grassroots level in the context of rural development. The changing roles of NGO could be traced from charity in 1960s, to handle welfare and relief activities during 1970s, to initiate development process in 1980s, during 1990s and onwards emerged and also engaged in the Advocacy role.[7]

Social mobilization process has to result in organizing the people, keeping in mind various socio-economic dimensions at the grassroots level. Once people are organized, capacity building of such organization becomes necessary with a view to change the culture of dependency to a culture of self-reliance. The NGOs are also involved in organizing community into various organizations at grassroots level that include–women, farmers, youth and also users of various "Resources and Services" like land, water, health, education. The NGOs role in organizing the people is aimed at enabling them to come together to work for effective use of resources and services. The NGOs mobilize local resources[8] and also raise sizable external resources from outside for the welfare and development action at grassroots level. During the last five decades, several measures have been taken up to address the different aspects in the development process. The yesteryears are marked with full of new beginning, shift in the policies and approaches towards developing self-contained communities. The development is understood as a transformation of society through new social and economic organizations, deviating from old ways of thinking.[9] The new thinking on development has laid much emphasis on a change in the people think and the way societies functioning. At the same time Dani Rodrik[10] observed that as part of the development strategies for the 21st Century, ".... Learning and imitating from aboard are important elements of a successful development strategy. But imported blueprints need to be filtered through local experiences....". India has experimented with any ways and means for achieving development during the last several years. In this process, many issues have come up while focusing on the development. In this book, attempts have been made to document the narrations on such experiments and experiences gained over the period of last five decades.

Literacy and Education

The need for adult education evolved and unfolded itself with the realization that it is the key factor to the future and progress of mankind. While this is common with the world as such, for a country like India, with all its socio-economic, geographical and linguistic diversity, it is a primary task of the state to provide and promote the literacy that could ultimately vanish the all kind of illness. This is the fundamental idea that has led to the launching of series of Adult Literacy Programme in India. The Indian Government in 1988 has launched the National Literacy Mission keeping in view the correlation between literacy and socio-economic development. The mission is now engaged in the task of imparting functional literacy to persons in the 15-35 age group. The focus in the Tenth Plan has shifted towards residual illiteracy and catering to difficult segment of the population. Literacy is a crucial input in the learning process and opens up a gateway for participation in the social, cultural, political and economic life. Level of literacy is considered as one of the determinants of Human Development Index. Higher level of literacy leads to more amount of awareness and results in the improvement in socio-economic and living conditions. It acts as a catalyst for social mobility of the people in the society.

Increased level of literacy also motivates indirectly migration of literate people to the urban centers in search of livelihood. At the same time, with existing level of education among the population that facilitates industrialization also leads to a situation that creates demand for schooling. Thus, education could be "means and also end" on its own that could influence the speed of the socio-economic development process. With increase in literacy, it is possible to transform the communities with science and technology inputs that could increase the range of development activities that result in heighten the employment and incomes in the rural areas and drives-away prevailing superstitions, prejudices, dogmas and narrow mindedness. Of course, increase in the literacy level, empowers the people who can apply the inputs of the science and technology for improving the efficiency and productivity. The section contains seven chapters on the various aspects of the development of literacy and education in the country. These chapters have discussed about the efforts made in the field of literacy and education. The discussion by various authors narrates experiences that could be useful for replication in different part of our country. The authors have also highlighted the present challenges and how that could be addressed.

The chapter Literacy and Development: Plan Initiatives by *Reddeppa Reddy* underscores the importance of the literacy in the context of socio-economic development. Author has also reviewed the initiatives made for eradication of illiteracy under the 10th Five Year Plan. He has discussed the role of education in the process of empowering individuals and more so, literacy can be one of the significant factors for motivating to People participates in development process. Participation of people is indispensable for the sustainable socio-economic transformation of the community. So, literacy could be instrumental for spreading required knowledge, particularly among women about education, health care, and nutrition, thereby enabling them to keep-up their families in better health and provide better care for their children through child health care and education.

The Akshara Sankranthi Programme started 2000 in the Andhra Pradesh marked a new era in eradication of women illiteracy. The chapter on Literacy Campaign for Women: Experience of Andhra Pradesh by *Vasudeva Rao, Prakash Rao* and *Gupta* discussed the performance of the Programme in Vishakapatnam district and also observed that during the implementation of the programme women learners have shown much interest only in thrift rather than attending the literacy class. Improvement of Literacy has progressed slowly and still adding to the illiterate population, specifically, among SC, ST and Women. The programme implementation was hampered by lack of effective supervision and monitoring, lack of material and incentives to instructors, etc. The chapter suggested that curriculum must be designed in a way, which may lead to their factual conditions, problems, and ways to solve these in tactful manner.

Elementary Education in India: Status and Issues by *Pulla Rao* has examined the effect of the initiatives of the government in the field of primary education in India. The trends were examined in primary education in terms of enrolment of children by sex, size of the teaching staff by sex, and (3) student-teacher ratio at the primary and upper primary stages. The chapter has observed that the quantitative growth of enrolment has been faster in the case of girls than in the case of boys throughout the period of five decades in both primary and upper primary education. Besides, the enrolment of students has increased at a higher rate than the number of schools and teachers. The quality of education is suffering with student-teacher ratio. As regards upper primary education, the situation has been relatively better as compared to primary education, most important reason of the downfall in the quality and standard of school education during the recent decades may be the uneven growth of enrolment, number of teachers and number of schools, the enrolment growing faster than the two.

The target of achieving universal elementary education also provided special assistance to encourage educational standard among tribal students. But it is seen that a number of unidentified and identified factors are acting as constraints in achieving the aspired goal. The local languages must be taken into consideration. Otherwise the students would not show interest, which could be one of the reasons for their dropouts. *KANAV*—a kind of Ashram School was started in 1994 on experimental basis for educating the students of the *Kattunaicken* and *Pariyan* tribes in the Wayanad district. *Bindu Ramachandran* in her article Anthropological Analysis of "KANAV' An Alternative Approach to Tribal Curriculum discussed about this native approach for educational development of the tribal community.

Technology has large extent influence the education system of the country in more than one ways. The use of Information

Technology in education system has potential to raise achievement level of the learners. *Chakraborty* in his descriptive chapter on Internet and its Impact on Education provides some evidences of the impact of Internet on education, the role of government, the advantages and disadvantages in the use of Internet in the field of education. The chapter has accentuated need for Universities and Technology Institutes to become leaders in applying this latest technology in the field of education for effective learning. We have to realize that the information available in the websites represent a new environment for learning and teaching process. It provides greater and wide access to information available through Internet that plays a major role in education.

Residential school facility is one of the significant pulling factors that could influence the educational development of the tribal community. Many States Governments have established and running the Ashram Schools with hostels facility in collaboration with Central Government. The Perspective and Paradoxes of Tribal Education: Experience of Rajasthan by *Seema Agrawal and Pankaj Agrawal* is based on a study in Dausa district, Rajasthan. In this district, tribe called *MINA are* found more and particularly in area of Ralawas, Bhanwata and Bhanwati. So, mostly in the Ashram School the MINA tribe occupies hostels. The authors have observed that tribal students are staying in the hostel, even though lack of some basic facilities. The study also shows that these Ashram Schools are very much popular among the tribes in this district. The schools have vital role to play in the development of certain qualities among tribal children. So, it is not necessarily to confine only to the formal education in their school, the activities of the school need to bring out the full potential of the students for their growth and development.

Success and performance of the literacy programme is sole depends on the role played by the Preraks as grassroots level functionaries. They are main actors in implementation of the various activities under the literacy programme. Base on a study, *Surendra* in his chapter entitled Community Opinion on the Performance of Preraks has presented various aspects of the performance of the Preraks. The chapter has enlisted and discussed the views expressed by the community representatives towards the Preraks. The author has observed that during the course of implementation of literacy programme, Preraks have experienced more problems than the neo-literates.

Rural Development and Extension

Efforts made for development in the last several decades include major shift in the approaches and strategies for rural development. Rural development is not merely development of rural areas but it should also result in the enrichment of living standards among the rural masses into self-reliant and self-sustaining communities. The critical point for rural development is to enthuse the people to take care of themselves and to place the instruments of change in their own hands. It is not enough to organize the poor, but it is equally important to give them a purposeful direction in combination with required power resource. Bottom line of the rural development is not a set of relief measures, but in increasing the capacity of the poor to meet their own needs.[11]

People's participation plays vital role in achieving comprehensive and sustainable rural development. Development without people's involvement and development not meant for people cannot be a development. It is the need of the hour to involve people in large-scale from grassroot level for the sustainable rural development. Development of rural area cannot be in total, which does empower people and mainly restrain them from silent participation. Hence, power to people with greater choice and voice is essential. Ultimately people should be allowed through different organizational structures like Panchayats, community based organizations, groups to choose and decide on their development and required intervention for the development. This section has four chapters that discussing on variety of rural development issues that are concern with good governance.

Education has a vital role to play in the development of a community. Education plays a significant role in the community to imbibe the desired values and attitudes among the community members and to have reciprocal relationship with the other members of the community. Further, it creates avenues opportunities to sustain in the community. No doubt, education is a pre-condition for the community development. Community building is the process of collective work of people to achieve the sustainable development. The pre-condition for community building is participation of community collectively, united in all stages of its development. The chapter on Community Building and Education: Role of Non-Government Organizations by *Uma Devi, Adinarayana Reddy* discussed the NGOs' role in the community building. Creation of awareness among the community about the various avenues and opportunities created by the government in the form of developmental programmes for the welfare of the wider community and empowering the community to demand their share is possibly only through the NGOs. Further, by empowering the community leads to the enhanced participation of the people in the community development activities conceive and implemented. The chapter suggested that Community education centres may be established in all the habitations by integrating the existing schools, crèche centres, EGS centres, Adult Literacy centres, Continuing Education centres etc., so as to increase the scope and coverage of the target. The community education centre needs to act as a communication centre for all the information relating to the developmental programmes. Such centres could be established and managed by the NGOs.

Marine fishing is an age-old and caste based activity and involves high risk with uncertainty of incomes. Often the fishermen households face cyclones, tidal waves, tsunamis and floods, which cause more damages to their properties and lives. *Surapa Raju* in his chapter Socio-Economic Conditions of Traditional Fishing Households in Andhra Pradesh analyzed the various aspects of the fishing as traditional occupation. The study reveals that traditional craft owners operate their crafts 196 days in a year and catch 2969 kgs of fish worth of Rs. 32,667. But their net income from fishing activity is only Rs. 8,111 per annum. The regression analysis suggests that more labour and capital are required to buy more length, width and quality crafts and more varieties of fishing gears to catch more varieties of fishes in different seasons to improve their incomes. But their present socio-economic conditions reveal that still they are living in below the poverty line. So government should give more motorized crafts and adequate nets to these fishing households by extending more subsidies, then only they will come out from the poverty.

Radio, as the development tool, can be effective in reaching wider audience at a low cost. The potentiality and scope of radio in reaching the mass audiences is relatively higher, where the conventional media channels did not meet the needs of information and education. Moreover, the number of radios is many times higher than the television sets in our country. In India, the concept of Community Radio Programme is not a new one. During the Green Revolution,

India experienced greater impact in the food production, especially in rice production through the use of hybrid variety of seeds, fertilizers and pesticides mainly due to the activated community radio programme. The radio programme could reach the nook and corner of the country and disseminate be able to the needed information with greater impact. Similarly health and family welfare messages have also reached many homes in all over the country through this users friendly medium of communication.

In this line, Population Foundation of India (PFI) New Delhi, a funding NGO at the national level working for the cause of population and development issues has conceived and promote a community radio programmes as a part of advocacy campaign. PFI launched its programme in the states of Karnataka, Uttar Pradesh and Madhya Pradesh through All India Radio (AIR). The radio programme is in the form of radio drama serial with 52 episodes of broadcasting. Each episode elaborates a topic in population and development issue with an absorbing story line. The script of the episodes is usually discussed at the scriptwriters' workshop, where the selected scriptwriters of native flavour, are oriented towards the subject. Subsequently the draft of the script is pre-tested improved, enacted and recorded. PFI purchased the slot from AIR and broadcast through local AIR station such as Mysore, Obra and Indore. To capture the broadcast in the villages, an NGO in the hinterland will do the spadework at grassroots level, so that the target audience will effectively listen to the programme. During the broadcast time, NGO workers will visit the villagers and observe the listeners and discussed about the radio programme after the broadcast. The Community Radio Programme has been monitored and evaluated.

The chapter on Community Radio, Reproductive and Child Health: Experience of a Backward District of Uttar Pradesh by *Thaigarajan* presents details of such programme in enhancing the knowledge of Reproductive Health in one of the districts of the Uttar Pradesh. The radio programme was aired through AIR, Obra through FM channel. The local NGO for the implementation at the grassroots level was 'Banvasi Seva Ashram', Sonbhadra. In this programme, 52 episodes were prepared and aired. The main RCH issues broadcast were on age at marriage, female feticide, population issues, small family size norm, antenatal care, safe delivery post natal care and contraceptives. During the programme, AIR Obra received a number of letters and a content analysis was carried. In addition, an end line evaluation was also carried using WHO cluster sampling method to identify the listeners in the district. The encouraging results show that the information could reach to the remotest areas of the country. The participation and involvement of NGOs at the grassroots level enhanced the listenership in the rural areas. The listeners could gain instant knowledge about RCH issues, as the basic knowledge. The mindsets of the listeners are gradually changing towards the critical issues of coverage such as adolescent health, immunization and age at marriage.

Rural Development and Decentralization are inter-related and also much discussed topics in the context of bringing together local initiatives and local knowledge for the socio-economic development. At grassroots level, Panchayats as elected bodies and Non-Governmental Organizations (NGOs) are also working for the rural development. The NGOs mobilize local resources and also raise sizable external resources from outside for the welfare and development action at grassroots level. It has resulted in emerge of village level organizations and user groups to manage various resources at local level. The linkages between CBOs and Panchayats can enable "convergence" of various facilities and services at village level. Community, CBOs and Panchayats has access to natural resources of land, water, forest etc. in the rural areas. The Panchayat has constituted the Village Education Committees (VEC), which is responsible for managing the delegated programmes for the development of Education at village level. The chapter on Grassroots Organization and Universities for Rural Development by *Venkata Ravi and Narayana Reddy* has highlighted that the Gram Panchayats need to have a forum at village level consisting of all CBOs working, local NGOs and government officials. This forum can prepare micro level plans for the development and welfare of the rural community. The Panchayats, NGOs and CBOs are working for the goal of rural development through effective organization and proper management of resources and services at different level. In this context, the Universities as professional institutes can play significantly to provide required support to the various grassroots organizations. The Universities are Think Tanks with a reservoir of professional expertise and technical knowledge in the various branches of knowledge. This team of faculties could be very useful to guide the organization and people to manage the development. The chapter has suggested various Models for Grassroots Partnership. As the situation emerges, wherein all these grassroots organizations–Panchayats, NGOs and People's organizations/community based organizations are equally important from the part of socio-economic development with social justice in the rural areas.

Employment and Social Security

In this section, four chapters that are presenting the different dimension of the employment and social security aspects in the context of the development.

Voluntary Retirement Scheme is usually referred as one of the strategies introduced in early 1980s in central PSUs to reduce the so-called surplus work force. It has gained wide publicity during nineties. The option to retire or remain in service is a matter of right to live with dignity. Hence, the trade unions have protested against forcible VRS. *Martina R. Noroha* in her chapter on Voluntary Retirement Scheme: Problems and Prospects observed that there are many instances where VRS has been implemented without proper manpower planning. The policy of the government has indicated that all the vacancies created on account of VRS would stand abolished. This has resulted in wasting precious human resources that could have been upgraded and modernized through re-training. On the other side, it is equally significant to focus on those who have opted for VRS and they are need to be given training and rehabilitation support. The chapter has highlighted key element for the success of VRS effective communication, building trust among employees about procedural justice and involvement of multiple stakeholders.

The female work participation is changing rapidly in developed countries, while it is taking place at a slower pace in the less developed countries. As a consequence, a study of female work participation has kindle considerable interest and large extent that influenced researchers and policymakers. Both economic and non-economic factors have dominated decision-making in this aspect. It is also equally significant to optimum utilization of female human resource for greater economic growth and development. In the chapter entitled Changing Female Workforce Structure in Karnataka State: A Post Reform Study by *Talwar Sabanna* has attempted to explain the changing female workforce structure in Karnataka state. Based on a study, author has noted that the labour market can affect the process of accumulation experience by the women workers. Therefore, share of women in employment compared to the male has been very small and accorded discriminatory treatment by creating set of socio-economic problems.

Labour force in agriculture and its allied sectors constitutes more than one-third of total work force; female workers are engaged in different activities of the agriculture sector, but their nature of work differs from region to region. The chapter on Determinants of Female Agricultural Wage: Evidences from Andhra Pradesh is based on a study in Ananthapur district of Andhra Pradesh by *Venkata Narayana Reddy* and *Satya Narayana Reddy*. While discussing the inter-regional variations in wage rates, also analysed various factors that influence the fixation of wage rates. Among the factors influencing the wage rates, factors such as cropping intensity, percentage of irrigated area, supply of labour, average size of operational holdings have significant relationship with wage rates of the female workers.

Family and friends constitute the world of the aged. They share their feelings with the close ones and also try to give something in return. However, with decline of joint family ties, mobility of the younger generation, deterioration of health conditions with age and demise of close ones gradually shrinks the circle of relatives and friends with whom and old can share his joys and tears. At this backdrop, Two-Way Flow of Family Support: A Study of Pensioners in Mumbai by *Aparajita Chattopadhyay* and *Roy* is an attempt to disclose the pattern of support system of two groups of educated pensioners of Mumbai who belong to two pre-retirement occupations namely, School teachers and Civil servants. Two hundred and forty eight teachers and 79 civil servants who have been selected scientifically were interviewed in the first half of 2000. The results indicate that economically better off civil servants depend less on others, especially on children for financial support, household chores and even for emotional confinement than teachers. The reciprocity of support is also less for the former group over the latter. If reciprocity of intimacy is looked into, it is balanced for offspring, weaker for spouse (especially for civil servants) and stronger for friends. Age is a significant determinant of the number of very close confidants (mainly family members) an elderly is having. Past occupation, type of family, present income, present work status and co-residence with child do matter the probability of having confidant in a significant manner. Presence of son or daughter in the household augments the chance of having very close confident as compared to those elderly who are not staying with or not having any child.

Environmental Management

Sustainable development primarily covers three elements such as economic, social and environmental in a balanced manner. From the economic point of view, environmental concern poses a significant threat to future economic activities and resultant comforts. From the environmental perspective the pollution and degradation of natural resources contribute to health problems. With the social incline, management of environmental issues has direct impact on health condition of the people and the same reflects mostly on the poor people as who are typically affected by any kind of crop-up of environment problems. Development is not a linear progress in various sectors, independent of each other but is an inter-dependent and integrated process in which environmental management needs to be given priority so as to preserve all the resources for future generations to come. This section has three chapters discussing on various facets of the environmental aspects of the development.

The disasters cause great damage or loss of life; it may be either natural, such as floods, droughts, cyclones and earthquakes or human made such as nots, conflicts, refugee situations, epidemics and accidents. In disaster management, our thrust was on crisis management and providing relief and emergencies. Now the focus shifted towards preparedness on pre-disaster planning, risk assessment, hazard zonation, land use regulation, prevention and mitigation. The policy shift in disaster management emphasizes on empowering community with various early warning systems calls for involvement of community in process of disaster management. *U.B. Singh* and *A.K. Singh* in their paper on Socio-Economic Dimensions of Natural Disasters in India: Strategies for Mitigations discussed India's efforts to meet exigencies as arisen by the natural disasters that affects the development. The paper has suggested that disaster management activities need to pay attention on meeting the local needs effectively. There are many shortcomings in the existing disaster management policy so as to overcome their problems; politico-administrative will is necessary for adopting sustainable practices. Authors have emphasized need for a specialized facility to provide professional training, education and management skills. An approach is essentially needs to focus on rehabilitation of disaster-affected population and for their overall development of the region in the post-disaster period.

There has been a growing awareness of global environment concerns such ozone depletion, the greenhouse effect, climate change and biological diversity. Indiscriminate use of pesticides and chemical fertilizers in cultivation of crops, results in environmental problems. But bio-fertilizers, bio-pesticides and over all bio-energy resources have direct and indirect environmental benefits and also socio-economic rewards. The article on People Participation in Environmental Conservation: A Case Study from Tamil Nadu by *Subbiah* is based on Research study on Environmental Conservation in Virudhunagar District, Tamil Nadu. This study has assessed the involvement of general public in environmental conversation in the study area. The chapter observed that though most of the farmers are aware that excessive use of chemical fertilizers and pesticides create environmental problems, they still apply chemical fertilizers and pesticides instead of using bio-fertilizers and bio-pesticides. In this chapter author has stressed need to create public awareness for involvement in environmental conservation. The chapter high-lighted the involvement of schools and colleges in the process of environmental education, possibly it would beneficial to introduce in large interest as a compulsory subject matter for student.

Water is most important natural resource. Its proper management is required for enhancing the effective use that would have relation with productivity and production in agriculture. Availability of surface water in rivers, lakes, tanks and canals depends on the rainfall and season in an area. The regular flow of surface water is influenced by so many factors and in turn pave way for sustainable faming. The activities in farming could directly and indirectly manipulate existing environmental resources. *Venkata Ramana Reddy and Satya Narayana Reddy* in their chapter on Surface Irrigation and its Determinants: A Study in Andhra Pradesh is based on their micro-study in Kurnool district. They have analysed the time series data on flow of water from different sources in the district.

Women Empowerment

Empowerment of Women in the context of gender and development is mostly defined as a process rather than end product; it is dynamic and changing and varies widely according to circumstances. Empowerment process will take a form which arises out of a particular cultural, ethnic, historical, economical, geographical, political and social context; out of an individuals place in the life cycle, specific life experience and out of the interaction of all the above with gender relations prevailing in society. Empowerment helps in gaining opportunity and strength to voice opinion, access to information, exposure to new ideas and experiences, taking responsibility to make decisions and taking risks. Empowerment of Women can be achieved through training, networking, evolving role that facilitating the process of enhancing capacity of individual and groups. It is to identify the needs, encourage commitment, ensure sustainability and personal development, create self-esteem and enable them to share power. This section has four chapters dealing with some selected aspects of the Women Empowerment.

In almost all countries, the Governments are providing special provisions for women's development and efforts are being made to extract maximum use of women's talent. Firstly, "empowerment of women" became a primary objective and secondly, the plan attempted "convergence of existing services" available in both women-specific and women related sectors. *Pulla Rao* in his paper on Problems of Women Entrepreneurship in India observed that the economic empowerment of women is possible only when women have full autonomy to spend their income and also control resources. Entrepreneurship development among women can be considered a possible approach to economic empowerment of women. In India, very few women entrepreneurs are in the big enterprises. In the SSI sector the participation of women can be classified into three types: Women as the owners of enterprises, Women as managers of enterprises, and Women as employees. Women entrepreneurship is the process where women take lead and organize a business or industry and provide employment opportunities to others.

The Government and Non-Government Organizations are giving more prominence to promote self-employment among women and build women entrepreneurship. *Reddappa* in his paper on Empowering Tribal Women: Experience of Andhra Pradesh observed that Building capacities of the women through imparting training to improve their technical skills and entrepreneurial abilities and improve their access to credit for creating income-generating assets to achieve economic independence can be achieved. The present chapter is an attempt to analyze the empowerment of women through provision of wage employment to the women SHGs. The government has also not made all out efforts for strengthening of women groups in tribal areas. The groups have improved their capability in identifying their community needs and priorities, and distribution of their group savings as a loan to the members for meeting their needs like health problems, agricultural credit, children education, marriage and other social functions depending on the availability of group savings. It is a positive sing in their positive sign in their mobility to achieve relative freedom form the domination by the women through wage employment under soil conservation works of the ITDA is motivating factor for women empowerment in tribal areas.

In Indian society, particularly in the rural areas, gender plays a dominant role in determining the education, status, training and all spheres of life of the women. The emergence of an increasingly knowledge-intensive society and the growth in Information and Communication Technologies require that women acquire appropriate education and vocational training to function in the contemporary society. Policies should be strengthened to make access to the quality education and vocational skills for the women. New strategies and approaches should be framed based on the needs of the women who need empowerment. *Uma Devi and Adinarayana Reddy* in their paper on Globalization and Women Empowerment discussed that the role of literacy in the process of development in the globalized society. Enable women to make informed choices in areas like education, employment and health, especially reproductive health in rural sector, the unemployment growth was 0.4 per cent during 1994-2000 as against 2.10 per cent in 1987-93. Strategies Environmental degradation has affected the women, particularly in the rural areas in adverse ways.

Development Policies and Issues

Social development cannot be achieved without economic development and *vice versa*. Development is a dynamic process of various social and economic processes interacting with each other. The process is based on various policies that determine the direction of the development. Use of various policies in given socio-economic and cultural setting for the development may come up with many issues in implementation of development strategies. Managing such development policies and related issues is part of the management of the development process. It is also possible that a cumulative effect of the development process in one sector may stimulate and also facilitates development in other areas. With lot many recent changes in the socio-economic development policies and its management in India is a learning experience. This section has five different chapters, which present variety of experiences on different aspects of development policies and related issues.

Children belong to an exclusive section in the society, which is sociologically termed as, a "dependent class" on family, community and society at large. Socialization, particularly through education is the initial process in the physico-mental development of the young generation. The chapter on Child Development in India: Some Economic Implications *Pandey* has noted that despite the efforts made by the State and Central Governments, to educate children, especially of weaker sections is yet to show desired level of results due to operation of various factors such as illiteracy, ignorance, lack of conscious awareness among the people. Some measures required for the healthy improvement of children are - involvement of NGOs in various efforts, minimization of social and economic deprivation, frequent visits by a team of child development experts, and by the doctors in the rural areas. The visits would be useful for creation of awareness among people on health practices related to the child development.

Studies on development problems in many countries recognize a close linkage between the effectiveness of development policies, prevailing attitudes and existing institutions. Involving people in the process of change that would make them to own the benefits can be achieved in the development process. The realization of Nation's aspirations requires rapid changes in the knowledge, skills, interests and values of the people. The chapter on Modernization: A Means of Development by *Satyanarayana Rao* says that development requires basically transformation and modernization in the society. The transformation is both "means" to the development and at the same time it could be ultimate 'goal' of the development process.

India has been witnessing significant changes in terms of social development. While, some indicators have shown improvement, others have highlighted the need for more attention. Governance plays a vital role in determining the direction and pace of social development. So, challenges to governance need to be recognized and managed that facilitates to achieve desired level of direction and level of development. An article by *Gunavathy* Social Development and Governance in India: Indicators and Challenges present analysis on social development indicators and measures of governance in the context of Indian situation. The author based on the analysis has highlighted the need for interventions in some of the areas to improve the situation. She has categorized the some indicators that have shown favourable situation and also enlisted certain indicators that work as impediments to effective governance.

Our country has been witnessing a rapid process of Globalisation. It is a process that emphasis for creating of 'one world order' across the national boundaries. Ultimately this process would result in opening of economy and at society level, exposure to the different cultures. The chapter on Globalization Versus Polarization in India: Emerging Concerns by *Gupta* observed that in India, major thrust has been on removing certain imbalances and restrictions that hamper the speedy economic development. The author has analyzed changing concepts in the context of Globalisation process in India and argued that it has led to the polarization in different forms in the economy and society. He has argued that opening up economy has increased the incidence of inequality and its consequences.

Commercial crops contribute a significantly to the growth of Indian economy and its development. Among the major commercial crops groundnut is a significant crop. Growing this crop in the rain fed and other condition considered as source of quick returns and also as livelihood option for the farmers. Cultivation of groundnut can have influence on the availability of oil for consumption. In the non-farm sector also the production of groundnut can trigger the activities relating to process and oil production. The chapter on Production Responses of Groundnut Crop in Andhra Pradesh: An Regional Analysis by *Usha Rani, Satyanarayana Reddy, Thulsai Naik* discussed the groundnut production in the context of increasing demand for oil. The authors have conducted a study on the production responses of groundnut in Andhra Pradesh. The chapter observed that area allocation decisions by the farmers depend on their expectations of rise in the price due to the effective demand. The analysis is confined to the secondary data for the period of thirty years from 1971 to 2001.

REFERENCES

1. COUNTRY BRIEF-INDIA accessed from http://www.world bank.org.in/.

2. This portion of information was derived from the document provided by the Government of India to the 5th Session of the United Nations Commission on Sustainable Development. It has been accessed from www.nic.in/Indiabudget/es97/Chapter10/html
3. Details are taken from a document presented for the discussion on Agenda 21 relating to the natural resource aspects of sustainable development in India; Accessed from www.un.org/esa/agenda21.
4. "Report on the University and Community Development Education and Training in Community Organization", Social Research and Development Project under the direction of the Centre for Coordination of Research of IFCU, St. John's National Academy of Health Sciences, Bangalore, Karnataka, India, 2000.
5. This part is largely based on the materials accessed on NGOs from http://www.worldbank.org/ngos.
6. Community Based Organizations (CBOs) refers to a group of beneficiaries organized. It can be Self-Help Group (SHG), Water User Association (WUA), Watershed Management Committee, Community Forest Management (CFM), Mothers Committee, Village Education Committees, Village Drinking Water and Sanitation Committee and any other similar at village level.
7. Chopra Ravi (2001) quoted in the "Drought 2002 – A Report", Ministry of Agriculture, Government of India, 2004.
8. Local resources include people contribution in terms of cash, materials and labour; and resources flowing under the various schemes of the Central and State Government welfare and development programmes. It also covers funds provided by the National Level Development Donors.
9. Joseph E. Stiglitz (2001) " Development Thinking at the Millennium" Key note Address delivered in the Annual World Bank Conference on Development Economics, 2000.
10. Dani Rodrik (2001), Development Strategies for the 21st Century, paper presenter in Annual World Bank Conference on Development Economics, 2000.
11. Venkata Ravi. R. Sunder Raj. D (2006) "Rural Development in India: An Overview" in Venkata Ravi. R. Siva Ram. P. Sunder Raj. D. [edited] "Empowering Rural India: Experiments and Experiences", Kanishka Publishers, Distributors, New Delhi, 2006.

Part–1
LITERACY AND EDUCATION

1

Literacy and Development: Initiatives Under Tenth Plan

M.C. Reddappa Reddy

Literacy was defined as a crucially important foundation for life-long learning and as a gateway to fuller participation in social, cultural, political and economic life. Literacy has been long perceived and projected as the indicator of a nation's progress. In fact, it is an important criterion for determination of human development index. Spread and diffusion of literacy is generally association with essential traits of today's civilization such as modernization, urbanization, industrialization, communication and commerce (DAE, 2002). Higher levels of education and literacy lead to greater awareness and contribute to improve economic conditions. It acts as a catalyst for social upliftment enhancing the return on investment made in almost every aspect of development effort, be it population control, health, hygiene, environmental degradation control, empowerment of women and weaker sections of the society (DAE, 2002). Reddy (1987) has established the relationship between literacy and socio-economic demographic factors in his study. Mukerji (1971) observed that the spatial patterns of literacy are directly related to the regional variations in the socio-economic development. The National Family Health reveals a very positive impact of literacy on socio-economic factors such as health, nutrition, childbirth and family planning, etc. Particularly in relation to women and it is seen that the literate women have advanced way ahead of her illiterate counter part. Raising the functional literacy level of women has led to a significant decline in fertility and infant mortality rates. This chapter attempts to explain the importance of the literacy in the context of socio-economic development. Further it has reviewed the efforts made for eradication of illiteracy and also stated the initiatives under the Tenth Plan.

Literacy and Empowerment of Individual

The role of literacy in the empowerment of an individual is a crucial issue. Literacy and education improve the social standing of an individual and contribute to his well-being. There are evidence to suggest that the education helps in the achievement of good health and prevention of diseases. Another reason why literacy is seen to enhance individual well-being is that it improves the self-esteem of people, makes them confident in their dealings with society and earns them the respect of their peers. It allows them to lead a dignified life. It allows an individual to develop knowledge and skills to capture economic opportunities and thus increase his or her income. This provides the basis to capture further opportunities. In addition, greater literacy and basic education help people to understand their needs and demand services. This expands facilities for the public and at the same time, improves the utilization of these facilities. Education, thus, empowers the individual.

Literacy and Strong Panchayat Raj System

Rise in rural literacy augurs well for our country as the majority of Indian's population lives in villages. More literate villagers mean more potential Panchayats – a certain fillip to the nation's endeavour towards a strong Panchayat Raj (DAE, 2001). People's participation is indispensable for the socio-economic transformation of the village community. Literacy can become a motivational factor in this respect.

Literacy and Status of Women

Literacy has found to have a direct impact on raising the status of women. Studies have shown that education women can take better decisions about nutrition and health care for their families. They are also more open to family planning and have fewer children. Studies show that an illiterate mother has six children on an average whereas a university level graduate mother has two children on an average. Literacy has helped spread knowledge about health care and nutrition, thereby enabling women to keep their families in better health and care better for the children. Moreover, an educated mother makes a tremendous difference to a child's health and education.

Literacy and Fertility

It has been widely documented that education depresses fertility. Cross-national multivariate analyses yield strong negative correlation between education and fertility (Bogue 1969 & Kasarda,

1971). Bogue's analysis, for example, revealed "educational level alone accounted for 56 per cent of the total variance in demographic transition. Adding all other variables managed to account for an additional 16" (1969:675). Country-specific studies also indicated inverse relation between education and fertility. In the limited states, for example, the commission on population growth and the American Future proclaimed "there is abundant evidence that higher educational attainment is associated with smaller families in the United States" (US Commission, 1972:155-156). In developing countries, however, the above results are not always found time at different stages of development. Based on 1968 Phillippine data, Encarnacion (1974:23) writes: "At the earlier stages of education merely aggravate population problem." This conclusion indirectly hints at the existence of a threshold level below which education has no discernible effect on fertility. Some supporting evidence comes from India where the effect of education, particularly of female on fertility is visible only at the levels of matriculation and above.

Literacy and Urbanisation

Literacy promotes migration of educated people flocked into cities / towns in search of jobs and other gainful employment. Further the urban areas themselves generate high proportion literates in view of better educational facilities. Still, the urban people adopt non-primary activities, which require the educational qualifications. Reddy (1987) has established significant positive relationship with literacy rate. High proportion of workers in non-agricultural activities implies high level of development in that particular region; and such development as also noted by Kundu & Rao (1986, p. 459), seems to have a significant impact on literacy.

Literacy and Industrialization

Literacy in an index of socio-economic development but also that it functions significantly in the transformation of underdeveloped countries into modern urban industrial nations. Because literacy and education stand in a mutually dependent relationship with other aspect of socio-economic development.

The relationship between industrialization and literacy seems to be dialectical, in that industrialization both requires more advanced and more widespread knowledge and skills, while certain level of education among broader sectors of population facilitates industrialization, which in turn creates conditions for and a need for more widespread schooling. Literacy and industrialization in 1950 correlate closely: the coefficient of correlation is 0.87 when industrialization is measured by the proportion of gainfully occupied males in non-agricultural pursuits, and 0.84 when measured by per capita income. The closeness of these relationships is further substantiated by historical data for individual countries. In England and Wales, for example, the growth of literacy has been closely associated with that of industrialism, as is confirmed here by a coefficient of correlation of 0.98.

Establishing the close interrelation of the diffusion of literacy and industrialization invites speculation on why it should exist: Literacy is not essential in the training for or the practice of traditional agriculture and its related handicraft occupations. These occupations can be learned through apprenticeship, by watching an experienced person, by attempting to imitate him by trial and error. The knowledge required for such work can be stored in a person's memory; the principles can be transmitted verbally as part of the apprenticeship process. Since neither business documents nor accounts need be kept, and since the work requires no blue prints, reading and writing are not essential to everyday life. When most parents follow these traditional occupations, they feel no strong incentive to send their children to school or to arrange somehow that the children acquire literacy skills (Golden, 1954).

Literacy and Productivity

Literate people use capital more efficiently, they think up new and better firms of production; and they enhance change and innovation faster and quickly learn new skills. Contribution of literacy in raising the Gross Domestic Product (GDP) has been established by research as reported in the World Development Report (1991) "Increasing the average amount of education of the labour force by one year raises the GDP by 9 per cent, three years of education as compared with none raises the GDP by 27 per cent. The return to an additional year of schooling then diminished to about 4 per cent a year." Further it was also proved that primary education causes an increase of 40 per cent in labour productivity, secondary education an increase of 10 per cent and the higher education of 300 per cent. The human capital model in theories of economic growth shows that a rise in the level of education brings a rise in the efficiency of all factors of production.

Literacy and Per Capita Income

According to Gunner Myrdal, 'Advances in literacy and advances in economic development are interconnected'. They influence on each other must be mutual and cumulative. Studies on pattern of literacy and economic development show possible correlations between literacy and per capita income. Among 24 countries with per capita incomes of $ 500, only 3 had literacy rates under 90 per cent. About 90 to 95 per cent is seen to accompany per capita income above $ 500 (UNESCO, 1968).

Literacy and Modernization

With literacy, it will become possible to transform modern science and technology into the villages and to increase the range of activities that can promote employment and higher incomes in the rural areas. Further, the science and technology drive away superstitions, prejudices, dogmas and narrow mindedness, which inhibit the development of the region along desired goals. Literacy also creates better consumer awareness, knowledge of food and health and the needs of the family. The World Education Report (1991) states, by improving people's ability to acquire and use information, education deepens their understanding of themselves and the world, enriches their minds by broadening their experience and improves choices, they make as consumers, producers and citizens.

Efforts Made for Eradication of Illiteracy

Keeping in view an almost perfect positive correlation between literacy and socio-economic development, Government of India launched a massive scheme of the National Adult Education Programme in 1978 besides the strengthening of Universalisation of Elementary Education. The need to further intensify the efforts for the eradication of illiteracy was felt and the National Literacy Mission was launched in 1988. Further, the NLM programme as revamped in 1999 to remove some lacunae in the original NLM while increasing the scope of the programme the parameters and norms of financial assistance of schemes under NLM were substantially enhanced. Under the NLM scheme, Total Literacy Campaigns, Post-Literacy Campaigns and Continuing Education Programmes are being implemented. The NLM has covered 96.64 million persons under various adult literacy schemes up to December 2001. At present, out of 593 districts in the country, 160 districts are covered under TLC, 264 under PLC (including 30 under the Rural

Functional Literacy Programme) and 152 under the Continuing Education Programme. NLM is now engaged in the task of imparting functional literacy to persons in the 15-35 age group and has set to achieve a sustainable threshold literacy of 75 per cent by 2005.

Initiatives under Tenth Plan

In the field level the illiterates to be motivated to participate in the adult education programme. It is, therefore, most important to ensure greater participation of these groups in future adult education programmes. This requires a focused attention to their needs and problems and to the adoption of specific measures to suit their requirements. The focus in the Tenth Plan would shift to residual illiteracy and catering to difficult segments of the population. This means that all the left-over districts and the left-over harder-to-reach groups would need to be targeted specifically.

REFERENCES

Hidla Hertz Golden (1954). Literacy and Social Change in underdeveloped countries, Bureau of Applied Social Research, Columbia University, New York.

National Literacy Mission. A Decade of Achievements: Literacy rates—An Analysis based on the National Family Health Survey (1998-99), Directorate of Adult Education, MHRD, Dept. of Elementary Education and Literacy, New Delhi.

Planning Commission. 10th Five Year Plan, (2002-07): Sectorial Policies and Programmes, Vol. II, Government of India, New Delhi.

Reddy, M.C.R. (1987). Spatial variations of literacy in Andhra Pradesh (unpublished Ph.D. Thesis), S.V. University, Tirupathi.

Reddy, M.C.R. (1991). Spatial variations of literacy in Andhra Pradesh, Ph.D. Thesis abstracts, Indian Educational Review, January 1991, pp. 76-83.

Reddy, M.C.R. (1993). Literacy and Socio-economic Development in Andhra Pradesh, Progressive Educational Herald, April 1993, pp. 31-37.

2

Literacy Campaign for Women: Experience of Andhra Pradesh

B.S. Vasudeva Rao, M.V.S.S. Prakash Rao and P. Viswanath Gupta

Universal literacy is recognized to be an important factor in contributing to social and economic development. The linkage between literacy on one hand and other aspects of social and economic development are quite strong. Literacy facilitates better and more effective communication of new technology in agriculture and extension agencies could work better in a climate of literacy environment. Illiteracy peasants rarely succeed in transforming co-operative environment such institutions are either controlled by bureaucrats or by exploitative landlords and usurers. The linkage between adoption of family planning and literacy are known to be even stronger. Adoption rates are higher among literate females as compared to illiterate females. Knowledge on nutrition, childcare, and health could be communicated better to literate as compared to illiterate people. Such strong linkage between literacy and other aspects of social development result in high benefits to investments in literacy, apart from the facts that universal literacy should be valued as an end in itself. Yet, this is an area in which achievements have lagged behind expectations. Literacy has progressed slowly, and the number of illiterates have been raising. Rates of illiterates continue to be high among scheduled castes, scheduled tribes and among females.

The need for adult education evolved and unfolded itself with the realisation of the fact that it is the key to the future and progress of mankind (Roy: 1967) while this is common with the world as such, a country like India, with all its manifestations of socio-economic and technical backwardness, has no other way but to take a serious view of the need for adult education and to implement it as a priority programme. It is to realized that led to the launching of adult education programme in India. The launching of Akshara Sankranthi Programme on 2nd October 2000 marked a new era in the education history of Andhra Pradesh towards eradication of women illiteracy.

Before initiating any mass programme one must identify the need and causes to implement the programme. Planners are some extent failed to identify the causes and hindrances before starting Akshara Sankranthi programme in Andhra Pradesh. Many research studies identify the following reasons of illiteracy among women. They are: (1) early marriage, (2) gender bias, (3) societal troubles, norms and customs, (4) religious inhibitions, (5) lack of awareness, (6) financial constraints, (7) poverty of the family, (8) lack of proximity to school, (9) girl child used as a unpaid servant at home and so on.

Kusum Vir (2001) feels that our women must frank out their chairs of ignorance and illiteracy and for this some solid measures are essential to be taken up. Smt. Vir suggested some of the necessaries worth while to discuss for future plan of action. The failures and success of the programme will give results depending upon the commitment and approach of implementing agency, attitude and positive response of the stakeholders.

The people's participation in any activity has different nature. The topology of participation may as follows: *(a)* passive participation *(b)* participation in information giving *(c)* participation by consultation *(d)* participation for material incentives *(e)* functional participation *(f)* interactive participation *(g)* self mobilization. The agencies must be in a position to assess the stakeholder's nature in participation before starting the programme or while surveying the area of operation.

For an example the nature of participation and the result can be observed from the Total Literacy campaign of Nellore district. In the third primes prepared by Z.S.S. contained a story called "Seethamma Katha." The story of Seethamma explains the problems faced by a family because of the drunken husband in detail. It is reflective of the tensions and stresses faced by many other women in their homes. The womenfolk under the leadership of the literates Seethamma organized a movement and forced the closure of the arrack (country liquor) shop in their village. The impact of this story can be understand only if one cares to examine the manner of which the women of Dubagunta village in Kolikiri Mandal of Nellore district reacted to the incidence that took place in 1993. This incident is about three men who consumed liquor at a local arrack shop and later drowned in the village tank. The village womenfolk marched down to the arrack shop, and forced its closure by blaming the shop owner for the incident. The message spread to the adjoining villages and more shops were close in the process. The political parties moved in and made a demand for the total prohibition in the state (Sandeep, 1994). This kind of participation gives substantial out come.

The Zilla Saksharatha Samithi of Visakhapatnam district has proposed to increase the illiteracy level from current 55.4 per cent to 95 per cent. The firm conclusion/decision of State Government to give a big trust to the "literacy drive" and which is a part towards realizing the goal, illiterates in self-groups of 31 plain Mandals and 2 municipalities. The programme is named as "Akshara Sankranthi" and launched the first phase on 2nd October 2000 and second phase on April 2001.

During the special drive launched in July, self-help groups that were interested in implementing the programme were identified along with the illiterates as well as volunteers using this as the base; it is proposed to expand the pilot phase to other areas of the district. In this process it is proposed to use the Continuing Education Centres as the focal points so that the post literacy phase is automatically linked to the basic literacy phase.

The Essential Features of the Programme

- Self-help group members will form the backbone of the target group of the programme. Other members will however be also being covered subject to their being willing and motivated and also on enable to close monitoring and supervision.
- The existing Continuing Education Centres will be the nodal points of activity.
- Programme main thrust is focused on women.
- Programme is linked to all existing activities already being under process by self-help groups with the involvement of other developmental departments..
- Teaching materials will be suitably modified to make it more relevant to the specific requirements of the group.

The duration of the programme was 90 days: the 40 days are devoted to teaching the alphabets and reading skills the next 40 days for writing practices, the last 10 days for numericals. In Visakhapatnam district 3 lakhs learners were enrolled, out of that 1,80,000 (60%) achieved the positive result. The total expenditure incurred by Z.S.S. in this district for the programme was Rs. 61,72,574. This means the project spent Rs. 20.64 per head to impart the literacy skills.

As per the internal assessment the literacy achievement of women learners in the district is 60 per cent. The council for Social Development (external agency) conducted a survey and identifiable that only 26 per cent become a literates among the target group.

Akshara Sankranthi Programme should play a pivotal role in achieving the literacy. In view of the importance of the programme, it is necessary to study the perception of the learners of the Akshara Sankranthi Programme about in performance and assessment of the programme. The variation of literacy percentage obtained by internal and external evaluations has significant difference. Hence the study was taken up in a Mandal only to find out the difference between the two evaluations. Keeping the above in view the present micro level study was formulated with following objectives.

Objectives of the Study

1. To analyze the social background of the learners enrolled in Akshara Sankranthi Programme.
2. To assess the literacy rate after the implementation of the Akshara Sankranthi Programme.
3. To assess the literacy programme i.e. the reading, writing and arithmetic skills of the learners.
4. To elucidate the views on relevance of this programme to their daily life.
5. To identify the strengths and weakness of the programme.

Sample

A sample is used to study the properties of a large group of which it is a part. The present study is proximal, time specific and context specific nature. Hence the investigator confined to micro level study in the Pendurthi Mandal. This Mandal comprises of 60 villages, and for the purpose of this study 12 villages were taken on random basis and from each village 10 learners were selected on random basis for data collection.

Administration of the Questionnaire

The investigator for the purpose of the data collection from the learners developed a questionnaire. It includes biographical information, the membership particulars and activities in self-help groups association with other social organizations. Their views, attitudes, suggestions, problems and benefits towards the programme. Besides this the observation method used during the data collection and their responses were recorded. And finally the literacy performance test conducted in reading, writing and arithmetic. The literacy test was prepared as per the NLM guidelines.

Profile of Sample Learners

The data was collected from Pendurthi Mandal to estimate the literacy achievement of Akshara Sankranthi learners. A total number of 120 learners were interviewed on sample basis from twelve villages. Only female learners were interviewed because the programme was designed to DWCRA groups.

In the Mandal, it was observed that learners 50 years were not enrolled. Majority 46 (38.33%) of the learners belong to 15-24 years and 40 (33.33%) learners from the age group of 25-34 years. 34 (28.33%) of the learners between the ages of 35-50 years. A glance at the social class of the learners show that majority of the participants 52 (43.33%) belong to backward classes. Learners belong to other social class are scheduled caste 30 (25.00%), other castes 34 (28.33%), and only 2 (3.33%) of the scheduled tribe learners enrolled. This is because the study are is rural. The marital status of the learners in the Mandal shows that majority 114 (95.00%) are married. This shows that the programme attracted the learners who are married and settled in life.

The learners under study as per their occupational background divided into five types viz., agriculturists, agricultural labour, labour, house wives and engaged in other occupations. In the Mandal shows majority of the learners are engaged as labour 52 (43.33%) and house wives 42 (35.00%) very few learners with other occupation joined programme, these are agriculturists 18 (15.00%) and others 6 (5.00%) and finally agricultural labour is 2 (1.67%).

Period of Association with DWCRA Group

The learners were asked about the joining particulars in development of women and children in rural areas (DWCRA) group. Among them 14 (11.66%) have joined one year back. Only 12 (10.00%) learners have associated with the group since four years, 44 (36.67%) learners and members of DWCRA group is 2 years. Majority 50 (41.66%) of the learners who are joined in literacy programme have experience in DWCRA activity since three years.

Participation in Government Welfare Programmes

It was observed that the majority 116 (96.67%) learners participated in DWCRA activities like meetings and other governmental activities. Only few learners 4 (3.33%) not participated due to personal and health problems. This indicates that though they are busy with family affairs, learners are also active in associating with developmental activities.

Activities of the DWCRA Group

The government is with an intention to impart literacy to members of DWCRA in specific and self-help groups in general on priority basis. Hence, only positive response was taken into consideration for analysis. They were asked about their activities like meeting of the group, savings, loan distribution and recovery, maintenance of records and participation of government meeting. The response was tremendous about 116 (96.50%) learners said all the activities are going very well. The results indicated the activities mainly at DWCRA group functioning as meetings 40 (33.33%), savings 56 (93.33%) loan distribution 114 (95.00%), loan recovery 114 (95.00%) maintenance of records 114 (95.00%).

Literacy Performance

Here is an attempt has been made to find out the impact of Akshara Sankranthi on the sample learners of Pendurthi Mandal under the study. The impact is analyzed with reference to the three major areas in literacy viz., reading, writing and arithmetic. The literacy rate of the learners was estimated as per the NLM norms. The learner is considered literate if she passes all the individual literacy rate (Reading 20 marks, writing 15 marks and arithmetic 15 marks) and other obtain a total score of 70 marks out of 100 marks and above in all the three tests taken together.

Out of 120 sample learners from Pendurthi Mandal 106 (88.33%) learners passed in reading test, 112 (93.30%) passed in arithmetic. But in regard to their writing test performance only 20 (16.67%) have passed. The literacy rate in this Mandal is 16.67 per cent only as per the study.

Age and Literacy Performance

The learners belongs to the age group of 15-24 years have performed well than the other age groups. The performance of 15-24 years age group in reading 40 (33.33%), writing 12 (10.00%) and arithmetic 44 (36.67%). Age group 25-34 years performed in reading 36 (30.00%) writing 4 (3.33%) and arithmetic 36 (30.00%). Age group of 35-50 years performed in reading 30 (25.00%), writing 4 (3.33%) and arithmetic 32 (26.00%). The last age group 50 years and above learners are not available for the test. All learners failed to achieve good performance in writing skills. Generally it seems writing skills is a problem for all the learners for all age groups.

Social Class and Literacy Performance

There is a significant difference in literacy performance among social class (caste group). The backward class learners performed very well comparatively than other caste groups. The achievement of backward class learners in reading 44 (36.67%), writing 12 (10.00%) and arithmetic 46 (38.33%). The performance other caste groups scheduled caste learners performance in reading 24 (20.00%), writing 6 (5.00%) and arithmetic 28 (23.33%), scheduled tribes learners performance in reading 4 (3.33%), writing zero (0.00%), and in arithmetic 4 (3.33%) and other caste learners in reading 34 (28.33%), writing 2 (1.67%) and arithmetic 34 (8.33%). It shows all the learners in the sample performed poorly in writing test.

Marital Status and Literacy Performance

The performance of married learners in reading 100 (83.33%), writing 20 (16.67%) and arithmetic 106 (88.33%). Performance of the unmarried learners in reading 4 (3.33%), arithmetic 4 (3.33%) and nil performance in writing skills. The performance of the unmarried learners are very poor comparative to the married learners.

Occupation and Literacy Performance

In the sample learners that learners working as labourer have performed better than the other occupational group in all the individual literacy tests in the Mandal. Their achievement levels are in reading 46 (38.33%), writing 12 (10.00%) and arithmetic 50 (41.67%). Secondly learners as house wives marginally performed better than learners with occupation as agriculture, agriculture labour and other occupation.

Only 16.77 per cent have attained literacy rate as per N.L.M. norms. Majority of learners passed in arithmetic (93.33%), followed by reading (88.33%). Only a few sample learners passed in writing test. As per the internal evaluation of Z.S.S. Visakhapatnam the literacy achievement is 60 per cent and the results obtain to the investigator is 16 per cent only.

It was observed from the date obtained from the sample learners, that majority of learners between the age group of 15-24 years belongs backward class, married, daily wage earners and house wives performed better in literacy tests conducted by the investigators. The association with DWCRA group ranged from 2 to 4 years and majority are actively associated with welfare activities of government and DWCRA group.

Benefits in Joining Akshara Sankranthi Programme

The opinion of the learners was ascertained about the benefits acquired in joining in Akshara Sankranthi Programme. The following are the views and advantages expressed by them.

1. Able to recollect the previous learning.
2. Able to sign, write words and reading bus numbers and other wall posters.
3. Opportunity to learn at advanced age, which was missed in early childhood.
4. Useful in purchasing house hold items at market places.
5. Observing savings accounts and loan balance.
6. Acquired positive thinking.
7. Are able to understand the necessity of education, hence they are sending their children to school regularly and observing their learning activity at home.
8. Before they join in this programme they know only about their village only. Now, they know about their surroundings.

Benefits Acting as a Group in the Community

1. Cultivate the habit of saving.
2. Understand that unity is the strength.
3. Awareness about welfare programmes of the government.
4. Opportunity to attend the participate in the official and non-official activities.
5. Solving of immediate economic needs of the family.
6. Able to mingle with others.

7. Could go to offices and interact with officials without fear.
8. Solving internal disputes of family and society as a united group.

Bottlenecks of the Programme

1. The time period selected for the implementation of the programme inappropriate.
2. It was observed the group members and learners are more interested in thrift rather than attending literacy class.
3. The learners are not in a position to attend centers daily because of *(a)* household work *(b)* child care *(c)* health problems *(d)* seasonal migration for work *(e)* social festivals and *(f)* getting fatigue after working in the field from morning to evening.
4. Lack of effective supervision and monitoring by the field functionaries and implementing agency.
5. Lack of identification of nature of participation group behaviour, their attitude and interest of the women learners in literacy training by the instructor and the organizers.
6. Lack of blackboard and teaching-learning materials at the Centre and non-payment of honorarium to the instructor.
7. An educated numbers from the DWCRA group was appointed as instructor to teach literacy. The instructor interested in thrift activity rather than organizing literacy class.
8. Teachers who are co-coordinators of the habitation are leaving the village in the evening and day time in school activity. So the centers could not be organized properly.

Suggestions for Better Implementation of the Programme

1. Explain to the womenfolk that all human beings are equal by birth. Caste inequalities have got to be eradicated.
2. It would be more successful if we can explain the women about the 'Rights they enjoy' and obligations they have to fulfill under the constitution.
3. Women must be made aware of power and value of their 'Vote', which will help to direct the country for real democracy in the country.
4. Illustrative feature films and slides of successful women would also be very effective for better motivation.
5. Involvement of leaders belonging to different political parties and community leaders in this programme would also yield better results.

6. The women should be made to realize the necessity of participating in the development programmes.
7. They have to organize made to volunteer corps to render Shramadhan to construct roads, cleaning the village-wells, cattle-sheds and removing dung hills.
8. The women must be aware that a sick person should be given medical treatment instead of resorting to witch-craft and use of mystical threads and beads.
9. The women folk must know their minimum needs, and their area needs – proper roads, a school, the streets lighting and medical units and children education.
10. The masses must understand the value of recreation entertainment and games in their life and organize activities like Bhajans, Festivals, Plays, Sports and Games, Mahila Sangs and National Day celebrations.
11. Arrange programmes to educate and utilize the family welfare programmes like vasectomy, tubectomy and rebirth control devices according to their needs.
12. They have to made to understand what is meant by nutritious/balanced diet and include nutritious diet-items in their daily meals by using locally available food items.
13. And also the work done by different learners like Rajarammohan Roy, Veerasalingam Prakasam, Gandhi and Tagore, Smt. Durgabhai Deshmukh and others, towards their contribution, social reforms should also be explained.
14. The curriculum must be designed in a way, which may lead to their factual conditions, problems, and ways to solve these in tactful manner.

By implementing all these programmes the masses will certainly derive social and political consciousness and empowering themselves. The factors behind the success of the literacy programme identified by the research study (Vasudeva Rao, 1984) as follows:

1. A strong commitment on the part of the implementing agency towards Adult Education.
2. A strong will on the part of volunteers.
3. A strong zeal on the part of the learners.

The Akshara Sankranthi project in the mandal lagged to some extent in creating proper impact among the learners, in spite of its huge financial outlay, vast infrastructural facilities and experience.

There is a need to reconsider existing conditions of the functionaries, its method of approach, method of monitoring and evaluation practicing at present for effective implementation of future literacy campaigns like Akshara Sankranthi.

REFERENCES

Chaturveedhi, Y.S. (2002) Managing Continuing Education, NIRD, Hyderabad.

– – – – Directorate of Adult Education, Vol. 63, No. 4, October-December 2002, New Delhi.

Kusum Vir (2001), "Empowerment of Women Literacy", Indian Journal of Adult Education" No. 13, June.

Paulofreire (1976), "Prospects", Quarterly Review of Education, Vol. 1.

Roy Nikhal Ranjan (1967) "Adult Education in India and Abroad", S. Chand and Co., New Delhi.

Sandeep, P. (1994) "Seethamma Katha: Does Literacy Change, I.U.A.C.E., New Delhi.

Subba Rao D., Vasudevadas Rao, B.S. (1984) "Adult & Continuing Education: Some Perspectives", Rural Development Publishers, Andhra Pradesh.

Subba Rao, D. and Vasudeva Rao, B.S. (2002), "Evaluation of Total Literacy Campaign in A.P. Experience" Edited Vol., "Practice and Research in Literates", Sage Publication, New Delhi.

Suraparaju, S. (2002) "Akshara Sankranthi Programme Evaluation", Indian Journal of Adult Education, Vol. 63, No. 4, October-December 2002, New Delhi.

Vasudeva Rao B.S. (1988), "National Adult Education Programme in Visakhapatnam", Himalaya Publishing House, Bombay.

Vijaya Kumar S. (2003), "Capacity building of NGOs an application of participatory research for sustainable development for rural areas", Source Book, C.S.D., Hyderabad.

3

Elementary Education in India: Status and Issues

D. Pulla Rao

India is the largest democratic country in the World. Geographically, the country is vast spread over 329 million hectares of land and is supporting 1045 million people (2002 estimate), about 1.25 times the total population of Europe. During the last five decades, our number has tripled. With the birth of 48,000 children per day, 18 million are added every year to our population. This addition is more than the total population of Australia. With only 2.4 per cent of the total global land and 2 per cent of the total world's income, we bear the burden of 16.7 per cent of the total population of the World. We are essentially the land of youth and children as about 50 per cent of Indians are below the age of 20 years. Population explosion is one of the most serious problems facing our nation, which tends to nullify our progress on several socio-economic fronts. Even after 50 years of sustained efforts to develop and expand education, about 35 per cent of the people are illiterate. The corresponding figure for women is 46 per cent. According to NSSO Report (1999-2000), 26 per cent of our people live under the poverty line.

One of the important characteristic features of democracy is that it presupposes an educated and enlightened society. Democracy, both as a form of the government and as a way of life, cannot function when the society is uneducated and ignorant. Education and modernization are the two wheels of the same cart. Both, when combined together, lead to a rapid socio-economic development of a nation.

Economists have been arguing with sufficient empirical evidence that education contributes positively to development. A number of studies have been undertaken by researchers to establish the relationship between literacy and socio-economic development. It is, however, necessary to remember that primary education is pivotal for achieving literacy. Primary education constitutes a very important part of the entire structure of education. It is at this stage, the child starts going to a formal institution and formal education starts. Primary education in India has been under the control of a number of agencies. It is still under the management of number of private agencies, though, the State is increasingly taking the responsibility of providing free and compulsory elementary education to all. Article 45 of the Constitution provides for free and compulsory education for all children in the age-group 6-14 years, up to a minimum level. The whole idea has been woven into the concept of Universalization of Elementary Education (UEE). The level of compulsory education as envisaged in this Article corresponds to the elementary education of eight year's duration from Class I to Class VIII for the children aged 6-14 years. The universalization of Elementary Education has been recognized as a constitutional obligation in India by the year 1960 but the target has not been achieved even after 44 years of the target year. Now the government's target is, that all children should complete five years of primary schooling by 2007, and eight years of elementary schooling by 2010.

Present Structure of School Education in India

India, being a union of states, has accepted a uniform structure of school and college education popularly known as 10+2+3 pattern of school and college education. This pattern visualized 10 years of general education including 8 years of elementary followed by 2 years of secondary education; 2 years of senior secondary followed by 3 years of college education leading to the award of the first degree. Until recently there existed several different patterns such as 8+3+3, 10+1+3, or 10+2+2. But, in pursuance of the recommendations of the Education Commission (1964-66) and the proposals of the National Policy on Education, 1968, most of the States have adopted 10+2+3 pattern. The National Policy on Education (NPE)-1986 also reiterated the need for adopting a common pattern, namely, the 10+2+3 in the whole country. The NPE-1986 also proposed adopt of a common structure of elementary education consisting of 8 years of schooling—5 years of primary and 3 years of upper primary education. Therefore, the present structure of school education can be represented as {(5+3)+2+2}. A child is admitted to Class I, normally, at the age of 6 years and is supposed to complete primary education up to Class V at the age of 11 years, and elementary education up to Class VIII, at the age of 14 years. Up to this stage the state is constitutionally obliged to provide for free and compulsory education to all children under Article 45 of the Constitution of India. Elementary education is followed by 2 years of secondary education popularly known as 'High School'.

Objectives

1. To examine the growth of enrollment of students in primary and upper primary schools by sex and the corresponding growth in the number of schools.
2. To estimate the trends in the student-teacher ratio in both primary and upper primary education.

The Data

The secondary data relating to the number of recognized schools, enrollment by sex and number of teachers appointed by sex in both primary and upper primary schools for selected years of five decades period from 1950-51 to 1999-2000 are obtained from annual reports for various years, Ministry of Human Resource Development, Government of India and from Selected Educational Statistics for various years, Ministry of Human Resource Development, Government of India. In as much as the terminal year of our study is 1999-2000, it cannot adequately reflect upon the phenomenal changes that have taken place in the primary educational set up in the more recent past. This is a limitation of the study.

The progress of UEE in India may be analysed in terms of three identifiable periods in history after independence such as Before Education Commission (1966); Between Education Commission and the National Policy on Education–1986, and After National Policy on Education–1986. On the basis of the above identifiable periods, our study period (1950-51 to 1999-2000) has been divided into 3 phases for estimation of annual compound growth rate of schools, enrollment and teachers by sex. The phases are: Phase-I 1950-51 to 1965-66; Phase-II 1970-71 to 1985-86; Phase-III 1990-91 to 1999-2000.

Progress of Primary Education

In Table-1, the growth of the number of primary schools and the enrollment into primary education (schools), and the number of children per school for selected years during the period of our study is provided. The First Five Year Plan (1951-56) began on 1st April, 1951. At the beginning of the First Plan in 1950-51, there were 2,09,671 primary schools in the country. By 1965-66, when the education commission submitted its report, the number of primary schools had increased to 3,91,064. When the progress was reviewed in 1985-86, it was found that the number of primary schools had increased to 5,28,872. The period from 1986 onwards has been the period of implementation of the NPE-1986. Therefore, it is expected that elementary education might have developed considerably, both qualitatively and quantitatively. The total number of primary schools stood at 6,41,695 in 1999-2000. It is better not to over emphasize changes in growth rates over different phases because for reasons of arithmetical property, when one starts with a low base (as in 1951) the period immediately succeeding 1951 will have high rate and the subsequent periods lower rates. But comparison between the growth rates of boys and girls in any one phase assumes importance. In the analysis below, the differences in the growth rates of boys and girls receive greater attention compared to differences between periods. The index of growth of schools taking 1950-51 as the base shows that the increase is not substantial as compared to the enrollment of children in primary schools. The annual compound growth rate of primary schools over a period of our study recorded 2.26 per cent. But the annual compound growth rate of primary schools in first phase is recorded 4.24 per cent, it is much higher than that of second phase (1.74%) and in third phase (1.35%). The total enrollment in primary schools in the year 1950-51 was 19.2 million children of which 13.8 million were boys and 5.4 million were girls. It constitutes 28.12 per cent of the enrollment of girls to the total enrollment. The enrollment had increased to 50.5 million children in 1965-66. The enrollment of girls was 18.3 million, which constituted 36.24 per cent of the total enrollment. The total enrollment in primary schools had increased to 87.4 million children in 1985-86 of which 52.2 million boys and 35.2 million girls. The girls enrolled constituted 40.27 per cent to the total enrollment. Ultimately in 1999-2000 the total enrollment of children stood at 113.6 million of which 64.1 million were boys and 49.5 million were girls. Here the girls enrolled constituted 43.57 per cent to the total enrollment. An interesting trend which can easily be observed is that enrollment of girls has grown at a higher rate than that of boys during the entire period of study. The annual compound growth rate of enrollment of total students was 6.66 per cent in first phase. This rate is much higher than that of the second and the third phases. The growth rate of enrollment in the case of girls is much higher than in the case of boys over the period of our study, in all the phases. The enrollment of students has increased at a higher rate than the number of schools and teachers.

Increase in Number of Students Per Teacher in Primary Schools

So far, we have examined the size and growth of primary education in the country during the period of five decades. But, they do not really indicate the quality of education. One indicator of the quality is the student-teacher ratio. So we, as a first step examine the number of teachers employed in the primary schools in the country and the rate of growth of the teachers by sex during the period of the study.

Table-2 shows that there were 5,38,000 teachers employed in primary schools in 1950-51 of which 15.24 per cent were women. By 1999-2000, the total number of teachers posted in primary schools increased to 19,19,000 of which 35.80 per cent were female. It is interesting that the index of female teachers increased at higher rate than that of male teachers through out the period under study. The annual compound growth rate of total teachers in the first phase recorded 3.82 per cent, then the growth rate decreased gradually in second and third phases. The growth rate of female teachers was 5.38 per cent in the first phase against the growth rate of 3.50 per cent for male teachers. The growth rate of female teachers was much higher than that of male teachers in all the phases as well as for the total study period.

Note, however, that the number of teachers has not increased in the country in consonance with the increase in the number of students enrolled. This has resulted in an increase in student-teacher ratio over time except in 1955-56, 1975-76 and 1999-2000. It shows that the ratio was 36:1 in 1950-51 and the ratio was constant in 1955-56. Later it increased to 54:1 in 1970-71 then the ratio continuously increased to 60:1 in 1990-91. Later it was constant in 1995-96 and it reached to 59:1 in 1999-2000. Though the government has been insisting on a student-teacher ratio of 40 students per teacher for aided schools, it has never been possible for the government to achieve this objective. The data presented in Table-2 indicates only the country's average, but in most of the schools, the student-teacher ratio is observed to be more than 100:1. This adversely affects the quality of education at primary level, because the school teacher does not find any motive to teach such a huge number, let alone paying the much needed individual attention at the stage of primary education.

Progress of Upper Primary (Middle) Education

From Table-3 it may be observed that there were only 13,596 upper primary schools in the country in 1950-51 and this number continuously increased to 1,98,004 in 1999-2000. The index of upper primary schools recorded a much higher increase than that of index of primary schools. The annual compound growth rate of upper primary schools was 5.50 per cent for the entire period of study. The rate is much higher in phase one (12.14%) than in phase two (2.68%) and in phase three (2.72%).

There were 3.1 million children enrolled in upper primary schools in 1950-51, of which 0.5 million were girls. They constituted only 16.13 per cent of total enrollment. Later the total enrollment raised to 10.5 million in 1965-66. The enrollment of girls was 2.8 million, or 26.67 per cent of the total enrollment. The total enrollment in these schools had increased to 27.3 million in 1985-86 in which they were 17.7 million boys and 9.6 million girls. The enrollment in upper primary schools ultimately reached to 42.1 million in 1999-2000, of which 17.0 million were girls or 40.38 per cent of the total enrollment. An interesting trend which can easily be observed is that enrollment of girls has grown at a higher rate than boys during the period of study in upper primary education. It is emphasized that the index of girls' enrollment in upper primary education is much higher than that of index of girls' enrollment in primary education. It is a positive sign and shows the improvement of upper primary education in the country during the study period. The annual compound growth rate of enrollment of total children in phase one was 8.47 per cent and it is much higher than that of the growth rate in phase two (4.91%) and phase three (2.16%). It is interesting that the growth rate of enrollment in the case of girls is more than that of boys over the period.

Student-Teacher Ratio in Upper Primary Schools

As noted earlier, the student-teacher ratio shows the quality of education. Here, we examine the growth in the number of teachers employed in the upper primary schools in the country during the period under study. The data are presented in Table-4. It is observed that there were 86,000 teachers employed in upper primary schools in 1950-51, of which 13,000 were women, or 15.12 per cent of the total. By 1999-2000 the total number of teachers in upper primary schools increased to 12,98,000.

The number of women teachers reached on all time high in 1999-2000 (4,69,000) and they constituted 36.13 per cent of the total teachers, indicating that women teaching community has been on the increase all through. One should consider this to be a healthy sign for the reasons (1) that it contributes to gender equality and (2) that women teachers exhibit care and patience, their general traits, in teaching children. The number of both in male and female teachers in upper primary schools shows an increasing trend over the period of our study. The index of female teachers recorded a much higher increase than that of the male teaches. This may be due to implementation of reservation policies in some states in the country in favour of women.

The annual compound growth rate of total teachers was 12.86 per cent in first phase. It is higher than the growth rate of second phase (2.82%) and third phase (1.92%). It is interesting that the recorded growth rate of female teachers at 17.11 per cent was higher than that of the male teachers at 11.80 per cent in phase one. The growth rates gradually decreased in phase two and phase three among both male and female teachers, but the growth rates of female teachers have been higher than that of male teachers in all the phases.

During the period under study, the increase in the number of teachers was 12,12,000 (12,98,000-86,000). As the enrollment in upper primary schools showed an increasing trend, it resulted in a favourable change in student-teacher ratio. It is observed that the ratio was 36:1 in 1950-51 and it decreased to 19:1 in 1960-61. Later the ratio gradually increased to 35:1 in 1995-96. By 1999-2000 the ratio decreased and stood at 32:1 in 1999-2000. Anyhow this figure is less than the student-teacher ratio of 40 recommended by the government for aided schools.

Conclusion

It is common knowledge that India achieved freedom from the British imperialism on 15th August, 1947. Many decades have elapsed since. Yet in matters of education in general and primary education in particular the country is enviably placed. Economic backwardness of the country may have to do with mass illiteracy and ignorance of the people. But economic backwardness alone cannot explain educational backwardness. Kerala, though not particularly a rich state in the country, has achieved the objective of universalisation of primary education. The population explosion in the country could not have been unrelated to the illiteracy of its people.

We examined here the effect of the initiatives of the government in the field of primary education. More specifically, we examined the trends in primary education in particular since 1950-51. The focus is on (1) enrollment of children by sex (2) size of the teaching staff by sex, and (3) student-teacher ratio at the primary and upper primary stages.

Our data on the trends in the enrollment of children at the primary level showed that it was not commensurate with the growth of population in the relevant age group, notwithstanding the fact that universalization of primary education has been the avowed objective of the government. The quantitative growth of enrollment has been faster in the case of girls than in the case of boys throughout the period of five decades in both primary and upper primary education. Besides, the enrollment of students has increased at a higher rate than the number of schools and teachers.

To reflect upon the quality of education we arrived at student-teacher ratios. Let it be told that the significance of women teachers has been increasing over time and this should contribute positively to the growth and development of children. The student-teacher ratio at the primary level as it stood in 1999-2000 was 59:1 and this compares highly unfavourably with the accepted norm of 40:1 ratio. What is more, in some schools the student-teacher ratio is in excess of 100:1. The outcome of such ratio would be that the quality of education suffers.

As regards upper primary education the situation has been relatively better as compared to primary education. Even the student-teacher ratio on an average for the latest year of the survey is 32:1 This no doubt augurs well for upper primary education. There is, however a further need to effect improvements in upper primary education. As the child goes into the upper primary set up from primary set up there will be greater demands on the quality of teachers, of school buildings, of other infrastructure including toilets. These need to be strengthened. Mere increase in the number of teachers does not satisfy the demands of the pupils. This aspect has to be borne in mind if we want to ensure that the upper primary set up expands fast.

The expansion of both primary and upper primary education had been the highest during the 1st phase than 2nd and 3rd phases in enrollment, teachers and schools. One important reason of the downfall in the quality and standard of school education during the recent decades may be the uneven growth of enrollment, number of teachers and number of schools, the enrollment growing faster than the other two.

As a conservative estimate, the population of children in the age group 6-14 years, at present, may be about 200 million of which about 160 million (2001-02 estimate) might be attending elementary schools. This leads to the conclusion that about 40 million children are still out of school, which constitute about 20 per cent of the relevant age group. It is reported that 22 per cent of the total out of school children of the world are in India.

According to our study, we have not been able to achieve the goal of the UEE as guaranteed in Article 45 of our Constitution. Though, there has been a massive expansion of schooling facilities during the last 50 years, the goal has moved farther with the number of out of schools children increasing. Moreover, there are glaring disparities in what has been achieved, which are based on caste, sex, religion, and rural-urban areas. There are good reasons to believe that India will not be able to achieve this goal of UEE even by 2030 unless some effective and efficient alternative strategies are planned and implemented.

REFERENCES

Anand, C.L. (1983), "The Constitution of India in the Teacher and Education in Emerging Indian Society", NCERT, New Delhi.

Gadgil, V.R. and Dandekar, V.M. (1955): Report of two investigators: primary education in Satara District, Gokhale Institute of Politics and Economics, Poona.

George Psacharopoulous (1987): "Economics of Education Research and Studies", Pergamon Press, Oxford.

Gopalan, K (1996): Education for all - new initiatives, University News, AIU, January 1, New Delhi.

Gopinathan Nair, P.R. (1981): "Primary education, population growth and socio-economic change", Allied Publishers, New Delhi.

Government of India (1969): "Education and National Development", NCERT, New Delhi.

Government of India (1994): 'Development of Education in India (1993-94)', MHRD, New Delhi.

Govinda, R. (2002): "India education report: A profile of basic education", NIEPA, Oxford, New Delhi.

Govinda, R. and Varghese (1992): "Quality of primary education: an empirical study", Journal of Educational Planning and Administration, Vol. 6, No. 1, January, New Delhi.

Govinda, R. and Varghese, N.V. (1993): "Quality of primary schooling in India: A case study of Madhya Pradesh", International Institute for Educational Planning, Paris and National Institute of Educational Planning and Administration, New Delhi.

Naik, J.P. (1975), "Elementary Education in India—A promise to keep", Allied Publishers, Bombay.

NIEPA (1990): "Development of Education in India 1988-90", MHRD, Government of India, New Delhi.

NIEPA (1990): "Education for All by 2000 A.D.", New Delhi.

Rajput, J.S. (1994): "Elementary Education - Alternative Strategies", The Hindustan Times, June 10, New Delhi.

Saini, S,K. (1980): "Development of Education in India", Cosmo Publications, New Delhi.

Saiyadain, K.G. *et al.*, (1966), "Compulsory Education in India", Universal Book House, New Delhi.

Table-1
Enrollment and Number of Recognized Primary Schools in India, 1950-51 to 1999-2000

Years	Primary Schools	Index	% Growth Rate over Previous Period	No. of Boys Enrolled (6-11 years) (in millions)	Index	% Growth Rate over Previous Period	No. of Girls Enrolled (6-11 years) (in millions)	Index	% Growth Rate over Previous Period	Total Enroll-ment (in millions)	Index	% Growth Rate over Previous Period	No. of Children Per School
1950-51	209671	100	–	13.8	100		5.4	100		19.2	100		91
1955-56	278135	133	32.65	17.1	124	23.91	7.5	139	38.89	24.6	128	28.12	88
1960-61	330399	157	18.79	23.6	171	38.01	11.4	211	52.00	35.0	182	42.28	106
1965-66	391064	186	18.36	32.2	233	36.44	18.3	339	60.53	50.5	263	44.28	129
1970-71	408378	195	4.43	35.7	259	10.87	21.3	394	16.39	57.0	297	12.87	139
1975-76	454270	217	11.24	40.6	294	13.72	25.0	463	17.37	65.6	342	15.09	144
1980-81	494305	236	8.81	45.3	328	11.58	28.5	528	14.00	73.8	384	12.50	149
1985-86	528872	252	6.99	52.2	378	15.23	35.2	652	23.51	87.4	455	18.43	165
1990-91	560935	267	6.06	57.0	413	9.19	40.4	748	14.77	97.4	507	11.44	174
1995-96	590421	281	5.26	62.4	452	9.47	47.4	878	17.33	109.8	572	12.73	186
1999-2000	641695	306	8.68	64.1	464	2.72	49.5	917	4.43	113.6	592	3.46	177

Contd...

Years	Primary Schools	Index	% Growth Rate over Previous Period	No. of Boys Enrolled (6-11 years) (in millions)	Index	% Growth Rate over Previous Period	No. of Girls Enrolled (6-11 years) (in millions)	Index	% Growth Rate over Previous Period	Total Enroll-ment (in millions)	Index	% Growth Rate over Previous Period	No. of Children Per School
Annual Compound Growth Rate													
1st phase	4.24			5.81			8.48			6.66			
2nd phase	1.74			2.56			3.40			2.89			
3rd phase	1.35			1.18			2.05			1.55			
Total period	2.26			3.12			4.53			3.62			

Sources: 1. Annual Reports of Ministry of Human Resource Development, Government of India.

2. Selected Educational Statistics, Ministry of Human Resource Development, Government of India.

Table-2
Number of Teachers Employed by Sex in Primary Schools in India, 1950-51 to 1999-2000

(in 000s)

Years	*Male*	*Index*	*% Growth Rate over Previous Period*	*Female*	*Index*	*% Growth Rate over Previous Period*	*Total*	*Index*	*% Growth Rate over Previous Period*	*Student-Teacher-Ratio*
1950-51	456	100		82	100		538	100		36
1955-56	574	126	25.88	117	143	42.68	691	128	28.25	36
1960-61	615	135	7.14	127	155	8.55	742	138	7.38	47
1965-66	764	167	24.23	180	219	41.73	944	175	27.22	53
1970-71	835	183	9.29	225	274	25.00	1060	197	12.29	54
1975-76	965	212	15.57	283	345	25.78	1248	232	17.73	53
1980-81	1021	224	5.80	342	417	20.85	1363	253	9.21	54
1985-86	1094	240	7.15	402	490	17.54	1496	278	9.76	58
1990-91	1143	251	4.48	473	577	17.66	1616	300	8.02	60
1995-96	1187	260	3.85	553	674	16.91	1740	323	7.67	60
1999-2000	1232	270	3.80	687	838	24.23	1919	357	10.29	59
Annual Compound Growth Rate										
1st phase	3.50			5.38			3.82			
2nd phase	1.82			3.94			2.32			
3rd phase	0.75			3.80			1.73			
Total period	2.01			4.34			2.58			

Sources: 1. Annual Reports of Ministry of Human Resource Development, Government of India.

2. Selected Educational Statistics, Ministry of Human Resource Development, Government of India.

Table–3

Enrollment and Number of Recognized Upper Primary Schools in India, 1950-51 to 1999-2000

Years	Upper Primary Schools	Index	% Growth Rate over Previous Period	No. Boys Enrolled (11-14 years) (in millions)	Index	% Growth Rate over Previous Period	No. of Girls Enrolled (11-14 years) (in millions)	Index	% Growth Rate over Previous Period	Total Enrollment (in millions)	Index	% Growth Rate over Previous Period	No. of Children Per School
1950-51	13596	100		2.6	100		0.5	100		3.1	100		228
1955-56	21730	160	59.83	3.8	146	46.15	1	200	100.00	4.8	155	54.84	221
1960-61	49663	365	128.54	5.1	196	34.21	1.6	320	60.00	6.7	216	39.58	135
1965-66	75798	557	52.62	7.7	296	50.98	2.8	560	75.00	10.5	339	56.72	138
1970-71	90621	666	19.55	9.4	361	22.08	3.9	780	39.28	13.3	429	26.67	147
1975-76	106571	784	17.60	11	423	17.02	5	1000	28.20	16	516	20.30	150
1980-81	118571	872	11.26	13.9	535	26.36	6.8	1360	36.00	20.7	668	29.37	174
1985-86	134846	992	13.72	17.7	681	27.34	9.6	1920	41.18	27.3	881	31.88	202
1990-91	151456	1114	12.32	21.5	827	21.47	12.5	2500	30.21	34	1097	24.54	224
1995-96	171216	1259	13.05	25	961	16.28	16	3200	28.00	41	1322	20.59	239
1999-2000	198004	1456	15.64	25.1	965	0.40	17	3400	6.25	42.1	1358	2.68	212

Contd...

Years	Upper Primary Schools	Index	% Growth Rate over Previous Period	No. Boys Enrolled (11-14 years) (in millions)	Index	% Growth Rate over Previous Period	No. of Girls Enrolled (11-14 years) (in millions)	Index	% Growth Rate over Previous Period	Total Enrollment (in millions)	Index	% Growth Rate over Previous Period	No. of Children Per School
Annual Compound Growth Rate													
1st phase	12.14			7.51			12.17			8.47			
2nd phase	2.68			4.31			6.19			4.91			
3rd phase	2.72			1.56			3.12			2.16			
Total period	5.50			4.64			7.31			5.35			

Sources: 1. Annual Reports of Ministry of Human Resource Development, Government of India.

2. Selected Educational Statistics, Ministry of Human Resource Development, Government of India.

Table-4
No. of Teachers Employed by Sex in Upper Primary Schools in India, 1950-51 to 1999-2000

(in 000s)

Years	*Male*	*Index*	*% Growth Rate over Previous Period*	*Female*	*Index*	*% Growth Rate over Previous Period*	*Total*	*Index*	*% Growth Rate over Previous Period*	*Student-Teacher Ratio*
1950-51	73	100		13	100		86	100		36
1955-56	132	181	80.82	19	146	46.15	151	175	75.58	32
1960-61	262	359	98.48	83	638	336.84	345	401	128.48	19
1965-66	389	533	48.47	139	1069	67.47	528	614	53.04	20
1970-71	463	634	19.02	175	1346	25.90	638	742	20.83	21
1975-76	554	759	19.65	224	1723	28.00	778	905	21.94	21
1980-81	598	819	7.94	253	1946	12.95	851	989	9.38	24
1985-86	663	908	10.87	305	2346	20.55	968	1125	13.75	28
1990-91	717	982	8.14	356	2738	16.72	1073	1248	10.85	32
1995-96	756	1036	5.44	409	3146	14.89	1165	1355	8.57	35
1999-2000	829	1136	9.66	469	3608	14.67	1298	1509	11.42	32

Contd...

Years	Male	Index	% Growth Rate over Previous Period	Female	Index	% Growth Rate over Previous Period	Total	Index	% Growth Rate over Previous Period	Student-Teacher Ratio
Annual Compound Growth Rate										
1st phase	11.80			17.11			12.86			
2nd phase	2.42			3.77			2.82			
3rd phase	1.46			2.79			1.92			
Total period	4.98			7.43			5.58			

Sources: 1. Annual Reports of Ministry of Human Resource Development, Government of India.
2. Selected Educational Statistics, Ministry of Human Resource Development, Government of India.

4

An Alternative Approach to Tribal Curriculum: Anthropological Analysis of 'KANAV'

Bindu Ramachandran

"Education is a cultural process which includes schooling as well as training by agencies other than school. In all the societies irrespective of whether they are tribal or highly civilized and modern, the chief aim of education is to impart knowledge, to pass it from generation to generation and to find out ways and means for improving upon the present one through different systems and institutions"(Rami Reddi 1997). Indian Constitution provides free and compulsory education to all children up to 14 years of age. The target of achieving universal elementary education also provided special assistance to encourage educational standard among tribal students. Free education, distribution of books, fee for tuition and other items, reservation of seats...etc. are part of such facilities granted to tribal students as part of encouragement to achieve a greater development in the field of their education. But it is seen that a number of unidentified and identified factors are acting as constraints in achieving the goal.

To begin with language Verrier Elwin writes—"an important reason why the school do not fulfill the real function in tribal society is the astonishing indifference on the part of educationists to the local languages" (1960; 90). The Dhebar Commission had proposed that the first two classes be taught in the local tribal dialect and from the third standard on the classes be in the regional language (1962:226). Moreover the other internal constraints in the present system and socio-cultural context of the community have also been neglected. These are some of the reasons for dropout and stagnation among tribal students.

Tribal Education in Wayanad

The Wayanad district in Kerala state is a tri-junction of three linguistic traditions i.e. Tamil, Malayalam and Kannada. There are about 10 different tribal groups in the same district speaking their own language but they can communicate with the non-tribes of the area in local language of Malayalam. Tamil and Kannada mixtures are predominant in their dialect. A scrutiny on the educational status shows that in Wayanad educational developments of the tribes do not come up with the all round educational facilities available. Some of the groups (Kattunaicken, Paniyan,) have late enrolment in schools. Detailed investigation on the school going children (data collected for DPEP Project 2000-01) and academic performances revealed that their standard is poor and dropout rate and stagnation is very high.

Dropout of Tribal Students—Wayanad 1996-2000

Name of Block Resource Centres	*Total ST Students*				*Dropouts*			
	M	*%*	*FM*	*%*	*M*	*%*	*FM*	*%*
Mananthavady	1230	16.43	1638	27.26	3642	36.31	1091	11.75
Vythiri	1439	29.44	3171	38.83	41	49	210	13.66
Sulthan Batheri	1633	70	63	60	157	22.5	2142	56.67

Here, Sulthan Batheri Block Resource Centre has the highest percentage of dropout for both males and females. When we look into the distribution of tribal communities in this area it is found that primitive groups like Kattunaicken and Paniyan are numerically predominant in the case of dropout.

'Kanav'—An Alternative Approach to Tribal Curriculum

A kind of Ashram school "Kanav" was started in 1994, on experimental basis for educating the students from Kattunaicken and Paniyan tribes. The organizer of this school is a native of Wayanad who is well aware of the educational status of the tribes and the various problems they are facing in the field of education. This Ashram school is financed by voluntary organizations inside and outside the state. The school campus consisted of a library, mess hall, art's theatre, classrooms, teacher's accommodations, student's hostel and a separate shed for training martial arts, dance, music etc. All the buildings were constructed in the style of traditional tribal huts, and at first sight it looks like a traditional tribal settlement.

School Planning and Management

At the time of data collection, Kanav consisted of a number of 63 students among which 35 are girls and 28 are boys. Community wise distribution showed that 49 students are from Paniyan and 14 are from Kattunaicken. Students were from four tribal settlements (Pathirambam Naicka colony, Perur Paniya colony, Neykuppa Paniya colony, Ayinimala Paniya colony) of Nadavayal Panchayat. Curriculum frame of Kanav consisted of six teachers from various disciplines. Among them two are postgraduates, and one with teacher's training degree. English, Malayalam, Mathematics, History and Agriculture are the main subjects for study. In addition to the teachers here, experts from various other fields such as doctors, health workers and technical experts like electricians and plumbers also take classes on free service. In addition to the academic disciplines students are also given training in music, dance, martial arts and drama.

Student group consisted of children between the age group of 3-16. Students are divided into 6 groups excluding the nursery students. These groups are named according to the subjects such as Malayalam group, English group, History group, Agriculture group, and a general group depending on the teacher with whom they are attending. Each group consisted of 6-8 students, which also may vary. Members of each group belong to different age groups and the senior most is selected as the leader of that group.

Classes begins from 9'O clock in the morning and each group has to attend 40 minutes class with each teacher. After that they are shifted to the next teacher in the next class. Teachers are sitting in the same class and only the students are moving from each class. This movement helps them to get rid of their sleepy mood after each class.

Nursery students are also divided into three batches based on their degree of knowledge and maturity in behaviour. Nursery education consists of simple drawings, plays, preparation of flowers with plastic sheets and papers and the like. The school authorities maintain a file for each student and record all the activities and improvements of the student including their creative and artistic talents. At the time of data collection, 20 students are studying in the nursery class in three batches.

Students are given an interval of 20 minutes at 11'O clock. The classes windup at 1'O clock. In the afternoon they are engaged in other activities like collection of firewood from the nearby forest, cultivation of vegetables, cleaning , washing, musical class, library work...etc. In the evening each student has to report the activities of that day in the general assembly. Presentation of daily activity report in front of the colleagues helps them to remove their introvert nature and also encourage them to speak fluently in front of others. The literary activities of the students are also encouraged and given time in time in the afternoon. Library is in-charge of Malayalam teacher. In addition to the academic groups, the whole students and teachers are divided into one more group for the preparation of food. It is the duty of that particular group to decide the menu and prepare food for the whole day.

Methods of Study and Materials

Pre-school training is essential for early compensatory education. Here in pre-school or nursery is a play school where children are stimulated through the use of play materials, pictorial presentations, maps, simple scientific equipments...etc. so that their natural curiosity and abilities can be developed. If they are placed in such an enriched environment for at least one year they may be adequately equipped to enter primary school with other children. After the completion of pre-school training from 'Kanav', the students can easily grasp the information compared to other tribal students. Here things are introduced at first through their own language and then the equivalent Malayalam and English terms are given. Fairy tales, rhymes, myths, riddles that are associated with morality are presented along with simple passages. Here much emphasis is given to the face-to-face interaction between the child and the teacher.

'Kanav' follows no particular syllabus for teaching. Learning is an active process of understanding. They are allowed to do their own activities for learning. Through this method of experimental participation in learning activities the students become aware of their own capacity, which helps them to develop self-confidence and curiosity for more knowledge. Some of the tribal students in Kanav show confidence to attempt school final exams through this method of study.

For teaching History, the teacher at first teaches them the historical position, importance and physical features of that district. They are given information about the various Panchayats, Taluks, and villages of their home district along with the demographic particulars, flora, fauna, topography and the cultural details of the inhabitants. The teachers in Kanav opined that there is no meaning in teaching world History without basic knowledge in one's own village. Maps, figures ...etc. are used for teaching and the students are shown the slides of various places, which are historically significant . Opportunities are also made to visit some places every year, so that the student can have proper understanding of life situations in the context of curriculum content. After visiting an area the students are instructed to write notes on that particular topic. At first the content is given in their oral language and students are permitted to write the matter in the own local language so that they will get a clear idea of presentation. In the place of elementary science and social science, the children here are taught about the tribal life and culture highlighting the myths, history and achievements of the tribal people to create interest in the curriculum. However, general idea about science is also given starting from the study of nature.

Student-Teacher Relationship

The National Policy on Education, 1986 has said about the role of teacher. The status of the teacher reflects the socio-cultural ethos of a society, it is said that no people can rise above the level of its teacher. The Government and the community should endeavour to create condition, which will help, motivate and inspire teachers on constructive and creative lines. Teachers should have the freedom to innovate to the needs and capabilities and the concerns of the community.

Co-operation among children is as important as it is with teachers and other adults. Social interaction among children in schools should be developed as a permanent educational programme. This will lead to peer teaching learning situations in later years. (Kamii 1974; 99-215). Here in 'Kanav' the students are free to mingle with their teachers and they can clear their doubts at any time without any hesitation. Students are not tied within the four walls of the classroom, but they can freely read, write or engage in literary works. Teacher here is a friend and guide. They are not imposing anything on the child. He/she chooses any cultural activity depending on his aptitude. Even tribal students who discontinued their studies from schools found joined in Kanav and studying happily. They opined that they are fully satisfied with the education system in

'Kanav' rather than a school where they are subjected to various discriminations.

A tribal student after completing pre-school from 'Kanav' can easily pull on his studies with other tribal and non-tribal students if he is admitted in a school. As far as a primitive tribe like Kattunaicken is concerned, an institution like 'Kanav' can certainly a lot in the improvement and interest in primary education. This type of a curriculum along with the technical education is an encouraging step and the students can divert their interests in making money rather than sitting idle after formal education.

REFERENCES

Buddhadeb Chaudhuri (1982) Tribal Development in India; New Delhi: Inter-India Publications.

Godfrey & Monica Wilson (1968) The Analysis of Social Change; Cambridge University Press.

Hasnain, Nadeem (1983) Tribal India Today; New Delhi: Harnam Publications.

Hochings, Paul (Year unavailable) The Blue Mountains-Ethnography and Biogeography of a South Indian Region; New Delhi: Oxford University Press.

Kattakayam, John Jacob (1983) Social Structure and Change among the Tribals; New Delhi: D.K. Publications.

Mathur, P.R.G. (1977) Tribal Situation in Kerala; TVM: Kerala Historical Society.

-------- (1994) Applied Anthropology and Challenges of Development in India.; Calcutta: Punthi-Pustak.

Mann, R.S. (1984) Anthropological and Sociological Theory (Approaches and Applications); Jaipur: Rawat Publications.

Misra, Rajalakshmi (1971) Mullukurumbas of Kappala; Calcutta: Anthropological Survey of India.

Ramachandran, Bindu (2001) Impact of DPEP interventions on Tribal Education in Kerala. (Unpublished project report submitted to Department of Education, Government of Kerala).

Vidyarthi, L.P (Ed). 1981. Tribal Development and its Administration; New Delhi: Concept Publishing CO.

----------- (Ed). 1968. Applied Anthropology in India; Allahabad: Kitab Mahal.

5

Internet and its Impact on Education

M. Chakraborty

Development of IT in the past years has been drastic. Changes have been reflected on the present school system. In the past sharing of information between the schools was very slow and limited. Many schools used a typewriter instead of computer. Access to library books, museums and other educational recourses were limited and in some regions were none. Internet is spreading into the schools curriculum. The schools used them as tools in regular school subjects. This enables students to used Internet as part of their lessons. Teachers put their lectures on the Net so that the students can access any lecture that they might have missed. New and emerging technologies can be proved powerful tools to improve teaching and learning.

"NETSCAPE COMMUNICATOR" and "INTERNET EXPLORER" is the software's that most schools use. Main feature of the Internet is e-mail. Electronic mail (e-mail) enables students to communicate with other students and teachers. These mails can be send and received globally. Students submit their assignments through e-mail. The student's ability to search on the Net enables them to go way beyond the expectations of the teachers and look for more information if they want to. The FCC (Federation of Computer Communication) has established new telecommunication discount that will let schools and libraries obtain new services for local networking and Internet access. This will give a tremendous impact on learning.

A group of innovative executives from the computer industry is planning to develop a nationwide computer network to enable public school students, their parents and teachers to interact with each other. The new network called "Education Dashboard" will enable parents to check student's grades and attendance, and also communicate with teachers, arrange computer-based tutoring and participate in chat sessions.

This way of communication will specially help parents to see the progress of their children through the period of time. On the other hand this type of project has difficulties because lots of people have not got computers at their home. But the way technology is growing this will be achieved in a few year times. Nowaday's people organise themselves in a more effective way. Lot of things can be done through the Internet. People can do shopping, consult their doctor, send messages etc. The way Internet is growing it will become the dominant factor for education and research.

What is Internet?

Describing Internet is like describing a city. Confusing because it is different from anything they are used to. It is neither a programme, nor a piece of hardware, it is not software, but a place where you can get information, make information available, and a place where you can meet people. Simply, we can say that the Internet is a global computer network allowing communication with millions of computer users and access to resources from around the world. It doesn't matter what type of matter what type of computer is used for connection to the Internet. It was conceived by the Advance Research Project Agency (ARPA) of the U.S. Government in 1969 and was known as Advance Research Project Agency Network (ARPANET). The original aim was to create a network that would allow users of a research computer at one university to be able to "talk to" research computers at other universities. A side benefit of ARPANet's design was that, because messages could be routed or rerouted in more than one direction, the network could continue to function even if parts of it were destroyed in the event of a military attack or other disaster.

Today, the Internet is a public, cooperative and self-sustaining facility accessible to hundreds of millions of people worldwide. Physically, the Internet uses a portion of the total resources of the currently existing public telecommunication networks. Technically, what distinguishes the Internet is its use of a set of protocols called TCP/IP (Transmission Control Protocol/Internet Protocol). Two recent adaptation of Internet Technology, the Intranet and the

Extranet, also make use of the TCP/IP protocol. For many Internet users, e-mail has practically replaced the postal service. Electronic mail is the most widely used application the Net. One can also carry on live "conversations" with other computer users, using Internet Relay chat. More recently, Internet telephony hardware and software allows real-time voice conversations.

The most widely used part of the Internet is the World Wide Web (WWW or called "the web"). Its outstanding feature is hypertext, a method of instant cross-referencing. In most Websites, certain words or phrases appear in text of a different colour than the rest; often this text is also underlined. When you select one of these words or phrases, you will be transferred to the site or page that is relevant to this word or phrase. Sometimes there are buttons, images or portion of images that are "clickable." If you move the mouse pointer over a spot on a Website and the pointer changes into a hand, this indicates that you can click and transferred to another site. Using the Web, you have access to millions of pages of information. Web "surf" is done with a Web browser like Netscape Navigator and Internet Explorer.

Current Scenario

Many believe a revolution is taking place in education in the way people learn and the way the instruction is given. The education community has been hearing of reforms and revolutions for the past few decades, but most of them have been non-existent or without any long-term merit or real value. Some believe the method of an instructor lecturing which students listen and "absorb" is really the only viable way to teach or learn. About two decades ago, when Personal Computer (PC) started to become affordable, many thoughts that computer would revolutionize education, that Computer Based Teaching (CBT) and Computer Aided Learning (CAL) would become the saviour of education. This has never really happened. Over the past two decades, many teachers have successfully prepared students, some with computers in the classroom and some without. Teachers could avoid computers, either because they chose not to learn how to use them or because they had none in their classrooms or school to use.

In India, Internet has been in existence for almost last five years and began to extend into schools; it was first introduced in Institutes, Universities and other big organizations. Did the Internet revolutionize education? Well, not exactly. It did provide an opportunity to expand learning options for teachers and students who were fortunate enough to have Internet access. These types of facilities are only available in few places. There are many factors affecting this slow implementation of computing and communication technology in schools, including administrations with no knowledge of its value or no willingness to realign school budget to include computational technology; insufficient in-service professionals development programmes for teachers; a lack of specific curriculum benefits or of resources for teachers to use in their courses; and deficient pre-service preparation of teachers in technology or computation.

In November 1993, the Nation Centre for Supercomputing Applications (NCSA) released Mosaic, the first World Wide Web (WWW) browser for all three computing platforms (UNIX, PC, and Macintosh). The Internet had become the World Wide Web, and now Mosaic allowed anyone who knows the basics about using a computer. Text, images, sound and video could come to the desktop and be used by students from kindergarten to Ph.D. level. Files rapidly become hypermedia text pages.

The Future

Using electronic mail and surfing for information with a browser, such as Netscape Communicator and Internet Explorer, involve communicating with others and local information. Communication via e-mail is a form of asynchronous collaboration. People enter messages that are sent to other people who read them. Desktop video teleconferencing, on the other hand, allows real-time, synchronous collaboration. Chat sessions are a text-based version of synchronous collaboration. A traditional videoconferencing can be installed in classrooms and some students can get benefit from this technology. All the desktops will be connected through Internet. An instructor can sit at a desktop workstation and communicate with a classroom of students, each of whom has a workstation and communicate with a classroom of students, each of whom has a workstation in front of him and a connection to the Internet. The students no longer have to be in the same room; they can interact with other students and teachers in different locations.

For example, those children who are born in the next year (2001) or so will complete college around the year 2020. Although we cannot know what learning system will best prepare this generation for careers extending well into the middle of next century, we can nevertheless say with some certainly that all the possibilities will be include technology, particularly networking technologies.

In USA the administration is committed to make full technology into classrooms and use the power of IT to improve teaching and learning. Also, administration has committed that every classroom must be connected to the information superhighway with computers and good software and well trained teachers. At present statistics indicate that 50 per cent of schools have some type of access to the Internet. In India, only Convent and Public Schools have IT infrastructure and access to Internet is available only in few public schools, mostly in big cities. Even before all schools are connected to the Internet, we must think about how they can use this connectivity effectively. What kinds of new tools will students have access to? What materials will they find online? What possibilities will arise for students to learn and use information in new and untold ways? And how will networking technologies enable students to meet high standards of achievements?

Impact of Internet on Education

How powerful is the Net as an educational tool? Are teachers prepared to utilize this technology? Does the Internet create better students? Will the Internet access truly change the way students learn? The Net will ultimately become much more than just another multimedia tools in the learning process. Educators, Administrators and Policy Makers have the following conceptions on Internet Education. Nowaday's schools, students and teachers have begun to develop the Internet into a major educational resource. Within the community of educational researchers, the Internet is now an accepted standard. Network use is also growing rapidly throughout the larger educational community, but several factors have placed practical limits on its growth. Some of the reasons that move forward use of Internet in education are:

Isolation

Wide area computer networks can help end the isolation of students and teachers in the traditional classrooms. Of course, networks will accomplish this end only if they are inexpensive enough to make available to all students and teachers.

Equity

Connecting all schools to the Internet will provide equity of access to online information and create opportunities for all schools to publish online. This requires a reasonable priced infrastructure that all schools can afford to purchase, install and maintain.

Reform

Network can be a powerful tool in support of educational reform. A network with easy access to information servers and tools for placing resources on servers will allow students and teachers to produce online materials.

Is Networking Schools Worthwhile?

Net can engage students in the learning process, offer them to a vast universe of previously unavailable information, and teach them virtual navigation and information-processing skills that are increasingly important to success in the workplace. Net has the potential to change the way student learns.Technology is enormously powerful in terms of changing what the children believe they can do. To get this technology out to more students and to give training to teachers is very essential.

Is the Web Teacher OR Textbook?

There was significant disagreement about the benefits and liabilities of Web-assisted education. Many educators stressed that the Net has potentially endless benefits. It can link students to peer anywhere in the world, allow them to access classroom materials anywhere at any time, and help them to overcome structural barriers such as gender, race or socio-economic status. Some administrator suggested that Internet could be viewed as educational tool rather than Internet environment. It can only be used when student has been motivated.

Isn't the Web full of Misinformation?

Another aspect, which worry educators the quality of information available. Some experts say that Net is filled with inaccurate, misleading or incorporate information. Few experts felt that students should be blocked from accessing information. Majority of experts suggested that the nature of the Internet would increase the importance of teaching students the art of discriminating research. The most difficult challenge for the next generation will not be gaining access of information.

Building Information Driveway in Schools

How do provide affordable access to the Internet for school? There are two factors, which affect the performance and affordability of internetworking; these are cost and bandwidth (speed of the network). Schools should choose their network technologies strategically. For example the commonly available digital telephone networking service known as Integrated Services Digital Network (ISDN) can provide economical connectivity at moderate bandwidths, as long as its tariffs are set at an affordable flat rate (with no time charges). When time charges are applied this service becomes uneconomical. Another network technology, which can be used, is Fibre Optic technology. Fibre brings vastly higher bandwidth. To get a connection of Internet at school the following is the requirements:

Hardware

1. Personal Computer (PC)
2. Modem
3. Telephone Connectivity.

Software

1. Windows 95/98
2. Browser (Netscape Communicator/Internet Explorer)
3. E-mail Client.

Internet Service Provider like VSNL (Videsh Sanchar Nigam Ltd.) needs to be contacted to get a TCP/IP connection. If there is Local Area Network (LAN) is available, then a Proxy Server is required for sharing the Modem Connection. New technologies with new applications will offer significant reduction in the cost of school networking and the capabilities of networks available to students and teachers. These economises will make it possible to provide universal access to educational networks.

Use of IT in Education

It is accepted that IT can prove a potential contribution to education. To use IT more effectively in education, a systematic planning is required. There should be direct access of IT equipment by students and teachers, so that they feel comfortable is using these latest technology. Sufficient time and opportunities should be given to teachers to become trained and comfortable in the use of these technologies. The issues involved in the use of IT in education are as follows:

Planning

To use IT more effectively in education, a detailed and systematic planning is required. A team of IT professionals first do the feasibility study. This study should be able to identify what type of technology is required for education. The team should identify the venders from where technology can be procured. Also, ensure that the technology, which is purchased, is appropriate to meet educational needs. Team should provide the guidelines for maintenance of technology, its Annual Maintenance Contract (AMC) and upgrade of technology. Proper training programmes should be there for teachers and students, so that they feel comfortable in using these latest technologies.

Access to Equipment

Students' access to IT equipment is the number of computers per student in schools. In considering access to equipment, it is necessary not only to consider the total number of computers per student, but also how access is distributed. With the use of information technology in education will lead to greater inequalities in knowledge and skills among different groups of students.

Students who have access to information technology equipment are more likely to gain the knowledge and information skills that are becoming increasingly essentials to employment. Students who do not have such access are less likely to find jobs, which in turn may perpetuate cycles of disadvantage within some families. Students whose family can afford computers have an enormous head start, through the provision of supplementary learning activities and additional encouragement and opportunities to do school work at home. The growing use of technologies that facilitate better links between school and home and increased parental involvement can also help to improve the learning opportunities of students who already have access to computers at home, while nothing to assist those who do not. The gap between different groups of students in access to technology at home reinforces the role and responsibility of schools to provide minimum level of access to all students. Information technology will only be successful in improving student achievement if teachers are able to facilitate its use in the classroom. Therefore, it is essential that teachers should given full-fledged IT training, so that they can use IT comfortably in during their classrooms.

Role of the Government

Government should give importance to use of IT in education. At present, huge range of hardware and software is available in the market, but there is a lack of IT skills and knowledge in schools. Government has to take initiative in the introduction of IT in schools. National Informatics Centre, Ministry of Information Technology, Government of India has its centres throughout India, i.e. in all district headquarters, all states headquarters and headquarter at Delhi. Schools can approach these NIC centres to seek their help in order to establish an IT infrastructure. There are some issues, which Government should consider as a matter of priority.

- Provision of guidelines on the use of IT in education.
- Provision of training programmes for teachers.
- Provision of technical advice, for example from National Informatics Centre, Ministry of Information and Technology, Government of India.
- Strategies to promote IT in higher education and distance education, especially in remote areas.

Using Internet in Education

There are positive and negative features of using Internet in education. Teachers also have benefits and shortcomings. Some advantages of using Internet in education given below:

1. Students using the Internet and the World Wide Web (WWW) will develop the technical skills required to use the Internet for communication and information gathering.
2. Students using the Internet and the World Wide Web (WWW) will acquire geographical awareness based on understanding the global nature of Internet connection and communications.
3. Students using the Internet and the World Wide Web (WWW) will improve their ability to learn and understand new and changing information technologies.
4. Students using the Internet and the World Wide Web (WWW) will learn to evaluate the validity of information acquired through Internet Resources.
5. Students using the Internet and the World Wide Web (WWW) will learn to integrate the data acquired through the Internet into a meaningful whole.
6. Students using the Internet and the World Wide Web (WWW)

will understand and know how to use at least one Web Browser.

7. Students using the Internet and the World Wide Web (WWW) will develop the skills required to rate information for relevance in meeting a specified need.
8. Students using the Internet and the World Wide Web (WWW) will understand differences and similarities among search engines and how to use a variety of search engines.
9. Students using the Internet and the World Wide Web (WWW) will develop strategies for finding and evaluating new Internet growth and use.
10. In the information age, student with access to Internet can explore extensive libraries and international resources on different subjects.
11. Through Internet students can share their work with learners of all ages.
12. Teachers who teach the severely handicapped may find themselves faced with students who have limited use of their arms and hands. With today's technology most of these students have other means of using a keyboard. Their horizons are opened and they are able to read and write through Internet. Even the blind students are able to use the Internet through speech recognition programmes and specially equipped computers.
13. By teleconferencing, in classes students can actually see and speak to each other in real time as they learn their lessons. The use of newsgroups and e-mail can both be incorporated into education.
14. The students can learn at their own pace. Services like e-mail and mailing lists can support communication between teacher and student. By using a combination of both e-mail and web, teachers and students can collaborate on research and projects even with those who don't live in the same city or country.
15. Automation recognition of speech in conferences and lesson plans with their translation into PC screen messages are a very good help for the deaf.
16. The places where facilities for higher education is not available, people can use Internet facility for their higher education. Some universities have started some higher-level

courses through Internet. So, if people have Internet access they can do their higher studies by accessing Internet. Many universities have launched many courses through Internet for example Indira Gandhi National Open University (IGNOU).

Limitations

1. Searching through the Net sometimes can lead children to the places that are not supposed to go such as: sex page, crime magazines, drug advices, etc. This is a major problem for teachers to keep children away from such pages.
2. With so many resources available to students in electronic form, they can quickly copy it. So, it is difficult to assess student.
3. It is not possible to keep students on task.
4. If students do not know how to use e-mail and browser (Netscape etc.), they cannot join e-mail groups, send mails and utilize online tutorials etc.
5. Computers can get viruses through Internet or E-mail.
6. Software often gets bugs and sometimes computer crash. In this situation students will left with nothing to do.
7. Some students spend too much time in playing games, which can be very violent.
8. Anyone can put information or images on the Internet, so criminals to communicate with each other or to send pornography can easily use it. There are no laws to stop this yet, and it is extremely difficult to ***Police*** the Internet.
9. A machine cannot give the necessary and meaningful personal attention to students.
10. Students will waste time if there is no teacher to check on them.
11. One student will be able to take the test of another student since no human will be checking.
12. Computers can be dangerous to the eyesight of students because of the need to read from the screen.

Conclusion

Technology is affecting education in revolutionary ways and the momentum towards these changes is irreversible. The use of information technology in education has potential to raise student's achievement. Teachers who have began to use the Web see this change occurring, even if they only have experience with static information-gathering and display capabilities. Most of these educators have not yet used or even seen the potential of technologies for their classroom and their school. Universities and Technology Institutes need to become leaders in applying this latest technology to education for learning. Colleges of education need to become leaders in applying computational and information technology for schools.

An obstacle that needs to be overcome is the views many hold that computers and Internet connectivity are tools for learning, and thus an increased grade point average or marks is only measure of value for these resources. A more important prospective is for administrators and school boards to realize that the Web represents a new environment for learning and teaching and that very soon every teacher and student will need access to information available on the Web. New technologies with new applications can significantly reduce the cost of school networking and significantly improve the networking capabilities available to students and teachers. These economies will make it possible to provide universal access to educational networks and ending the isolation of the traditional classrooms. Internet will play a major role in education in the near future.

REFERENCES

Hoffman Paul E., Internet Instant Reference, 1995, BPB Publications, New Delhi.
Goel M.K., Let's Learn Internet, Sterling Information Technologies, New Delhi.
Galla Preston, How the Internet Works : Millennium Edition, 1999, QUE.
Levine John R., The Internet for Dummies, 2000.

6

The Perspective and Paradoxes of Tribal Education: A Case of Rajasthan

Seema Agrawal and Pankaj Agrawal

Rajasthan exhibits significant growth in rate of literacy in the last decade (1991-2001), which has risen from 38.55 per cent to 61.03 per cent. It is noteworthy here that it consists of 12.5 per cent tribal of its total population. It is a fact that Scheduled Castes and the Scheduled Tribes are the poorest and the most backward section of the Indian population. They face enormous socio-economic constraints. Government of India has developed a number of plans and policies for enhancement of such communities. Response to such programmes varies from community to community. Hence they are at different levels of development. Some communities have now days accepted the process of development fully. Whereas other have adopted it half-heartedly or still bear the status of societies with simple technology. Development is associated with social change. August Comte argued that social change is the outcome of intellectual development. Intellectual progress causes moral development thereby setting in change in social institutions. Education is the best medium for the purpose.[1] It is only through education that tribals can fully utilize the opportunities for socio-economic development. It not only provides knowledge and skills but also inculcates values, training of instincts, fostering right attitudes and habits.[2] Education is proving quite instrumental in bringing the tribes in mainstream and nation building. The states are provided with necessary directives for providing free and compulsory education to the children up to 14 years. Article 46 of the Constitution envisages that–

The state shall promote with special care the educational and economic interests of the weaker sections of the people and in particular of the Scheduled Castes and the Scheduled Tribes and shall protect them from social injustice and all forms of exploitation.

To fulfill the constitutional the Central and State Governments are adopting directions measures. The special programmes and intervention strategies for the educational progress can broadly be categorized into 3 types, viz.[3]

1. Welfare measures and incentive schemes like scholarships, mid-day meals, supply of free uniforms, fee concession etc., and the welfare measures are indirect economic support to motivate the families to send their children to school.
2. Special institutional arrangements and concessions like separate hostels in ST and SC habitations. Hostels, ashram hostels, mobile hostels, non-formal education centers, reservation of seats in educational institution, relaxation of age and qualifying levels, etc.
3. Direct input for the teaching learning process in the form of free textbooks and writing materials.

The study pertains to ashram hostels in Rajasthan. The concept of ashram hostel originated in Gujarat when in 1922 Thakkar Bappa initiated ashram schools in Panchamahal hills for the benefit of tribal children. After independence, an attempt was made by Government of India to open such schools during First Five-Year Plan. The working pattern, structure and level of education in ashram schools differ widely among the states. In Rajasthan and West Bengal the ashram hostels are there are students study in the general schools along with the children of other castes. In Maharashtra, Gujarat and Andhra Pradesh ashram schools are co-educational whereas in Orissa, Rajasthan and Madhya Pradesh these schools are separate for girls and boys.[4] Mina, Bhil, Garasia and Saharia are major tribal communities of the state. The most populous and prosperous tribe Mina inhabits in Jaipur, Tonk and Swaimadhopur districts. Southern part is known as homeland of Bhils and Garasia. Saharia is the only PTG of the state residing in Baaran. On April 1, 1951, the First Five-Year Plans were launched and a lump sum provision was made for the schemes for weaker sections including STs. Since then, special emphasis was given on provisions and policies related to tribals. The State Government has established a Tribal Development Department in 1975. Fifth Five-Year Plan may be termed as a landmark in development planning for the tribals. The entire tribal population whether living in the areas of the concentration or outside were covered by suitable approaches. Tribal sub-plan, Modified Area Development Approach, MADA cluster and Scattered Tribal Population Area etc., were designed on these bases during Five-Year Plans.

This study focuses on introduction of Ashram hostels under MADA scheme. 34 Ashram hostels are being run for ST students in 12 districts under this scheme. Two Ashram hostels of Ralawas and Bhanwata Bhanwati in Dausa district have been focused. State Government in collaboration with Central Government runs ashram hostels. This fieldwork was conducted in 2003-04. It is an exploratory study, which emphasizes to know that whether available infrastructure facilities have been in accordance with the rules and needs of ashramites? Does staying at ashram hostels cultivate some notable qualities in their personalities? Can ashram hostels be pursued as one of the instruments for increase in rate of literacy among tribals?

About the Study

There are 8 ashram hostels in Dausa district named after Kalipahadi, Vilonalakala, Ghumer, Nihalpura, Ukrund, Ralawas, Bhanwata Bhanwati and Nandri villages. First 6 ashram hostels are meant for boys and last 2 for the girls. Since majority of population is Mina, so Mina students are found primarily in these ashram hostels. Both of the ashram hostels are housed in pucca buildings. 50 ashramites each from both of the ashram hostels were interviewed. Non-participant observation method and interview technique was used to collect qualitative data. Group discussions were organized with teachers and students whenever necessary.

Observations

Mina population of the two villages namely Ralawas and Bhanwata Bhanwati is 72 per cent and 55 per cent respectively. Ralawas ashram hostel is for the students of upper primary school and in Bhanwata Bhanwati the students of secondary level are admitted. Ashramites of Ralawas and Bhanwata Bhanwati go to upper primary and secondary level government schools situated nearby. Students from all sections of the society like ST, SC, OBC, minor and general study in these schools. Capacity of both ashram hostels is 100 students each. In Ralawas and Bhanwata Bhanwati there are 97 and 100 students respectively. Thus almost cent per cent occupancy of ashram hostels show that this policy is very popular among tribals. Only 3 students at Ralawas hostel were not able to follow the rules and regulations due to some socio-economic pressures. Hence, their names were ticked off from the register of ashram hostel. 58.76 per cent and 55 students are from BPL families in Ralawas and Bhanwata hostels respectively.

In Ralawas students belong to 9 to 13 years of age group whereas in Bhanwata Bhanwati the age group ranges from 10 to 17 years. In Ralawas 22 per cent students belong to age group of 9-10 years whereas 34 per cent and 14 per cent students fall in the age group of 14-15 years and 16-17 years respectively. It is revealed that in Ralawas ashram hostel 44 per cent students were the freshers. Only 2 per cent students have been studying there for last 4 years. 24 per cent and 30 per cent students were those who have been studying there for last 2 and 3 years respectively. Ashramites of Bhanwata Bhanwati show a little difference in this context. The percentage of the fresh student remains almost same (42%) as that of Ralawas. 16 per cent students have spent their 4 precious years in this hostel. Whereas 18 per cent and 24 per cent students have been staying there for last 2 and 3 years respectively. Thus there is an upward trend in the admission of the tribal students in ashram hostels in last five years. It is worthwhile to note here that policy of ashram hostel is becoming very popular. The admission committee of Ralawas has been conducting entrance exams for last two years due to overwhelming response of the aspirants.

The study reveals that an expenditure of Rupees 6750 is incurred per student in 10 months. This amount is spent on items of their daily needs and clothing. They get drinking water in their hostels from hand pumps. DRDA facilitated them with sumersible water pumps about 2 years back but electric connection for such pumps have not been provided so far. Students take bath under the hand pumps because both of the ashram hostels lack bathrooms. The toilets are in a bad condition. The ashramites get up early in the morning to cope up with the problem of short water supply and bathrooms. Full diet is provided to the students on the basis of weekly chart and their Superintendent also provides other facilities to them. Television, radio and telephonic facilities are not available in both of the hostels, libraries of both the hostels are poorly maintained. Students hardly get fresh magazines or books from there. No regular health check-up is done there.

The ashramites devote 3-4 hours daily to their studies. They do face some problems in doing the homework as there is no coach teacher. They expressed that their seniors and Superintendent of the hostel help them to overcome such problems. All students pray 'goddess Saraswati' collectively in the courtyard of the hostel. Students believe in their deities also. They worship the deities like Bhawani and Narsinghji etc. in their rooms at their personal level. The provision of taking the ashramites to some place once in two years is also followed. Students are allowed to visit their parents on Sundays and other state/national holidays.

Living rooms are large and airy. 8-9 students in collective share one room. It develops friendly relationship among students. Students believe that they are having not only personality developments but also experience positive changes in their family, political and religious spheres which would definitely help them in their over all development. The students of their own community come here from distant villages, which further encourages intra-cultural communication. The windows and doors were found in very bad condition. Almarahas provided to the ashramites in their rooms are not covered with doors. Therefore, there is always a possibility for the students to loose their belongings. Generally they doubt their roommates if such mishap occurs. Such incidents spoil the atmosphere of ashram hostels and also develop a tendency of unacceptable and unethical activities among ashramites. Superintendent is supposed to reside in the premise but Superintendent of Bhanwata Bhanwati doesn't follow it.

Results and Findings

Analysis of the data collected points out some important facts. They can be described as below.

- *Increasing consciousness of other cultures:* By joining ashram hostel and relevant government school, the ashramites come in contact with members of other communities. They come to know about a new world with an entirely new value system, which they try to understand and adjust with it.
- *Development of a sense of community and nationality:* During process of socialization they knew only about their deities like Bhomiyaji, Narsinghji and goddess Bhawani etc. Now they are well aware of national celebrities, festivals and cultural occasions also.

- *Knowledge of the surrounding environment:* Due to advent of communication and transportation the tribals got exposed to non-tribals like caste Hindus. Consequently a number of social evils like veil system, child marriage and dowry etc. had crept in. It appears that getting education through ashram hostels may prove instrumental in eradication of social malpractices because the students collectively think to oppose such malpractices. At first instance such thoughts might appear emotional, ineffective or illogical but one cannot deny the fact that such childhood thoughts can bring revolutionary changes in the society in future.
- *Developing of personality:* Since 8-9 students share one room they develop a feeling of discipline, adjustment and tolerance for each other. It also helps them in development of quality of leadership and dynamism.
- *Change in family atmosphere:* Tremendous changes in a student's all round personality forces his/her parents and family to come out of their age old practices, for example parents of some of the students wear shirts and trousers in case of males and saris in case of married females. They are well conversant with Hindi now. Whenever they visit their family they speak Hindi to impress others. Their acquaintances also try to learn and speak Hindi from them. In a way the ashramites are the example setters in their residential areas. They act as motivational factors for other parents to send their sons and daughters to get admitted in ashram hostels. Special facilities provided by ashram hostel motivate other relatives and friends also.
- *Preparation for bright career:* Earlier their model personalities used to be some member of the family or political party of the village. Now they have come out of that narrow circle while studying at ashram hostel. They are quite aware of national and international celebrities, which could prove instrumental in their personality development. Simultaneously they are quite capable now to plan for their bright future and some of them act accordingly.

Paradoxes

- Rules for admission in ashram hostels are not fully justifiable. Only those students get the admission that lack primary/middle/secondary level schools in the periphery of 1.5/3/5 kms. of their home range. Ashram hostels are generally situated in tribal villages. Therefore students of that particular village are not eligible to seek admission in such ashram hostels. It is true that government provides free education to the children of scheduled tribes through various policies but in certain circumstances where family atmosphere is sometimes quite tense, children of such families look for residential facilities for education so that they can be away from their homes. Hence, there is a dire need of formulation of some policy through which such students could get boarding facilities.

- Intercultural contacts are feasible during school hours only. For rest of the time they have to interact within their group only. It creates a kind of ghetoisation among them. Sachchidananda also started that it is our experience that putting up separate hostels for SC and ST students has led to the persistence of exclusiveness and hindered their mingling with other sections of population[5] in this case the situation gets more critical when other students and teachers look upon them as most privileged students because of free boarding facilities.
- Ashram hostels were introduced for enhancement of education among tribals. For that matter there is provision of a coach teacher who would help them in solving their syllabi problems. Both of the ashram hostels lack coach teachers.
- Absence of Superintendent from girls' hostel brings bad name to the security of ashramites. There is no other facility like telephone or watchman to help students to overcome an unseen problem. It is a serious drawback of the ashram hostel scheme, which can be a major reason for low rate of literacy among tribal women in future.

Recommendations

- There is a dire need to review admission rules for ashram hostels so that students of the same village where the hostel is situated can also get admission.
- Arrangement of infrastructure facilities like toilets, drinking water, electricity and a cook also to create a favourable atmosphere for the study.

- Timely recruitment of the staff and regular monitoring of ashram hostels' functioning and activities of the ashramites is most desirable.
- Appointment of a coach teacher and his regular presence is a must to sort out the problems.
- Regular interaction between parents and the Superintendent would help in smooth functioning of the hostel.
- Arrangement of vocational/occupational training to the ashramites can make this scheme more beneficial.
- Since many students share one room, they should be provided with basic facilities. Every effort should be made to prevent ashramites from indulging in bad habits.
- Post modern society is passing through globalization and information technology. Therefore ashramites should also be motivated to learn computers and have access to Internet, through which they can learn more about the outer world. Also use of latest technology would create a certain kind of self-confidence among them, which further helps them to compete with urban students.

Conclusions

Analysis of the study suggests that at large infrastructure facilities were in accordance with the rules and meet with the needs of ashramites. Favourable family atmosphere is desirable to send tribal students to ashram hostels. Almost 100 per cent occupancy of ashram hostels indicate that this type of policies are very popular among tribals and tribal parents are willing to take maximum benefit of such facilities despite lack of some basic amenities. The schemes like residence-cum-school may play a vital role in development of some basic qualities in personality of tribal children. Ashram hostels can produce better results if the occupants are not confined to gain formal education only.

REFERENCES

1. Mann, R.S., 1994, Social Change and Social Research: An Indian Perspective, Concept Publishing Company, New Delhi, pp. 32-33.
2. Chandra, S.S. and Sharma, Rajendra, K., 2004, Sociology of Education, Atlantic Publishers and Distributors, New Delhi, p. 1.
3. Sujatha, K., 1999, Education of Weaker Sections in India in Indian Education: Development since Independent Ed. By Mukhopadhyay, M. and Parhar, M. Vikas Publishing House, New Delhi, p. 83.

4. Nagi, B.S., 2000, Educating Tribals in India: A Study of Ashram Schools, Kanishka Publishers, Distributors, New Delhi, p. 23.
5. Sachchidananda, 1999, Education of Scheduled Castes and Scheduled Tribes in Indian Education: Development since Independence Ed. by Mukhopadhyay, M. and Parhar, M., Vikas Publishing House, New Delhi, p. 88.

7

Performance of Preraks and Community Opinion: A Study in Andhra Pradesh

G. Surendra

In the present study an attempt is made to know the positive and negative opinions of the representatives of the community towards continuing education. The attitude score obtained by the community representatives are categorized into two groups based upon mean ± ½ standard deviation. The items on which the community representatives have obtained scores equivalent and above mean + ½ standard deviation are treated as those possessing high positive opinion and the scores equivalent and below the range of mean - ½ standard deviation are treated as those representing negative opinion. Out of 45 items on 19 items, the opinion is positive and on 26 items the opinion is negative.

Positive Opinion of Community Representatives

It is evident from the Table 1, the community feels that, the Preraks are good with regard to the aspect such as creation of awareness about DWCEA, CMEY, TRYSEM and Deepam, organizing literacy awareness programmes through kalajathas, street plays, dances, slogans and folk arts, discussion about individual development of the neo-literates, social evils and dowry. Further, community opinion is positive on the organization of programmes related to literacy and development, organizing discussion groups on safe drinking water, health, diseases and traffic rules, conducting short-term training programmes like leadership qualities, right to vote, agriculture, animal husbandry, embroidery and tailoring, organizing cycle rallies in the village, facilitating the neo-literates participation in group discussion, improving the literacy skills in the evening classes of neo-literates, helping self-help groups to acquire literacy, organizing activities related to individual members, singing competitions and vocational training programmes. Community opinion is also favourable in the following functions of the Preraks like, taking steps to maintain the records and reports such as forwarding different types of reports to Nodal Prerak, recording information about village and maintaining records and registers in the centre. Preraks participation in the review meetings and training programmes and collection of corpus fund through village education committees.

Table–1
Positive Opinion and their Respective Mean Values Checked by the Community Representatives

Sl. No.	*Positive Opinion*	*Mean Value*
1.	Creating awareness about DWCRA, CMEY, TRYSEM and Deepam	1230.00
2.	Organisation of discussion groups (drinking water, health, diseases and traffic rules)	1182.00
3.	Organising cycle rallies in the village	1182.00
4.	Organising short-term training programmes (leadership, qualities, right to vote, agriculture, embroidery and tailoring)	1126.00
5.	Organizing literacy awareness through kalajathas, street plays, dances and slogans	1100.00
6.	Forwarding different types of reports to Nodal Prerak	1052.00
7.	Facilitating neo-literates participation in group discussion	1036.00
8.	Recording information about the village	1018.00
9.	Maintaining records and registers in the centre	1008.00
10.	Organizing vocational training programmes	1000.00
11.	Improving literacy skills of neo-literates in the evening classes	992.00
12.	Collection of corpus fund through village education committees	990.00
13.	Helping self-help groups to acquire literacy	986.00
14.	Organizing activities related to development as per the desire of the individuals	946.00
15.	Organising singing competition	922.00
16.	Creating awareness on folk arts	912.00
17.	Discussion about individual development of the neo-literates	910.00
18.	Discussion on social evils and dowry	902.00
19.	Participation in the review meetings and training programmes	894.00

Negative Opinion of the Community Representatives

Out of 45 items, on 26 items, the community has negative opinion as shown in Table 2.

Table–2
Negative Opinion and their Respective Mean Values Checked by the Community Representatives

Sl. No.	*Negative Opinion*	*Mean Value*
1.	Organising equivalency programmes	888.00
2.	Providing minimum facilities to the neo-literates	886.00
3.	Arranging cultural programmes with the help of local cultural troops	880.00
4.	Organising quality of life improvement programmes	872.00
5.	Supplying daily newspapers, monthly and fortnight magazines to the centre	866.00
6.	Discussion about the individual and village issues	856.00
7.	Identification the learning needs of the neo-literates and preparing a plan to meet these needs	854.00
8.	Motivating the neo-literates to participate in games and sports	840.00
9.	Creating conducive educational environment in the centre	826.00
10.	Collecting the information about development programmes	814.00
11.	Discussion about the population, family planning and pollution	810.00
12.	Collection of the funds and books to organize the library	800.00
13.	Organizing self-employment programmes	794.00
14.	Keeping records in continuing education centres about literacy and illiteracy in the village	794.00
15.	Organizing recreational activities	784.00
16.	Running the centre for six days in a week	780.00
17.	Organizing continuing education centre programmes through the village education committees	778.00
18.	Teaching the importance of games and sports to neo-literates	764.00
19.	Running the library and reading room	762.00
20.	Conducting sports and games competitions	742.00
21.	Running the information centre	740.00
22.	Getting help from Mandal Literacy Organizers and supervisors in organizing the continuing education centre activities	734.00
23.	Collection of books related to social, scientific, art and history	712.00
24.	Evaluating the progress of the centres	696.00
25.	Arranging audio-visual aids	690.00
26.	Making aware of the uses of the games and sports	676.00

The community representatives feel that, the performance of Preraks is poor in issues related to provision of minimum facilities in the centre, supply of daily newspapers, weekly, monthly magazines, collection of books related to social, scientific, art and history and in arranging the audio-visual aids. The communities opinion is also poor on the activities like organizing equivalency programmes, quality life improvement programmes, self-employment programmes, continuing education centre programmes through village education committees, arranging cultural programmes with the help of local cultural troops and recreational activities, discussion about the individual and village issues, population, pollution, family planning and national values, identifying the learning-needs of the neo-literates and preparing a plan to meet these needs, collection of information about development programmes, keeping the records in continuing education centers about literacy and illiteracy in the village, running the library and reading room in the centre, conducting the sports and games competitions, running the information centre and evaluating the progress of the centers, collection of finances to organize the library.

Table-3
Means, Standard Deviation, and 't' Test for the Community Opinion of Community Representatives

Sl. No.	*Community Opinion*	*N*	*Mean*	*SD*	*'t*
1.	Positive	160	120.83	7.96	22.64**
2.	Negative	200	103.46	6.20	

** Significant at 0.01 level.

The Table 3 clearly shows that 44 (160) per cent of the community representatives opined that the Preraks performance was good in all respects of continuing education centres. On the other hand, 56 (200) per cent of the community representatives have negative opinion about the capacity of the Preraks. Based on the opinion, the community representatives are categorized into two groups viz., positive and negative attitude members and their attitude scores are calculated and presented in the Table 3. The trend of the obtained mean scores of the community representatives and difference between the positive and negative groups and 't' test is found that there is significant different at 0.01 level. The second group of community representatives expressed poor opinion against the Preraks. Hence, the hypothesis "there is no significant difference between the positive and negative opinions on the performance of Preraks" is not accepted.

Field Situation

In order to understand, the relationship between performance and problems of the Preraks and neo-literates. In order to study the Preraks/neo-literates are categorized into two groups based on their mean scores. The Table 4 shows that the mean scores, Standard Deviation obtained by the Preraks/neo-literates and their respective 't' values.

Table-4
Mean Performance Scores, Standard Deviation Obtained by the Preraks and Neo-Literates Along with 't' Test in the Areas of Performance

Sl. No.	*Community Opinion*	*N*	*Mean*	*SD*	*'t'*
1.	Preraks performance	120	126.80	8.23	66.10**
2.	Neo-literates performance	360	67.67	9.19	

** Significant at 0.01 level.

Preraks Performance *Vs.* Neo-Literates

In order to measure the performance of two groups viz., Preraks and neo-literates and their respective mean performance scores are calculated. The trend of the mean performance scores shows that the Preraks have obtained better performance than the neo-literates performance. In addition, the 't' test result shows that the difference between the Preraks and neo-literates performance is significant at 0.01 levels. Hence, the hypothesis "there is no significant difference between the Preraks and neo-literates performance" is not accepted. Hence, the Preraks performed their specific functions properly viz., organization of evening classes, maintaining the library and reading room, conducting training programmes of short duration, organizing charcha mandal, conducting sports and games, recreational and cultural activities, and acted as a information window and communication centre.

Preraks Problems *Vs.* Neo-Literates

The trend of the mean problem scores illustrates that the neo-literates are facing fewer problems than the Preraks and 't' test is applied to find out the difference between these two groups and it is significant at 0.01 level. Hence, the hypothesis "there is no significant difference between the Prerak problems and neo-literates problems" is not accepted. Preraks are facing innumerable problems of personal and programme related, while the neo-literates are facing less problems than the Preraks.

Preraks Performance *Vs.* Community Representative Opinion

In order to measure the Preraks performance and community representatives opinions and their respective mean scores are calculated. The trend of the mean scores shows that the Preraks have obtained better performance scores than the community representatives. In addition, the 't' result shows that the difference between the Preraks and community representatives opinion is significant at 0.01 level. Hence, the hypothesis "there is no significant difference between the Preraks performance and community representatives opinion" is not accepted.

Literacy is one of the key elements of human resource development. In order to improve the quality of human resources of the country, the Government of India has launched a number of adult education programmes for the promotion of literacy. As a result, a large pool of newly made literates was created. In order to prevent them to relapse into illiteracy and institutionalize continuing education programme, the scheme of continuing education centres were launched throughout the country.

- Positive opinion of the community representatives on the performance of Preraks is found in the sphere of organizing literacy awareness programmes, creation of awareness about self-help groups, organizing group discussions, organization of programmes related to literacy and development, maintaining records and registers and collection of corpus fund through village education committees.
- Negative opinion of the community representatives on the performance of Preraks is poor on issues related to provision of minimum facilities, supply of magazines, arranging audio-visual aids, lack of library and reading facilities, organization of continuing education programmes, lack of teaching-learning materials, collection of information on developmental programmes and conducting sports and games in the centre.

- 44 per cent of the community representatives opined that the Preraks performance was good in all aspects of continuing education centres. On the other hand, 56 per cent of the community representatives have negative opinion about the capacity of the Preraks.
- There is a significant difference between the Preraks performance and neo-literates performance.
- There is a significant different between the Preraks problems and neo-literate problems.
- There is a significant difference between the Preraks performance and community opinion.

Community participation is crucial implementing the continuing education programme. It was observed in the present study that the community members expressed a low profile on issues like organizing equivalency programmes, providing minimum facilities to the neo-literates, arranging cultural programmes with the help of local cultural troupes, organizing quality of life improvement programmes, supplying daily newspapers, monthly and fortnightly magazines to the centre, discussion about the individual and village issues, identification the learning needs of the neo-literates and preparing a plan to meet these needs, motivating the neo-literates to participate in games and sports, creating conducive educational environment in the centre, collecting the information about development programmes, discussion about the population, family planning and pollution, collection of the funds and books to organize the library, organizing self-employment programmes, keeping records in continuing education centres about literacy and illiteracy in the village, organizing recreational activities, running the centre for six days in a week, organizing continuing education centre programmes through the village education committees, teaching the importance of games and sports to neo-literates, running the library and reading room, conducting sports and games competitions, running the information centre, getting help from Mandal Literacy Organizers and supervisors in organizing the continuing education centre activities, collection of books related to social, scientific, art and history, evaluating the progress of the centres, arranging audio-visual aids, making aware of the uses of the games and sports. The district administration has to take steps to enhance that participation of the community so that the programme can be made successful.

Part–2
RURAL DEVELOPMENT AND EXTENSION

8

Education and Community Building: Role of NGOs

D. Uma Devi and P. Adinarayana Reddy

Community is an aggregate of population with unity of consciousness, shares common mode of life, with historical heritage and act in a co-operative manner and with special features. It is a permanent local aggregation of people having diversified as well as common interests and served as a constellation of institutions. According to Maclever and Page "wherever the members of any group, small or large live together in such a way that they share nor this or that particular interest, but the basic condition of common life is a community." According to Dawson and Gettys "A community is a unit of territory within which is distributed a population which possessed the basic institution in their simple and more specialized form by means a common life is made possible."

In every community, there is a power system through which people share the authority and try to manage the affairs. All these things are possible only when the community has the necessary human resources to keep itself going. Education is the one of the agency designed by the community to train its members as socially acceptable persons and helps them in acquiring required skills and abilities to lead a comfortable life.

Education has a vital role to play in the development of a community. Education plays a significant role in the community to imbibe the desired values and attitudes among the community members and to have reciprocal relationship with the other members of the community. Further, it enables the members of the community to participate in all spheres of life and activities initiated by the authority for their own development. The community education should help to preserve and promote the culture and traditions of the society for the future generations.

Education in the present day context of the community is the important means for individuals to improve their capacities, skills and abilities to not only to overcome the constraints created by the system but also for the well-being of the individual. Further, it creates avenues opportunities to sustain in the community. It is a powerful instrument for bringing about socio-economic and political changes in the society and to integrate the individual in the community effectively. Hence, the process of education has a pervasive impact on all spheres of life. The level and spread of education has not only been an important pre-condition for sustained economic growth, both in the developed and developing countries, but it also plays a critical facilitative role in the demographic, social and political transition of the societies, creation, appreciation and adaptation of new technologies. No doubt, education is a pre-condition for the community development.

Role of Education in Community Building

Community building is the process of collective work of people to achieve the sustainable development. The elements of community building include education, training, leadership, natural resources and using all these for the promotion of well-being of the individual through the practice of values and traditions. The pre-condition for community building is participation of community collectively, unitedly in all stages of its development.

Realizing the relationship between the literacy and community building, the Government of India has launched a number of programmes such as adult education programmes, total literacy campaigns, continuing education centres, education guarantee schemes in non formal sector and Sarva Shiksha Abhiyan under DPEP, formal schooling etc., in the formal stream of education for the eradication of the illiteracy among the people. Inspite of all the efforts of the Government for promotion of education among the masses to enhance their participation in community building could not reach the level expected due to slow growth of literacy, ignorance of their role in the development process. Keeping the limitation of the Government in penetration in the community, has paved a way for the genesis of alternative strategies.

NGOs in Community Building

The failure of the government in reaching the downtrodden and effective implementation of the developmental programmes resulted in the establishment of alternative agencies namely the Non-Governmental Organization. The NGOs are the democratic institutions formed out of a union of like-minded people with a set of objectives and a set of regulations to govern themselves. The capacity of the NGOs in reaching the target for whom the programmes are formulated and implemented are found to be more effective than the Governmental Institutions which has hierarchically arranged administration and rigid in formalities. As a result of the smooth functioning and ability in reaching the target by the NGOs, the government has encouraged the participation of NGOs in the implementation of various initiatives of the government.

The NGOs are involved in all spheres of life of an individual starting from womb to tomb. In other words they are capable of pertaining into various sections of the society to accelerate their pace of development. The NGOs are involved in the areas of health, education, welfare, skill development, income-generation, old aged, physically handicap, social defense etc. It also involved in target-oriented programmes such as women welfare, tribal welfare, BC & SC welfare, aged, pre-school children etc. The above is an indication to show that NGOs apart from the government is one of the biggest network created for covering all the sections of the population by the community as an alternative to the government for its own welfare.

The NGOs can play a pivotal role in the community building. Creation of awareness among the community about the various avenues and opportunities created by the government in the form of developmental programmes for the welfare of the wider community and empowering the community to demand their share is possibly only through the NGOs. Further, by empowering the community leads to the enhanced participation of the people in the community development activities conceive and implemented. Further, it is rightly said that the NGOs conceive strategies for participation of the target before launching the programmes. As a result, they are able to attain the objectives.

The NGOs can co-ordinate all the agencies and programmes functioning at the community level to improve their efficiency and also to avoid duplication of efforts of the institutions such as schools,

SHGs, Youth Clubs, Women's Clubs, adult literacy centres, Education Guaranteed Scheme, Sarva Shiksha Abhiyan etc., for the welfare of the community.

No doubt, the NGOs too have inherited problems of recognization from the community and the government. The community will recognize the institutions only if they believe that these institutions will solve their problems and assist them in difficult situations. Once the community recognizes the services of the agency, the community obeys the leadership of the NGOs.

In view of the recognization from the community, the NGOs should plan its activities in integrated programmes rather than isolated programmes at the community level. These agencies should create awareness among the community about the importance of the education in individual development and the overall development of the community as a whole. Further, they can take up the programmes to create awareness about the various developmental programmes initiated by the government for various groups enabling them to utilize the opportunities. A number of agencies are providing specialized services to the community and this information will enable the community to make use of the services effectively.

Suggestions

- Community education centres may be established in all the habitations by integrating the existing schools, crèche centres, EGS centres, Adult Literacy centres, Continuing Education centres etc., so as to increase the scope and coverage of the target.
- The community education centre should act as a single window for all the information relating to the developmental programmes.
- A community education centre should act as a communication centre for onward transmission of information from community to the Governmental Agencies and disseminate the information in the community, which was supplied by the government.
- The community education centres should have a library where all categories of people can use it according to their tastes and needs.
- It should act as a cultural and recreational centre where the community can display the cultural heritage of the

community for the benefit of the younger generations and it will be a centre for recreation for all age groups.

- It should create communal harmony, national integration among the people.
- Community Education Centres should be able to inculcate gender sensitive, gender biased attitudes among the people.
- They must be equipped to promote need based vocational education.

It is suggested that such centres may be created in all the habitations to make them more relevant and useful to the community. The NGOs are the suitable agencies to create such centres on experimental basis through its resources. On assessing the performance of these centres in the course of time there may be replicated to other areas by making suitable modifications in it's functioning. Then only the NGOs can play good role in community building. Further, to make any programme a success, the five Cs are essential. They are Commitment, Collectivity, Connectivity, Co-operation and Co-ordination. Then only any development can be achieved.

9

Socio-Economic Conditions of Traditional Fishing Households in Andhra Pradesh

S. Surapa Raju

Marine Fishing is an age-old and caste based activity and involves high risk with uncertainty of incomes. Often the fishermen households face cyclones, tidal waves and floods, which cause more damages to their properties and lives. This is evident from the recent tsunami, which hit on 26th of December 2004 caused ninety per cent of the human loss particularly from the Traditional fishermen households and more damage occurred to their fishing units and equipments, houses. Traditional fishermen households are defined as the households who operate small crafts without engines and in fishing operations they used to go into the sea either alone or accompanied by a few crewmembers. Hard and strenuous workers, adventurous sprit in going into the vast sea and sharing tendencies, characterize them but they are very poor in socio-economic and cultural aspects. They inherited high skills in fishing activity, but their standard of living is very poor despite of development in fisheries sector.

Over the years while the population of small-scale fishermen has increased by more than 20.8 per cent, the average production of each fishermen declined by more than half which resulted in 98.5 per cent of the fishermen population descending below the poverty line. While the traditional fishermen who constitute 89 per cent of the total fishermen households caught a negligible quantity of fish, the mechanized fish gear operators, who are very small in number have been taking away the bulk of the catch viz. more than 92 per cent. This is having a total effect upon the lives and economy of the traditional fishermen, giving rise to several incidents of breach of law and order (Kocherry). The present study aims to know the socio-economic conditions of the Traditional fishermen households in Gilakaladindi village in Krishna district of Andhra Pradesh. The major focus of the study is to study the investment, operational expenditure, and net income of the households; analyse scale of economies of the traditional craft; and also to study the socio-economic conditions of the sample households. Gilakaladindi village of Krishna district in Andhra Pradesh is selected for this study. It is located near Machilipatnam town, which is the district headquarter of Krishna district of Andhra Pradesh. This village consists of 984 households, of which 56 households own traditional fishing crafts. All the 56 households were interviewed and collected information with the help of the structured schedule.

Investment, Costs and Returns

Information was collected from the sample households on income, costs and returns to know the viability of the unit. Traditional fishing households need to invest some amounts on productive assets, which are very much essential to catch fish. On an average the traditional craft owners invested Rs. 25.036 to acquire the craft, gears and other equipment. Costs are two types namely fixed costs and variable costs. Fixed costs are defined that whether the craft is operated or not, the craft owner has to incurred some expenditure on few items such as depreciation on hull, gear & engine and insurance, interest on loans etc. where as in the case of variable costs the fisherman has to spend some amounts everyday to operate his craft, which are very much essential, and without these costs he could not go for fishing into the sea. These costs include ice/salt repairs and maintenance, food for crew, wages/share of the workers etc. The traditional craft owners spend the highest amount on wages (78%) to their total variable costs, since they operate the crafts manually. Due to use of inferior quality wood in craft leads to more repairs. Nearly 14 per cent of total operational expenditure is on repairs and maintenance. (Table-1).

The traditional fishermen obtained eight varieties of fish namely Pomfret, Seer, Shark, Hilsa, Rays, Milkfish, Anchovies and other miscellaneous varieties. Among these varieties, the fishermen netted more quantity of Rays (28%) and 29 per cent other varieties of fishes. In value terms, more money was obtained to Pomfret fishes and the least amount was obtained to anchovies. With regard to per kg value of fish, Rs. 23.2 and Rs. 21.2 were obtained to Pomfret and Hilsa fishes respectively (Table-2). During the period between July to October the fishermen households catch more quantity and value of fish (Table-3). On an average 2,969 kgs of fish captured in a year by the small-scale fisherman and its value was Rs. 32,667. They netted more value and quantity of fish during the period between July–October months (Table-3). On the whole the fisherman household gets Rs. 11.0 per kg of fish. The field observations revealed that these traditional fishing crafts got very low price per kg of fish may be due to many reasons; *(i)* lack of technology used in operation of the crafts which may results *(a)* less distance covered in the sea for fishing; *(b)* less quality and varieties of gears used; *(c)* more time taken for travel which may restrict their actual fishing time. *(ii)* perishable good; *(iii)* credit market linkages; *(iv)* failure of cooperative societies in marketing the fish; *(v)* lack of proper infrastructure facilities. The traditional craft owner gets only Rs. 8,111 annually for their fishing activity.

Table-1
Distribution of Component-wise Investment of Traditional Crafts

Investment	*Average (value in Rs.)*
Hull	10,486 (41.9)
Fish Gear	13,179 (52.6)
Others	1,371 (5.5)
Total	25,036 (100.0)
Fixed Costs	*Average (value in Rs.)*
Depreciation on Hull, Engine & Gear	2,138 (53.7)
Insurance	572 (14.4)
Interest on loans	1,249 (31.3)
Others	26 (0.6)
Total	3,985 (100.0)
Variable Cost	*Average (value in Rs.)*
Ice/Salt	1,743 (8.5)
Repairs and maintenance	2,805 (13.6)
Wages/share of the worker	16,023 (77.9)
Total	20,571 (100.0)
Total Cost	*Average (value in Rs.)*
Fixed costs	3985 (16.2)
Variable costs	20571 (83.8)
Total costs	24,556 (100.0)

Table-2
Variety Wise Catch Particulars of Traditional Fishermen Households

Sl. No.	*Fish Varieties*	*Quantity (in Kgs.)*	*Value (in Rs.)*	*Per kg Value of Fish (in Rs.)*
1.	Pomfret	330 (11.12)	7663 (23.45)	23.2
2.	Seer	236 (7.95)	4619 (14.14)	19.6
3.	Shark	376 (12.66)	6422 (19.66)	17.1
4.	Hilsa	254 (8.54)	5389 (16.50)	21.2
5.	Rays	831 (27.99)	3203 (9.80)	3.8
6.	Milk Fish	43 (1.45)	545 (1.67)	12.7
7.	Anchovies	46 (1.55)	469 (1.43)	10.2
8.	Others	853 (28.73)	4357 (13.34)	5.1
	Total	2969 (100.0)	32,667 (100.0)	11.0

Table-3
Period, Quantity and Value Wise Catch Particulars of Fishermen Households

Sl. No.	*Periods*	*Quantity (in Kgs.)*	*Value (in Rs.)*	*Per kg Value of Fish (in Rs.)*
1.	November-February	990 (33.3)	10,922 (33.4)	11.0
2.	March-June	486 (16.4)	5035 (15.4)	10.4
3.	July-October	1,493 (50.3)	16,710 (51.2)	11.2
	Total	2969 (100.0)	32,667 (100.0)	11.0

Table-4
Input *vs.* Out Put

Particulars		*Rs.*
Total value of fish catch		32,667
Investment		25,036
Output/Input	(32.667/25036)	1.30
Net profit		8,111

Relationship Among the Selected Variables

Seven characteristics of the craft was identified namely length, distance, fishing days, fishing hours, gear value, age of the craft and value of the catch. Among the selected characteristics (variables), craft length with distance and value of catch were having a positive relationship at one per cent significant level. Generally, the fishermen operate their traditional craft with manual labour, which needs more crew to operate the boat and nets. Lengthy craft can also carry more water, more ice, more crew, more nets etc., which enable the fishermen to go to far off fishing grounds. When the length of the craft increases, the value of the catch also increases for the traditional craft, as it carries more workers, covers more fishing areas, more variety of nets etc., which enable the craft to get more catches and more value. A Positive and significant correlation (at 1% level) was noticed between the distance covered in the sea with fishing days, gear value, workers and catch value. It is found that a 0.62 correlation co-efficient is observed between the distance covered and the number of fishing days. Similarly, between the distance covered and with the catch value, there is a positive correlation (0.76) at one per cent significance level, as more coverage of fishing area helps the fishermen to get higher returns.

Distance covered by the traditional craft with variables like fishing time and age of the craft shows a negative correlation. As the coverage of distance increases, the fishing time or effort decreases which may be due to more time taken for travel to cover long distance by manual operation and this reduces the actual time for fishing. A negative correlation is also observed between distance and age of the craft. It is obvious that the age-old crafts cover less distance. As the age of the craft increases, the distance covered in the sea decreases due to unexpected breakdowns.

Positive correlation at one per cent significant level was observed for all variables with fishing days except for age of the craft. As the number of fishing days increases, the fishing time also increases which can lead to more attempts at fishing. A positive relationship was noticed between the fishing days and the gear value, which was calculated on the basis of net length, width and type of nets, material used in the nets etc. Traditional craft owners are using more nets and various varieties of nets to catch fish in different seasons. The traditional crafts required more number of crew to operate boats as well as nets besides increase in the number of fishing days to catch fish. It is obvious that the increased number of fishing days had led to more catches. The correlation between the fishing days and age of the craft is negative at one per cent level of significance.

Table–5
Matrix of Correlation Co-efficients on Characteristics of the Traditional Craft

Variables	*Length of the Craft*	*Distance Covered*	*Days of Fishing*	*Fishing Hours*	*Gear Value*	*Age of the Craft*	*Catch Value*
Length of the Craft	1.00	0 .64**	0.37	0.31	0.26	-0.34	0.42**
Distance Covered		1.00	0.62**	-0.68**	0.59**	-0.48**	0 .76**
No. of Fishing Days			1.00	0 .80**	0 .47**	-0.53**	0 .78**
Total Fishing Hours				1.00	0.57**	-0.43**	0 .82**
Gear Value					1.00	-0.42**	0 .78**
Age of the Craft						1.00	-0.49**
Value of the Catch							1.00

Note: ** Denotes significant at 1 per cent level.

In other words, with an increase in the age of the craft, the efficiency of the craft decreases due to the possibility of frequent breakdowns and repairs.

Regression Analysis

An attempt is made to identify the factors associated with the value of catch obtained to the traditional craft. Like in agricultural production, marine fish production requires land, capital and labour. In this context, sea is treated as land, fishermen as labour and crafts and gears as capital inputs. There is some similarity between agriculture production and marine fish production. In the case of land, there is gestation period for the crop; where as in sea, fish is already available in the form of a ready crop. In the case of agriculture production, there is some time lag to get the crop. To catch marine fish, craft & gear and labour are the inputs, which indicate 'Capital' and 'Labour'. Land (sea) is not required to purchase and it is available as a free gift for marine fishermen. Explanatory variables (inputs) such as craft and gear (capital), crew (workers) and fuel (energy) are selected for this regression analysis to estimate the ***Cobb-Douglas Production***.

The functional form is:

$Y = A\ K^{á}\ L^{a}\ E^{ā}$

$\ln y = \ln a + b \ln K + c \ln L + d \ln E$

Where,

Y = Value of catch per day (Rs.)

K = Value of craft and gear and other equipment (capital)

L = Number of workers per day employed (labour/crew)

E = Value of oil consumption per day (energy)

Table-6
Estimated Production Function by Craft Technology

Variables	*Particulars*
Capital	0.320* (9.308)
Labour	0.732* (5.755)
Energy	–
Constant	1.764
R^2	0.87
'F' Value	187.294*
Return to scale	1.052

Note: Brackets in the parenthesis indicate T Ratios.

* Indicates those regression co-efficients are Significant at 5 per cent level.

Actually, three essential inputs are required for the fishermen to catch fish, namely *(i)* capital (craft, gears and equipment); *(ii)* labour (crew); and *(iii)* energy (oil). But in the case of traditional craft owner, fishermen require only two inputs namely capital and labour to capture the fish (production) and not using the third input as they are not using any mechanical devices, which require energy (oil).

The R^2 of 0.87 gives 87 per cent of variation in the output explained by the regression analysis. Both the capital and labour are found to be positively and statistically significant at 5 per cent level on per day value of catch. Both these independent variables are positive and significant and the values indicate that there is scope for increasing per day value of catch by increasing the level of their inputs. Investment on craft was observed to be significant, as it requires more quality wood, length, width etc. to carry more crew, nets, water, ice etc. More varieties of gears require for them to catch different varieties of fish in different seasons (Raju; 2001). The elasticity of capital is 0.32 indicating one per cent increase in capital, as a result of which, the expected percentage of increase in the value of fish catch would be 0.32. The elasticity of labour is 0.73, which indicates a one per cent increase in workers, as a result of which; the expected percentage of increase in the value of fish catch would be 0.73.

The analysis suggests that more labour and capital are required to buy more length, width and quality crafts and more varieties of fishing gear to catch more varieties of fish and thereby they may get more value for their fish catch. Returns to scale are observed for this technology at 1.052, say that increasing returns to scale exist. So we have to conduct a test by estimating the equation log viz., $Y/L = \mu$.

$\text{Log } y = \mu + B_1 \log C + B_2 \log L$ unrestricted Cobb-Douglas production function

If $B_1 + B_2 > 1$	increasing returns to scale
$B_1 + B_2 < 1$	decreasing returns to scale
If $B_1 + B_2 = 1$	constant returns to scale

$B_1 + B_2 = 1.052$ to say that increasing returns to scale is existing; we have to conduct a test. We estimate the equation $\text{Log } Y/L = á + B_1 \log C/L$ constant returns to scale to except this F value > Table value

Note that $\text{Log } Y/L = \log Y - \log L$

$$\text{Log } C/L = \log C - \log L$$

Now R^2 from both the Regressions.

$$F = \frac{(R^2_{unres} - R^2_{res}) / m}{R^2_{unres} / N - K} = \frac{0.876 - 0.794}{0.876 / 56 - 3} = 4.82$$

R^2 Unrestricted	=	0.876
R^2 Restricted	=	0.794
N (sample)	=	56
K (parameters)	=	3
M	=	number of restrictions

Critical value of F for 1,53 and the difference is 4.02

F value = 4.82

Since estimated F is greater than the table value, we reject the hypothesis therefore, Increasing Returns to Scale operate.

Socio-Economic Conditions

Data collected and tabulated on socio-economic conditions of sample households in the selected village. It deals with the basic information about the individual as well as household particulars of the traditional craft owners. Age, marital status, educational status, occupation, etc. are collected and tabulated in the personal data and type of family, type of house, source of lighting, source of drinking water, assets owned, average number of earners, family size, average income from fisheries, income from other than fishing, total household income, per capita income and indebtedness are collected and tabulated under the household data.

Most of the traditional fishing households are in the age group of 31-50 years. 89 per cent of the total sample households are married and the rest of them are widowers. 64 per cent of the sample households are illiterate and among the literate households 90 per cent of them studied up to primary level and only 10 per cent of them reached to high school level. Fishing is the primary occupation of sample households and to supplement their incomes they are engaging in fish trade and labourers in aquaculture.

With regard to type family 77 per cent of the total households live in joint family. 23 per cent of the total sample households live in kutcha houses and still 20 per cent of the households are using kerosene for the lighting purposes. Most of the sample households use the common piped water for the drinking purposes. The average family size is 5.90 and 3.52 members are earners. Fishing is the primary activity for the households and they earn income of Rs. 8,111 from this activity.

Conclusions

The traditional craft owners operate their crafts in 196 days in a year and catch 2969 kgs of fish worth of Rs. 32,667. But their net income from fishing activity is only Rs. 8,111per year. The regression analysis suggests that more labour and capital are required to buy more length, width and quality crafts and more varieties of fishing gears to catch more varieties of fishes in different seasons to improve their incomes. But their present socio-economic conditions reveal that still they are living below the poverty line. So government should give more motorized crafts and adequate nets to these fishing households by extending more subsidies, then only they will come out from the poverty.

Table-7
Socio-Economic Conditions of Sample Households

Personal Data of the Sample Households	*Total*	*Percentage*
Age		
21–30	5	0.9
31–40	17	30.4
41–50	19	33.9
51–60	14	25.0
Above 60	1	1.8
Total	**56**	**100.0**
Marital Status		
Married	50	89.3
Widower	6	10.7
Total	**56**	**100.0**
Educational Status		
Illiterate	36	64.3
Literate	20	35.7
Total	**56**	**100.0**
Primary	18	2
Secondary	90.0	10.0
Total	**20**	**100.0**
Occupation		
Primary Occupation	56	100.0
(Fisheries)	32	57.1
Secondary	18	56.3
Workers Fish Trading	14	43.7
Total	**32**	**100.0**

Table–8
Household Data of the Sample Traditional Craft Owners

Household Data of the Sample Traditional Craft Owners	*Total*	*Percentage*
Type of Family		
Nuclear	13	23.2
Joint	43	76.8
Total	**56**	**100.0**
Type of House		
Pucca	14	25.0
Semi-pucca	29	51.8
Kutcha	13	23.2
Total	**56**	**100.0**
Source of Lighting		
Electricity	45	80.4
Kerosene	11	19.6
Total	**56**	**100.0**
Source of Drinking Water		
Tap water common source	41	73.2
Bore well	15	26.8
Total	**56**	**100.0**
Average number of earners	3.52	
Average number of dependents	2.38	
Average family size	5.90	

REFERENCES

Apostle, *et.al.*, (1998), *Community, State and Market on the Atlantic Rim: Challenges to Modernity in the Fisheries*, University of Toronto Press, Toronto.

Bailey, C. (1982), *Small Scale Fisheries of San Miguel Bay*, Philippines, ICLARM Technical Paper 10, Manila.

Council for Social Development (1988), *A Report on Techno-Socio Economic Survey of Fishermen Community in Andhra Pradesh*, A Government of India Project, sponsored by Directorate of Fisheries, Andhra Pradesh.

Emerson, D.K. (1980), *Rethinking Artisanal Fisheries Development: Western Concepts, Asian Experiences*, World Bank Staff Working Paper No. 423, World Bank Publication, Washington DC.

F.A.O. (2000), *Poverty in Coastal Fishing Communities. An Advisory Committee on Fishery Research*, Third Session, December 5-8, 2000, Food and Agricultural organization, Rome.
Http: //WWW. FAO. Org/DOCRELP/MEETING/003X8905E. html.

Kocherry, Thomas (1998), *Indian Fisheries over 50 Years*, published by Books for Change (A Unit of Action Aid Karnataka Projects), Bangalore.

Raju, S. Surapa (2001), "Beach Landing Craft Scheme: A Boon or Burden?", in Indian Economic Panorama, Vol. 10, No. 4, pp. 56-60, January 2001.

Raju, S. Surapa (2004), "Empowerment of Fishing Households through Technology", R. Venkat Ravi *et.al.*, (eds.), *Empowerment of People, Grassroots Strategies and Issues*, Kanishka Publishers, New Delhi.

Raju, S. Surapa (2003), "Economics of Fishing Crafts: A Comparative Study in Andhra Pradesh", *Journal of Fisheries Economics and Development*, Vol. V, No. 1, January-June, pp. 1-14.

Raju, S. Surapa (2004), "Impact of Craft Technology on Marine Fishermen Households" *Man and Development*, Vol. XXVI, No. 2, June, pp. 93-104.

Sinha, N.K. (2000), "Code of Conduct for Responsible Fisheries", *Bay of Bengal News*, Vol. 11, No. 18, September.

Thorpe, Andy *et.al.*, (2000), "The New Economic Model and Marine Fisheries Development in Latin America", *World Development*, Vol. 28, No. 9, pp. 1689-1702.

10

Community Radio, Reproductive and Child Health: Experience of a Backward District of Uttar Pradesh

B.P. Thaigarajan

In many ways, communication is at the heart of development. There is a lack of awareness of the value of communications, particularly radio, in development. Radio, as the development tool, can be effective in reaching wider audience at a low cost. The potentiality and scope of radio in reaching the mass audiences is relatively higher, where the conventional media channels did not meet the needs of information and education. In the past 25 years, there has been a sevenfold increase in the number of radios in the developing world. The figure is now estimated to be 500 million – ten times the number of television sets (Sarah Shuffell, 2003). It was also pointed out that the fifty per cent illiteracy among women in low-income countries that puts newspapers beyond their reach, radio might be their only source of unbiased information. In India, the number of radios is many times higher than the television sets. Moreover, radio can serve as an important agent of social change with appropriate message production and reception factors.

In India, the concept of Community Radio Programme is not a new one. During the Green Revolution, India experienced greater impact in the food production, especially in rice production through the use of hybrid variety of seeds, fertilizers and pesticides mainly due to the activated community radio programme. The radio programme could reach the nook and corner of the country and disseminate be able to the needed information with greater impact. Similarly health and family welfare messages have also reached many homes in all over the country through this users' friendly medium of communication.

Community Radio Approach

In this line, Population Foundation of India (PFI) New Delhi, a funding NGO at the national level working for the cause of population and development issues has conceived and promote a community radio programmes as the part of advocacy campaign. PFI launched its first radio programme, namely *DEHLEEZ (Threshold)* way back in 1993 as an entertainment-education for the adolescents. The community radio programme was again started by the Foundation in a soap opera style to bring reproductive health message alive in 2000. The radio programmes were started in the States of Karnataka, Uttar Pradesh and Madhya Pradesh through All India Radio (AIR) in that chronology order. The target segments for the radio programmes were Soliga tribal community in Mysore district, tribal and rural community of Sonbhadra and Indore districts. PFI purchased the slot from AIR and broadcast through local AIR station such as Mysore (Karnataka), Obra (Uttar Pradesh) and Indore (Madhya Pradesh).

Strategy for the Community Radio Programme

The main approach by PFI is that the experts for the community produce the community radio programme with the interactive inputs from the community members and writers. It is produced in the form of radio drama serial with 52 episodes of broadcasting. Each episode elaborates a topic in population and development issue with an absorbing story line. The script of the episodes is usually discussed at the scriptwriters' workshop, where the selected scriptwriters of native flavour, are oriented towards the subject. Topics and their ways of representation are discussed in detail with the writers, keeping in mind the cultural milieu and dialects involved, so that relevant topics and themes emerge. Subsequently the draft of the script is pre-tested improved, enacted and recorded. As a reception factor in order to capture the broadcast in the villages, an NGO in the hinterland will do the spadework at grassroot level, so that the target audience will effectively listen to the programme. During the broadcast time, NGO workers will visit the villagers and observe the listeners and discussed about the radio programme after the broadcast. The Community Radio Programme has been monitored and evaluated.

Community Radio Programme in Uttar Pradesh

In Uttar Pradesh, the district Sonbhadra was selected for this programme implementation due to its relative backwardness in the state in terms of RCH and other related indicators such as low female literacy, low coverage of child immunization, high proportion of girls marrying below 18 years and low population density (Table 1).

Table-1
Comparative Status of Sonbhadra District with Uttar Pradesh

Indicators	*Uttar Pradesh*	*Sonbhadra*
Total Population	166,052,859	1,463,468
% Decadal growth rate	25.8	36.1
Population Density	70.5	21.6
Female Literacy	43.0	34.3
% girls married below 18 years	45.5	67.0
Birth order 3 and above	58.1	60.5
Total unmet need	32.5	32.2
Per cent current user	31.3	30.5
Complete ANC	12.8	8.8
Safe Delivery	32.8	24.4
Complete Immunization	46.3	18.8
Knowledge of AIDS of females	24.3	11.6

The location of the district was also an added attraction for implementation, since Sonbhadra is surrounded by the three other backward states, namely, Jharkhand, Bihar and Chhattisgarh.

SONBHADRA MAP

In Uttar Pradesh, the radio programme was called as 'UJALA' (Brightness). The radio programme was aired through AIR, Obra's Frequency Modulation channel. The local NGO at the grassroot level was 'Banvasi Seva Ashram', (BSA) Govindpur, Sonbhadra. In this programme, 52 episodes, 30 minutes duration each, were prepared and aired. The main RCH issues broadcast were on age at marriage, female feticide, population issues, small family size norm, antenatal care, safe delivery, post natal care and contraceptives. Other topics covered in the radio programme are role and responsibilities of members of Panchayat Raj Institutions, empowerment of women, literacy and education, common communicable diseases and their prevention and water supply and sanitation and food and nutrition.

UJALA was launched on March 19, 2001, after the two-day scrip-writing workshop held at BSA UJALA was broadcast in every Monday at 7.30 p.m. for 30 minutes. The produced programme comprised of 30 episodes and this programme was aired for 52 weeks, which includes repeat broadcast. The advocacy message styles in the UJALA programme were more of rational appeals than emotional appeals. It has both negative and positive appeals in the story line. It has more of individual appeals than mass appeals that had repetitive in nature. UJALA radio programme emphasized the definite conclusions rather than open conclusions.

Evaluation of UJALA Radio Programme

In order to evaluate the radio programme, a household survey was conducted in May 2002, covering 1707 households immediately after the completion of broadcast of all the episodes in Sonbhadra district. The evaluation was carried out with using 20 cluster sampling procedure and it aimed to have a five programme listeners in each cluster. In other words, in each sampled village/cluster, the search for UJALA programme listener was carried out from one household to other, till the required number of five UJALA listeners was reached. The media reach of UJALA programme was estimated as the percentage of total programme listeners to the total number of households searched to get the total listeners.

The procedure for searching the programme listeners was as follows: After reaching the village, the village was hypothetically divided into four parts. In each part, the search for UJALA listener began from randomly selected first household. In the first household, anybody in the household ever listened to UJALA programme in the past year was enquired. If identified, further detailed questioning was carried out to know the effectiveness of the programme. Otherwise, the household details like household number, door number name of the head of the household, number of adult members (aged 18+) were asked and noted down. Then the next household was searched for the programme listeners. Once the first segment of the village is completed, the investigator moved into the next segment. Likewise the investigator covered the whole village in order to get the target of 5 programme listeners. In case, the target listeners could not be reached in the village, there was no replacement of village. The investigator subsequently moved into the next sample village for searching the new 5 programme listeners of the village.

It was decided that the 5 programme listeners in each cluster/village would be searched in 20 sampled cluster/villages to search a total of 100 programme listeners in Sonbhadra district. The required number of villages (20) was selected from the list of villages of 1991 Census, following Population Proportion to Size (PPS) sampling procedure. In order to get the Media Reach of UJALA programme, details of all the households contacted were separately noted with minimum details. Once the listener is identified, detailed questionnaire on the Impact/Effectiveness of UJALA programme was administered and responses were recorded for later analysis. Apart from this household survey the evaluation team also took some of the letters received by AIR Obra about the UJALA programme and verified them to check that these letters were not fake.

Results of the Evaluation Study

The targeted sample size was 100 listeners of UJALA programme but evaluation team could interview only 53 listeners (49 complete and 4 partial interviews) after listing the 1707 households. These 4 partial interviews were not included in the analysis because of missing information.

Table-2
Percentage Reach of UJALA Community Radio Programme in Various Sampled Villages of Sonbhadra District, Uttar Pradesh

PSU No.	*Village Name*	*Listeners Interviewed*	*Total Number of Households Searched to get Required Listeners*	*No. of Houses Searched per Listener*
1.	Conga	4	66	16.50
2.	Majhouli	5	104	20.80
3.	Aura Dand	1	67	67.00
4.	Anapara	1	87	87.00
5.	Kirwil	4	95	23.75
6.	Jamshila	0	96	–
7.	Dadihara	3	91	30.33

Contd...

PSU No.	Village Name	Listeners Interviewed	Total Number of Households Searched to get Required Listeners	No. of Houses Searched per Listener
8.	Kushmaha	4	83	20.75
9.	Ramgarh	2	115	57.50
10.	Siltham	1	137	137.00
11.	Jugali	5	87	17.40
12.	Belwania	3	84	28.00
13.	Raiwari	0	39	–
14.	Sirvit	0	115	–
15.	Raiya	1	92	92.00
16.	Belach 4	88	22.00	
17.	Lashara	4	66	16.50
18.	Bahuarah	2	58	29.00
19.	Bahura	3	105	35.00
20.	Tiara	2	32	16.00
	Total	**49**	**1707**	**34.84**

Among these 20 villages selected for the evaluation purpose 8 villages were from lower Sone area of South of Sone, where BSA is working. The rest 12 villages were from Upper Sone or Northern part of Sone, where BSA is not working.

Major Findings

Particulars about the respondents, media habits, knowledge level of UJALA, opinion of the radio programme mainly on the contents and overall reaction to the programme, any change after listening to the programme were discussed.

Profile of Respondents

The sample size was 49 spread across 20 villages in Sonbhadra district. Out of 49 respondents 79.6 per cent were males and 20.6 per cent were females. Most of the respondents (63%) were young in the age group of below 30 years. Majority of the respondents i.e. 85.7 per cent (42) belong to Hindu religion. Distribution of caste reveals that the majority of the respondents 59.2 per cent belong to Backward Castes, 22.4 were Scheduled Castes, 8.2 per cent were Scheduled Caste and 10.2 per cent were General Caste. Regarding educational attainment, 22 per cent were illiterates, 14 per cent were below primary education and the remaining (64%) was above primary level of education.

Media at Home

Radio continues to dominate the lives of the respondents in villages where almost 90 per cent of the respondents had a radio set in their house and only 10 per cent respondents did not have a radio set in their home. Because of high illiteracy newspaper and magazine reading was very poor and only 12.2 per cent and 34.7 per cent respondents read newspaper and magazine respectively at their home.Television was available in 32.7 per cent households and Cable TV was available in only 4 per cent households. Regular radio listening habit (6-7 days per week) was found among 80 per cent of the respondents.

Listening Pattern of UJALA Programme

As mentioned earlier, 52 episodes of UJALA were broadcast during March to November 2001 that includes 30 original and 22 repeat broadcast. Listeners were asked about number of episodes broadcast and number of episodes they listened to. If the number(s) of episodes listened to was less than 30, they were further asked about the reasons of not listening to the remaining episodes.

Majority of the programme listeners i.e. 71.4 per cent had no idea about the total number of episodes broadcast and only one-sixth of them could tell that 30 original episodes were broadcast. Approximately 6 per cent listeners told that 10 or fewer episodes were broadcast and only one listener told that more than 30 episodes were aired. Every respondent was able to listen to at least a few episodes of UJALA only 10.2 per cent did not remember the exact number of episodes they were able to listen. 28.6 per cent listeners could manage to listen 5 or less episodes and 24.5 per cent listeners could listen 6-10 episodes of the programme and about 28 per cent listeners were able to listen more than 20 episodes of UJALA. The reasons cited by the listeners for not listening to all the episodes of UJALA were busy with work or study, out of home for some time, FM band radio was not available before and purchased it very late, lack of proper electric supply and frequent power failure and radio was out of order or under repair.

Recall of Programme Timings

UJALA programme was broadcast once a week on every Monday from 7.30 – 8.00 p.m. for half and hour. The programme listeners were asked to recall the exact day and timings of UJALA broadcast. A significant number of programme listeners were able to recall that UJALA was broadcast on Monday and only 28.6 per cent listeners wrongly informed the day of UJALA broadcast.

Overall Reaction to the Programme

The findings substantiate the immense interest it generated among the programme listeners. A very high proportion of listeners i.e. 92 per cent have rated the programme as very interesting, and 96 per cent listeners have correctly identified the programme format as drama or noutanki. It is very interesting to know that all the 49 listeners have found the programme timing suitable and convenient. It is to be mentioned that in a predominantly agricultural household, it is difficult for a person, especially women, to find timings other than evenings or leisurely listening. The language of any programme and performance of the artist's is certainly the key factors, which makes the programme very popular and easily understandable. All the listeners have found the UJALA programmes as very informative, its language used as of understandable nature. Performance of artists worked in various episodes was very good as well as story line was also quite interesting for all the 49 listeners.

Knowledge about Specific Issues of Broadcast

The respondents were asked to give specific information about the programme to know whether they really understood the programme.

Table-3
Did UJALA Broadcast the Following Issues

S.No.	*Issues*	*Yes*		*No*		*Can't Say*	
		N	*%*	*N*	*%*	*N*	*%*
1.	Abolition of dowry	44	89.8	3	6.12	2	89.8
2.	About terrorism	4	8.16	43	87.76	2	89.8
3.	Education of girl child	42	85.7	5	10.2	2	89.8
4.	Adolescent problems	29	59.18	17	34.69	3	6.12
5.	Agricultural problems	25	51.02	21	42.86	3	6.12
6.	Age at marriage	41	83.67	5	10.2	3	6.12

Contd...

S.No.	Issues	Yes		No		Can't Say	
		N	%	N	%	N	%
7.	Cotton cultivation	3	6.12	43	87.76	3	6.12
8.	About panchayats members	33	67.35	13	26.53	3	6.12
9.	About electricity	8	16.33	38	77.55	3	6.12
10.	Family planning	42	85.71	4	8.16	3	6.12
11.	About revolution	12	24.49	34	69.39	3	6.12
12.	Female foeticide	32	65.31	14	28.57	3	6.12
13.	Prenatal & postnatal care	33	67.35	13	26.53	3	6.12
14.	About fertilizers	7	14.29	39	79.59	3	6.12
15.	Population problems	39	79.59	7	14.29	3	6.12
16.	Prevention of diseases	38	77.55	8	16.33	3	6.12
17.	Safe delivery	37	75.51	9	18.37	3	6.12
18.	Self employment for women	31	63.27	15	30.61	3	6.12
19.	Women education	39	79.59	7	14.29	3	6.12

When asked to name the specific issues of broadcast, a majority of the listeners reported (89.8%) abolition of dowry as a major issue, followed by education of girl child and family planning 85.7 per cent each, age at marriage 83.7 per cent, population problems and women education 79.6 per cent each; prevention of diseases 77.5 per cent, and safe delivery 75.5 per cent respondents. Most of the respondents could identify the correct issues of UJALA broadcast and very few of them identified some wrong issues.

Impact of UJALA Programme

The community radio programme greatly enhanced the knowledge on RCH issues of the listeners in the villages. Most of the listeners (86%) considered that UJALA was not only entertaining them but at the same time it was also giving some useful information. Respondents were also asked whether UJALA changed their views about Reproductive and Child Health issues. Three-fourths affirmed that it changed their ideas, whereas 10 per cent of listeners told that there is no change in their ideas about RCH after listening to UJALA and about 16 per cent listeners did not reply to this question. A very significant proportion of the respondents (93.9%) considered the information presented in this programme as very useful. Majority of the listeners (85.7%) considered that UJALA was definitely trying to persuade trying to persuade them to change their ideas/views about certain issues.

Conclusions

The media reach of UJALA radio programme was around three per cent in the sample villages. Compared to the vast hinterland of radio station, this media reach is very small. However the main reasons for the low media reach are widespread poverty in the region resulting people did not have money to buy radio and time to listen radio programmes. In addition, very high illiteracy in this area hurdled the people not to listen any informative programme, but to listen to popular song based programmes. The role of BSA, as the grassroot level NGO in popularizing UJALA was noticeable. It was observed that in almost all the villages the field teams visited, they could see the penetration of BSA either through their centres or by seeing the villagers easily identifying the BSA volunteers. It was also reported that the listeners of BSA project villages got their initial knowledge about UJALA, through BSA only.

Frequency Modulation (FM) Channel: In this tribal prone low-density area, it was observed that possession of radio along with wristwatch and cycle is considered as the status symbol. Moreover, radio with OBRA Channel (FM channel is called here in this way) was mainly with well to do family. It has been noticed that on an average 10 persons possess the radio in a village and among them only 2 or 3 persons possessed the Obra channel. Some villagers pointed out that to have Obra channel is a costly affair and it costs around Rs. 110 that they cannot afford. Even the villagers mortgaged their radios for urgent money.

UJALA is not totally free from the drawbacks that other community radio programmes have. The main shortcoming is that radio programmes are mainly of awareness creation programme rather than persuasive in nature. Another limitation is that rigidity of replication of the community radio programme to other parts of the state since programmes are produced mainly to concentrate on dialect, problems and custom of local flavour. Radio programmes are usually more of production oriented as compared to recipients oriented programme. Methodological challenges of evaluating community radio programmes, such as, unable to identify an appropriate control group and to infer causal attribution, and lack of money to do adequate evaluation are usually the part of radio programmes. UJALA is also not free from these common points.

However, Sonbhadra area is well suited for the community radio programme. The community radio programme greatly enhanced the knowledge on RCH issues of the listeners in the villages. Radio is the only possible mass media channel that can reach these scattered villages. Moreover, the penetration of TV is almost nil in this area and may not be possible at least for the coming ten years due to its less number of villages with electricity connection. In this situation, if UJALA can be rebroadcast with suitable groundwork after adjusting for ground realities that would be a fine contribution to the rural folk.

Slick production and mass reach are the two eyes for the success of any radio programme. Population Foundation of India has notably succeeded in producing better community radio programme and some more focused efforts at the reception factors are needed to reach out the masses. The conventional community radio programme model can be revived, supplemented and followed. It can be supplemented by folklore so that sustainability of the programme might be feasible in future. Perhaps, more such types of folklore can be incorporated in the radio programme itself so that people will be able to identify the folklore with radio programme. In future, that particular folklore can be produced and shown in the villages.

Masses can sit together and listen to the radio programme during the time of broadcasting. If possible loudspeaker can be arranged so that all can hear together and discuss the matter after the programme is over. The concluding remarks are that community radio programmes strategically have to concentrate more on reception factors at the grassroot level than on sophisticated production factors. It is better to have a small and comfortable hut in the earth rather than building an enormous castle in the air.

11

Grassroots Organization and Universities for Rural Development

R. Venkata Ravi and V. Narayana Reddy

Rural Development and Decentralization are inter-related and also much discussed topics in the context of bringing together local initiatives and local knowledge for the socio-economic development. The process of decentralization is mainly for devolving of functions and authority that give opportunities for the people to play their role, which can ensure their initiatives and involvement in the development activities at grassroots level. In Indian context, constitutionally endowed democratic decentralization through Panchayat Raj Institutions[1] (henceforth known as Panchayats) is best suited to operate at and within the community level. Because, the PRIs enable involvement of the people representatives in the decision-making process related to the planning and implementation of activities for socio-economic development with social justice. The 73rd Constitutional Amendment (CA) has strengthened the PRI by granting the status of local self-government and they are brought to the center stage of the development administration in our country.

Besides, Panchayats as elected bodies, at grassroots level—Voluntary Organizations (VOs) or Non-Governmental Organizations[2] (NGOs) are also working for the rural development. The NGOs operate at the grassroots level, as catalyst for social mobilization and also bringing changes that are much needed for rural transformation. The NGOs have emerged as a suitable alternative for government in the area of development based on community initiatives by understanding the local needs, problems and resources (Joshi R.P. and Narwani G.S., 2002). They are also capable of involving local people and tapping their contribution to experiment with new approaches, strategies and programmes for sustainable rural development for which large scale expenditure/ investment is not required (Yatish Mishra, 2002).

Over a period of last five decades, the NGOs in India has gradually shifted their focus in their operations and have become one of the major stakeholders at the grassroots level in the context of rural development. The changing roles of NGO could be traced from charity in 1960s, to handle welfare and relief activities during 1970s, to initiate development process in 1980s, during 1990s and onwards emerged and also engaged in the Advocacy role (Chopra Ravi, 2001).

Social mobilization process has to result in organizing the people, keeping in mind various socio-economic dimensions at the grassroots level. Once people are organized, capacity building of such organization becomes necessary with a view to change the culture of dependency to a culture of self-reliance. In the decentralization efforts, Institutional strengthening of Panchayats is also a crucial strategy at the micro-level, in addition to the promotion of Community Based Organizations[3] (CBOs) and their capacity building for sustainable rural development. The NGOs are also involved in organizing community into various organizations at grassroots level that include—women, farmers, youth and also users of various "Resources and Services" like land, water, health, education. The NGOs role in organizing the people is aimed at enabling them to come together to work for effective use of resources and services. The NGOs mobilize local resources[4] and also raise sizable external resources from outside[5] for the welfare and development action at grassroots level.

Both government and non-governmental organizations have introduced a format where people are involved in decision-making (with democratic content) to have community control over decisions on use of resources and delivery of services. It has been done as part of the decentralization process with the aim of transferring responsibilities and sharing of power. It has resulted in emerge of village level organizations and user groups to manage various resources at local level. These Community Based Organizations (CBOs) like User Committees and Self-Help Groups (SHGs) have influence on local self-governance, as they exist parallel with the constitutionally established structure of Panchayat Raj Institutions.

On other hand, the Community Based Organizations have become new channel for enlisting people's participation and also to manage the resources and services in the rural areas (Benjamin Powis, 2003, emphasis is mine). Surfacing of this kind of grassroots organizations has created a new situation in process of decentralization in rural areas. The emergence of these organizations has created scope for horizontal linkages[6] among various organizations and also chance of confrontation cannot be ruled-out with each other in managing the development process in rural areas.

The present chapter is meant for discussing various aspects of the partnership between varieties of organizations working at the grassroots level for across purpose. The first part of this chapter is based on the available literature on the relationship among the Panchayats, NGOs and CBOs. Whereas in the second part of the information generated on the NGOs perception, experience and issues regarding the partnership is discussed.

Current Situation in Partnership

Currently, decentralization policies are being considered as instruments for promoting more Social Capital[7] formation at the local community level. So, the CBOs are not just user groups or committees, it is also a channel to bring the local community in achieving self-reliance and sustainability. The proponents of decentralization and local self-governance have argued for strengthening the CBOs. The social capital is developed through local associational activity that sets norms of reciprocity, trust and community involvement that ultimately results in organized demand for good governance. At the same time, building partnership for horizontal alliance between Panchayats and CBOs is viable strategy for achieving development in rural areas.

The literature on the subject is mostly scanty and available is only indicating the desired direction and also nature of partnership between these grassroots organizations for rural development. Andhra Pradesh[8] is unique in promoting the user groups and committees in the areas of education, water use, thrift, watershed, and youth employment at village level. The Self-Help Groups (SHGs) are organized not merely for saving and credit, but also to mobilize the women and empower them. As these organizations are becoming strong at grassroots level, there is lot of scope for an efficient interface between PRIs and SHG as both these organizations are focusing on "people-centered" development (Bandhyopadhyay *et. al.*, 2002).

The CBOs are different in many aspects from the Panchayat Raj Institutions (PRIs). Because, they are constitutionally mandated institution that has provision for bringing the people into the system under gender and caste based reservations, whereas the CBOs are not having any such reservations to bring the marginalized to the decision-making forum (Benjamin Powis, 2003). The linkages between CBOs and Panchayats can enable "convergence" of various facilities and services at village level. The idea of convergence between PRIs and CBOs is anchored on a "collaborative framework" that takes into account of the relative strengths of each other's. The CBOs could function as implementation agencies for the PRIs and also this approach may make "Panchayats" as without much functional role, but discharging responsibilities as local self-government (Venugopal and Annamalai, 2003).

It is also possible that the SHG in the form of Vigilance Committee at village level can supervise the execution and monitoring of rural development activities. This kind experiment is going on currently in some part of the Assam (Aziz Ahmed, 1999). This practice facilitates involvement of people not only in implementation of development programmes, but also monitoring the same. The system can help Panchayats to more closely work with the people and also for achieving the transparency in the programme management.

The Panchayat Raj System has two hierarchies – one is the elected leader and another is the official. The elected leaders are expected to make decisions and that need to be executed by the officials in the Panchayat Raj System. The system of Panchayat Secretary[9] (PS) introduced in the Andhra Pradesh in 2002. But this system is found in some form or other in Rajasthan, Uttar Pradesh, Madhya Pradesh, Kerala and Gujarat. The role of Panchayat Secretary (PS) has created that a new kind of challenge at the village level (Vijay Kumar and Sudhakar, 2003). As the PS is responsible for the promotion of SHG and other CBOs in the villages, it provides chance for direct interaction between the GP and CBOs at grassroots level. More so, in Andhra Pradesh, the government has also been promoting the user groups/committees at grassroots level to manage the various resources and services.

Community, CBOs and Panchayats has access to natural resources of land, water, forest etc. in the rural areas. The interest and preferences of members vary as they use the resources. Moreover, interest of the people is based on their resource endowment level and accessibility to land, water, livestock, and location of habitations. The existing kind of link with resource has influence on livelihood options for the people and on their interest in managing such resources. Access to the shared common resources is crucial to local livelihood, mainly for poor who depend directly on shared natural resources (Pari Baumann and John Farrington, 2003).

Whenever, the CBOs has backed the elected leadership in the Gram Panchayat, possibility of bringing together and working together arrangement between CBOs and Panchayat is more due to same leadership in both organizations.[10] This kind of leadership also paves way for required level of consultation with CBO in decision-making and in implementation of the programmes (Bhat and Venkata Ravi, 2003).

A study in Andhra Pradesh, Kerala and Madhya Pradesh[11] shows absence of convergence between CBOs and the Panchayats. At the same time not found any significant level of conflict between these two sets of grassroots organizations (Venugopal and Annamalai, 2003). But, these community based organizations are meant, on one hand, for organizing the people as users and on other hand to bring out capacity of the rural leadership for restructuring the channels of power and control the access to resources. At present a diversity of user groups/committees with beneficiaries of development programmes are found in the villages for managing natural resources and some of the vital service delivery. But these organizations are not elected by the village community, but often appointed by the development agencies to monitor the programme implementation (James Manor, 2001). In a sense, these organizations from socio-political perspective attempt to play the role of Panchayats in their capacity to control and manage the natural resources at village level.

A clear linkage and partnership amongst stakeholders is noticed in the health service delivery at village level in Madhya Pradesh. Because, from the planning stage, purposive strategy has been evolved to enlist people participation through partnership and networking in health service delivery at village level. Apart from officials, SHGs, PRI and village health committees have been involved as partners in the process. As the health service is significant to all the partners work together jointly in managing the delivery system (Durga Prasad and Madhuri, (2004). An experiment by M.S. Swaminathan Research Foundation (MSSRF) in Wynad District, Kerala is a unique in partnership building among local communities, SHGs, Government Officials, Farmers and People's Science Movement to preserve local level healthcare system (See: Durga Prasad and Madhuri, 2004). This partnership is focused on addressing livelihood issues and bio-diversity by bringing all the stakeholders together to have functional and resource convergence. The partnership is working effectively as the people's interest for livelihood is involved and their roles are clearly designated and also performed. But, the partnership is not for managing scare resource, more so to establish a resource base at village level.

The Report on Drought by the Government of India (2004) provides evidences for CBOs involvement in providing and managing the relief. In Orissa, a women group with 21 members in Koraput block with their accumulated fund of Rs. 25,000 as their strengths have taken up the responsibility of managing the Public Distribution System (PDS) and earned a considerable profit from the same. Learning from this experiment, the PDS outlets are operated by the Gram Panchayats are shifted to the SHG in the districts of Kalahandi, Bolangir and Koraput in Orissa.

In the case of Rajasthan, the PRIs have been entrusted the responsibility of executing the drought relief activities and made available needed resources. The SHGs have formed the basis for executing these relief activities for which the PRIs have provided required quantum of foodgrains. Moreover, the SHG have provided loans to its members for purchase of food and fodder to overcome the stress of the drought. In the meantime, the NGOs are involved in a large scale in Rajasthan in the drought relief activities and contributed in providing health care, drinking water, transportation facilities, cattle camps, fodder depots and also relief works. The PRIs have provided required infrastructure facilities and the NGOs have executed the activities with its network of CBO at grassroots.

The NGOs role is increasingly found many areas of development aspects related to watershed, forests, women, children, self-employment, and health sanitation. The Panchayat Raj Department through NGOs implements the UNICEF funded programmes on rural sanitation and safe drinking water. In the states like Andhra Pradesh and Rajasthan, watershed projects are executed by the NGOs (Joshi and Narwani, 2002).

The Panchayat has constituted the Village Education Committees (VEC), which is responsible for managing the delegated programmes for the development of education at village level. In many states, community participation in development programmes has been made possible through VEC for the primary education. The VEC is made up of representatives from all sections and organizations at grassroots level that include women groups and local NGOs (Manohar Lal, 2003). The crux of the whole emerging phenomenon is that the elected leaders in Panchayat are concerned about their present position and power, sustain the same even in future, but, the NGOs and CBOs are focusing on the betterment of people in the rural areas. Another aspect that needs to be considered is that functionaries in the Panchayat are often replaced or transferred that cause the disturbance in managing the grassroots level development. But, in the case of NGOs, experienced and skilled functionaries are continued relatively for a long period that has comparative advantage in management of the development activities.

It is observed that in the discussions with NGOs, that the relationship between NGOs and Panchayat is very much influenced by the perceptions on both sides that they are mutually interfering in each other sphere.[12] It is also noticed that NGOs have experienced non-cooperation from Panchayats in sharing data. Whereas, Panchayats pointed out the NGOs are not consulted while identification of problems and also target group for any programme in the village. In this line clash and conflict was recently seen in Rajasthan between NGO and villagers of its area verse state department of irrigation (see: Joshi and Naswani, 2002).

Though the multiple organizations can provide more scope for mobilization of community to respond to their needs in the villages, the domination of elite and power groups may exclude the socially marginalized people to advantage of these grassroots organizations (Eshman and Uphoff 1984; Benjamin Powis, 2003). These organizations are potential for emerge of new leadership in rural communities. Of course, it can result in changing the nature and direction of decentralization of power and access to resources. The NGOs are appropriate for motivating and organizing village communities, but limiting factor could the numerical strength of both NGOs and also CBOs promoted by them. It is not possible for the NGOs to effectively cover the vast geographical area and dealt with large number CBOs. In such context both people and Gram Panchayats are treating the NGOs as outsider to that area (Manish Tiwary, 2003). In this process who wins and who looses due to these organizational power need to be seen in the field.

Emerging Issues

Many NGOs are effective in the social sector like mobilization, awareness creation, capacity building, and health service and also involved to large extent in promotion of SHG and micro enterprises on a sustainable basis. In this aspect, the NGO and CBO have been working together to use the natural resources for creating livelihood opportunities. Most of the natural resources in the village fall under three categories of property region, like owned by the government, owned by the private and owned by the community. The claim over the natural resources and control same by different stakeholders for the utilization has potential for complexity. On event of emerging user groups related to these resources throws up new challenges at grassroots level and redefining the roles of the GP, NGOs and CBOs.

Emerging another dimension is that the NGOs that resent the emergence of Panchayats, particular Gram Panchayat, as they have to vacate space for these constitutional bodies. On the whole the Panchayats are replacing the NGO, as implementation agencies for government sponsored development programmes (Poornima and Vyasulu, 2000). With the devolution of powers and resources to the Panchayats, a cleavage is becoming visible in many areas between the NGOs and Panchayats. It is a matter of serious concern in the context of interface between these grassroots organizations needs to be continual for sustainable development (Joshi and Narwani, 2002). The Panchayats as local self-government dictate the term while the NGOs working on the common properties or of the government. However, common property resources provided sustenance to rural households in general and much more important to the poor in particular. In recent years, most of the village commons were degraded into open access situation with a weak property rights relations, institutional arrangements and break down of local authority system (Ratna Reddy, 2000). Simultaneously, the NGO and Panchayats can work together in partnership as many NGOs are involved in providing training to newly elected leaders of PRIs as part of their capacity building programme.

The grassroots level partnership has several implications that if the government services are not routed through CBOs, it is difficult to sustain the interest of the members. As a result the members of CBOs may develop negative attitude and withdraw from the organization (Yatish Mishra, 2002). So, absence of partnership with the various organizations, situation is potential for the dilution of the CBOs and gradually disappear that ultimately result in lack of community participation in development process.

The model for the partnership and linkages can vary according to the ground reality in rural areas. However, a collaborative model to converge the services/functions can be suitable. The Gram Panchayat needs to have a forum at village level consisting of all CBOs working in the village and local NGOs and government officials. The forum can prepare micro level plans for the development and welfare of the rural community. At the same time the CBOs can be implementation agencies in their respective field of interest. However, the NGO need to play a facilitating role and for advocacy. This forum can be as "Village Planning Committees" under leadership of the Gram Panchayat.

Suggested Model for Grassroots Partnership–1

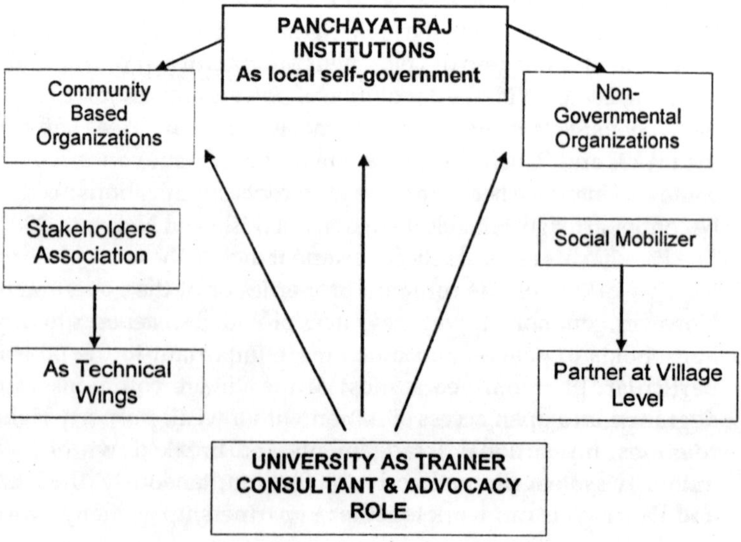

Tasks ahead in this connection are involving re-orientation of policies and resultant decisions related to autonomy for PRIs purely depend on the following by any State Government. They are like- making a clear decentralization policy, measures for strengthening the PRIs with more autonomy, micro level planning and collective action at grassroot level, change of attitude among all stakeholders and political willingness to make such objective decision for long lasting changes in administrative set-up and share in the power and authority along with financial resources.

As the situation emerges, wherein all these grassroot organizations – Panchayats, NGOs and People's organizations/ community based organizations are equally important from the part of socio-economic development with social justice in the rural areas. But, it needed of the hour that NGOs, PRIs have to give up the attitude of working in isolation, superiority complex and treating as competitors. It is very much required that mutually they could contribute in the development process. It is very important to rely on the each other's strength to make community based initiatives for the comprehensive development of rural areas.

Suggested Model for Grassroots Partnership-2

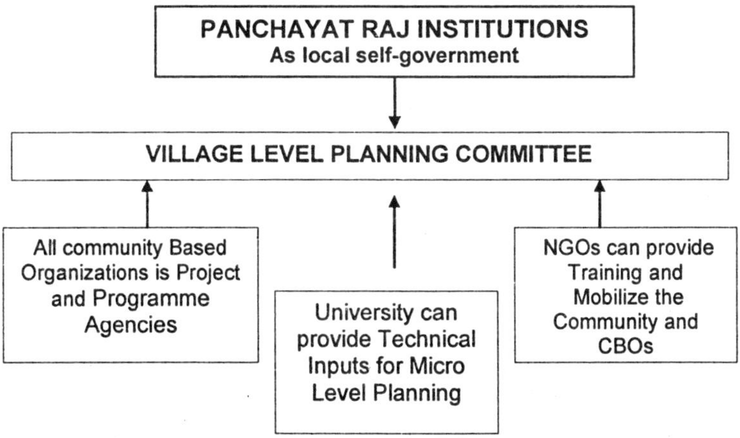

Common Goal

The Panchayats, NGOs and CBOs are working for the goal of rural development through effective organization and proper management of resources and services at different level. In the future, community initiatives in form of Users groups and

Stakeholders Association would play an important role in the area of decentralized management of development in rural areas. These grassroot organizations need adequate technical and professional support to perform their roles and discharge their responsibilities.

In this context the Universities as professional institutes can play significantly to provide required support to the various grassroots organizations. The Universities are Think Tanks with a reservoir of professional expertise and technical knowledge in the various branches of knowledge. This team of faculties could be very useful to guide the organization and people to manage the development.

Suggested Model for Grassroots Partnership-3

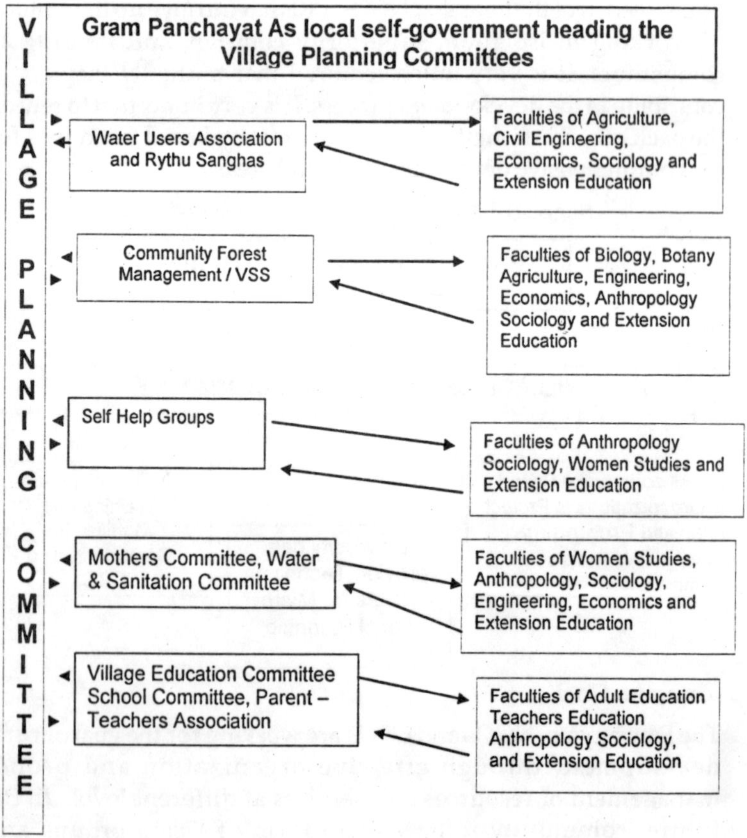

Partnership Among Grassroot Organizations

	Panchayats	*NGOs*	*CBOs*	*Universities*
Primary Role	Local Self-government work for the development at grassroot level	Development Agency work as Motivator, Trainer and facilitator	Channel for people participation & contribution	Provide the leading role as Think Tank to direct the development
Prime Responsibility	Providing the basic services for the community	Bringing people together and help the community and Panchayat	Making people to manage affairs of the community on their own	Providing all required technical inputs and know-how
Major Functions	Preparing time bound Micro Level Plans for the develop-ment of the community	Helping the Panchayat & community to work together	Manage various service delivery system and also resources	Analyzing the different delivery system operating and develop appro-priate system suitable for the community
Problem Identification	Through the participation of all stake-holders	NGOs could play major role in Systematic identification problems	Different Users Groups and Stakeholders Association work for Rapid Assessment of the situation	Can use the professional skill for this task
Client Identification	Approving in the selected list of persons and programmes	Facilitator to undertake such process	Service and Resource utilization status can be known from the CBOs	Can undertake required survey and Research for this purpose
Need Assessment	Consult and bring together al reports	Interface between Community (CBOs) Panchayat and University	Providing the information and express the felt needs and common needs	Can provide technical and professional know-how in this purpose

Contd...

	Panchayats	*NGOs*	*CBOs*	*Universities*
Planning the Action Programme	Primarily Planning for delivering basic services	Facilitator role	Providing information and sharing the available local knowledge	Providing the professional skills for planning process
Participatory Implemen-tation	Provide funds and Control the programme	Bring in the external resources to supplement the available resources	Technical Wings of the Panchayat and work as implementation agencies	Process Monitoring and providing project and programme management support
End Evaluation	Commission such evaluation and use the outcome of Evaluations	Information providers	Information providers	Take up Applied Research Project and provide feed back to the Panchayats & NGOs

On the whole the linkages between University – Panchayat - Communities is very much required in the present society as the development is mostly "Knowledge Based" and "People-Centered". Moreover, the current trend in the development administration is more focused on decentralisation, wherein scope for different partnership is increase. The University system is work on the three-pillars-namely Teaching, Research and Extension. Within this framework, "Social Capital of all " can be effective put into use for the overall development of the society. The linkages are necessary so as to share the available knowledge and experience in the affairs of the community in which we are all living.

REFERENCES

Moitree Bhattacharya (2002), "Panchayati Raj in West Bengal: Democratic Decentralization or Democratic Centralization", MANAK Publishers Private Limited, New Delhi.

Manoj Rai and Others (2001), "The State of Panchayats : A Participatory Perspective", SAMSKRITI, New Delhi, pp. 35-76, 105-130.

Aureliano Fernandes (2003), "Aggrandiser Government and Local Governance", *Economic and Political Weekly*, Vol. 38(27), pp. 2873-2879.

Shikha Jha (2002), "Strengthening Local Governments: Rural Fiscal Decentralization in India", *Economic and Political Weekly*, Vol. 37 (26), pp. 2611-2623.

Bandhyopadhyay D., Uganda B.N., and Amitava Mukherjee (2002), "Convergence of Programmes by Empowering SHG and PRIs", *Economic and Political Weekly*, Vol. 37(26), pp. 2556-2561.

Pattanaik B.K., (2004), "Community Participation, Panchayati Raj and Rural Health Care", *Kurukshetra*, Vol. 52(3), January, pp. 14-18.

Durga Prasad P., and Madhuri N.V., (2004), "Partnership and Networking for Health Development: Initiatives, Successes and Challenges", *Kurukshetra*, Vol. 52(3), January, pp. 4-13.

Vijaya Kumar A., and Sudhakar E., (2003), "Role of Panchayat Secretary in Andhra Pradesh—A Study" Indian Journal of Public Administration, Vol. XLIX (2), April-June, pp. 201-211.

Venugopal G., and Annamalai U., (2003), "Relationship Between PRIs and CBOs: Issues of Convergence", Journal of Rural Development, Vol. 22(4), pp. 455-486.

Vasudeva Rao D., (2003), "Emerging Leadership of Women in Institutions of Local Governance: A Study in Andhra Pradesh", *SOCIAL ACTION*, Vol. 53(2), April-June, pp. 159-168.

Vasudeva Rao D., (2001) "Democratic Common Interest Groups Foster Empowerment in Andhra Pradesh", *Social Welfare*, Vol. 47 (11), February, pp. 27-33.

Chopra Ravi (2001) quoted in the "Drought 2002—A Report", Ministry of Agriculture, Government of India, 2004.

"Drought 2002: A Report", Ministry of Agriculture, Government of India, 2004.

Joel S.G.R. Bhose (2003), "NGOs and Rural Development: Theory and Practice", Concept Publishing Company, New Delhi. 11-100-1005.

UNDP Document Community Based Pro-poor Initiatives Programme of Government of India, Sourced from www.undp.org.in/programme/propoor/apcdppi.htm

"Women's Political Participation and Good Governance: 21st Century Challenges", UNDP 2000, accessed from http://magnet.undp.org//

Manohar Lal (2003) "Community Participation through Village Education Committee in Primary Education in India" *Journal Social and Economic Studies*, Vol. XV, December, pp. 39-49.

Joshi. R.P. and Narwani. G.S. (2002), "Panchayat Raj in India: Emerging trends Across the States" Rawat Publications, New Delhi.

Yatish Misra (2002), " Empowering People: Grassroot Organizations and Rural Development", Kanishka Publications, New Delhi.

Manish Tiwary (2003) " NGOs in Joint Forest Management and Rural Development: Case Study in Jharkhand and West Bengal", *Economic and Political Weekly*, December, 27, pp. 5382-5390.

Eshman and Uphoff (1984) "Local Organization–Local Intermediaries in Rural Development, Cornell University Press.

Perspective on Grassroot Organizations and Rural Development, in (Ed.) D. Vasudeva Rao, S. Vijaya Kumar and R. Venkata Ravi, "Narratives on New Perspectives of Development", Book Enclave, Jaipur, 2005, pp. 77-90.

NOTES

1. Panchayat Raj Institutions refers to all the three tiers—Gram Panchayat, Panchayat Samiti and Zilla Parishad; in this paper all the three tiers are referred as Panchayat.
2. Voluntary Organizations and Non-Government Organizations referred to a registered society involved in taking up welfare and development activities at local level. However, cooperatives are not included in this type of Organizations.
3. Community Based Organizations (CBOs) refers to a group of beneficiaries organized. It can be Self-Help Group (SHGs), Water User Association (WUA), Watershed Management Committee, Community Forest Management (CFM), Mothers Committee, Village Education Committees, Village Drinking Water and Sanitation Committee and any other similar at village level.
4. Local resources include people contribution in terms of cash, materials and labour; and resources flowing under the various schemes of the Central and State Government welfare and development programmes. It also covers funds provided by the National Level Development Donors.
5. External Resources include mainly funds brought in from International Development Agencies and Donors.
6. Collaborations and cooperation between different organizations working at village level that primarily includes Panchayats, CBOs and NGOs in carrying out their major activities.
7. Social Capital denotes local wisdom and knowledge of the community.
8. Andhra Pradesh is one of the states where large number of SHGs and also User Committees have been organized for managing Water, Forest, Health Service, Education and etc. has been organized by the Government and NGOs.
9. During January 2002, the Government of Andhra Pradesh has made appointed of Panchayat Secretary to all Gram Panchayat according to the provisions of the Andhra Pradesh Panchayat Raj Act (1994). They are the Executive Officials to implement the decision made by the Gram Panchayat. The Panchayat Secretary is responsible in the Gram Panchayat area for both Development and Revenue functions, apart from assigned duties by the government machinery.
10. A study conducted by the Council for Social Development, Hyderabad during 2003 on functioning of Gram Panchayats after appointment of Panchayat Secretary in Andhra Pradesh, which shows that wherever, leaders of SHGs are elected as Sarpanch of the Gram Panchayat, and the collaboration between Panchayat and CBOs is made easy and has a constructive relationship.
11. The National Institute of Rural Development, Hyderabad has conducted a study on the Relationship Between PRIs and CBOs: Issues of Convergence.
12. It is noticed during the visit to some of the NGOs in Andhra Pradesh for Monitoring and Evaluation of their Programmes supported by the CAPART, Ministry of Rural Development, Government of India.

Part–3
EMPLOYMENT AND SOCIAL SECURITY

12

Voluntary Retirement Scheme: Problems and Prospects

Martina R. Noroha

Many companies across India are either shutting their shutters or shedding their excess flab i.e. staff strength. Established corporate houses opt for the Voluntary Retirement Scheme (VRS) route. Multinationals plead that after liberalization, units, which had been set up for backward integration and import substitution, have become redundant and competitors, who rely on cheaper imports, are out pricing them. Thus most companies have dangled the carrot in the form of VRS. They believe that attractive packages will tempt labour to go in for VRS and will help to improve efficiency and restore their health.

Meaning and Objective

Employers refer to VRS as the 'Golden Handshake'. Trade unions call it 'Voluntary Retrenchment Scheme' while for the government it is an 'Exit Policy'. VRS is one of the strategies introduced in early 1980s in central (PSU) to reduce the so-called surplus or redundant workforce. The Centre set up a National Renewal Fund (NRF) for downsizing in PSUs and Government Corporations. VRS gained publicity after the introduction of new economic policy in 1991. Liberalization adopted in 1992 formally blessed VRS. The main objective of VRS is to downsize surplus and unproductive labour force and thus achieve optimum manpower utilization. Also another objective of VRS is to improve the average age mix of the employees. It is a means to improve efficiency and thus restore the health of sick units.

VRS Offered by Various Enterprises

In the year 2003, many companies offered VRS to their employees and have met with considerable success. Cummins India Limited on March 25, 2003, has announced VRS for its employees as well as Subsidiary Cummins Diesel Sales & Service (India) Ltd. 1300 out of 8500 employees of Reliance Industries Ltd. opted for VRS in May 2003, at its Naroda Plant. 1600 employees of Indian Petro Chemicals Corporation Ltd. went in for VRS in June 2003. Maruti Udyog Ltd., had offered its maiden VRS in October 2001. 1050 employees or 19 Percentage of the workforce had opted for the scheme and the number of employees decreased to 4596. Again, on December 22, 2003, it retrenched 27 Percentage of its staff as part of its efforts, to control costs and improve profitability by having a younger workforce. 1251 employees opted for VRS in their 2nd VRS scheme out of 4606 employees. 1000 employees out of 3000 of Group C and D opted for VRS offered by VSNL in July 2003. VIP Industries Ltd., offered VRS at its manufacturing unit at Jalgaon on December 22, 2003. Colgate Palmolive (India) announced VRS for its manufacturing facility at Aurangabad on December 21, 2004. Bharat Petroleum Corporation Ltd. (BPCL) had 12433 employees. It has become trimmer by 445 people (120 from the management cadre, 70 from the clerical order and 255 from labour) after its VRS scheme closed on May 31, 2004. The company had targeted those near the 42-year age bracket. Indian Drugs Pharmaceuticals Ltd. (IDPL) was declared a sick company in 1992. The government offered VRS to the employees of IDPL and released funds to the extent of Rs. 470.63 crore till December 31, 2004. As a result of VRS, the total strength of 6592 employees (inclusive of both wholly owned subsidiaries as on December 31, 2002) has been reduced to 440 employees as on September 1, 2004. SAIL on January 13, 2005 has extended its VRS upto January 31, 2005. It has an overall target of bringing its employees from 129600 to 112000.

The banking industry in an attempt to optimize their efficiency decided to curtail their workforce, after tempting labour to go in for the golden handshake. State run banks that have already come out with VRS schemes include Bank of India, United Bank of India, Punjab National Bank, Bank of Maharashtra, Canara Bank, UBI, UCO Bank, Syndicate Bank and Indian Bank. About 22000 public sector bank employees have opted for VRS 2000 schemes i.e. almost 10 to 12 Percentage of their workforce. The Small Industries Development Bank of India (SIDBI) announced its VRS package on January 16, 2004 for employees above 40 years of age with at least 15 years of service. On December 14, 2004, IDBI accepted 415 applications of VRS including those of 246 officers involving an expenditure of Rs. 50 crores. While State Bank of India in consultation with the Ministry of Finance is again preparing an exit policy for its under performers which will curtail 10 to 12 Percentage of its total workforce. In the banking industry, about 120000 employees have been removed in the name of VRS.

Staff Strength in Banks (IBA)

	31-03-2000	*31-03-2001*	*31-03-2002*
Officers	241593	217041	209288
Clerks	438746	400176	373800
Sub-Staff	193130	180674	173960
Total	**873469**	**797891**	**757048**

The Insurance Sector was also not far behind. The Insurance VRS Scheme was intended by the government to bring the management ratios at par with the statutory norms of 19.5 Percentage. Of all the costs, wages comprise the highest component of high management ratios. At present, the management ratios of all the companies – New India Assurance Co. Ltd., United India Insurance Co. Ltd., National Insurance Co. Ltd. and Oriental Insurance Co. Ltd. are well in excess of these norms. The government is likely to launch another round of VRS for the four state owned general insurance companies at the end of this fiscal. The "Son Report" which was submitted to the Finance Ministry suggested that the four general insurance companies were over-staffed by about 10 Percentage. It also suggested that the average age of employees in these companies was significantly high. The last VRS, which was launched in January 2004, had received a lukewarm response with only 10 Percentage of the targeted number opting for the scheme. The government had allocated Rs. 500 crores for the scheme.

In January 2004, in a bid to bring down the average age of its operational staff, the Railways introduced a safety related VRS for loco pilots and trackmen. On December 16, 2004, the government approved VRS for the employees of Air India and its subsidiary HCL (Hotel Corporation of India). The Indian Airlines on February 23, 2004 had approved extension of VRS covering permanent employees of the company who had rendered a continuous service of not less than 10 years or have attained 40 years of age on the date of closure of the scheme. The state owned domestic carrier, besides deciding in 2000 to roll back the age of retirement from 60 to 58, had among other introduced VRS in 2003 also. These two measures had helped the airlines to reduce its manpower by about 850 and 450 respectively.

Observations

Unions have protested against forcible VRS. But recently, even the right to strike by Government Employees has been clipped by Supreme Court ruling. The option to retire or to remain in service is a matter of right to live with dignity. Dignity of life should not be put on the bargaining counter. In the health care industry, efficient and loyal staff is the greatest asset. The administration may be successful in cutting down the monetary cost but will end up losing more in terms of sincere and efficient staff. Trade Unions fear that the exodus may create a vacuum leading to an erosion of efficiency. There are certain banks that after offering VRS have been saddled with inadequate staff to meet customer service. Customer service has been badly affected. There are many instances where VRS has been implemented without proper manpower planning. Delhi Power Generation Karmachari Sangathan alleged that more than 6200 employees who availed of VRS have not been paid their terminal benefits and are running from pillar to post. United Bank of India is still struggling to find out ways of funding the VRS. Also employees availing VRS shall not be eligible for re-appointment under the State Government or any Public Sector Undertakings or any autonomous agency of the State Government. The government has indicated that all the posts created by the exits under VRS schemes would stand abolished. Composite growth rate of urban employment has declined from 2.9 Percentage to 1.27 Percentage. Rural employment also decreased from 3.1 Percentage to 1.6 Percentage. In the organized public and private sector, the growth rate in employment decreased from 1.44 Percentage to 0.04 Percentage. Thus liberalization policy in its anxiety to modernize, restructure and globalize the products of Indian Industry is wasting precious labour force that could have been modernized through re-training.

Is this justified? Behind the veil of announcements about efficiency drives, there lies a dormant volcano of social problems. Keeping the employable idle will not only be counter-productive but it can lead to many social problems. It is rightly said, an idle mind is a devil's workshop. Even from the taxation point of view, employees availing VRS is a loser to a certain extent. An employee taking VRS may find his normal salary earned up to retirement, when added to the taxable portion of VRS, brings his income under the head 'salaries' over 5 lakhs will also not be eligible for rebate under Section 88.Compensation up to 5 lakhs is free but any amount above that is fully taxable, even if it is received in subsequent years or even if it is received by way of LIC annuity or a Co-Pension Plan.

Conclusions

Those who opt for VRS should be given training and rehabilitation support. Social welfare facilities should be adequately provided. Social safety programmes should be started with an aim to address the impact of job-loss trauma, which is an outcome of downsizing of enterprises. It should focus on skill improvement and prepare the retired staff to take self-employed projects. Andhra Pradesh has started social safety net programmes, which has covered 5500 people so far. Other states should follow suit. For a person opting for VRS regular returns along with safety of capital will be his investment objective. Mutual Funds do provide benefits according to their requirements. It is necessary that awareness about this should be created among the investors. The success of VRS scheme depends upon how the scheme is implemented and the perceptions of the persons opting for VRS and the survivors. The key concerns for the success of VRS are effective communication, building trust among employees about procedural justice and involvement of multiple stakeholders.

13

Changing Female Workforce Structure in Karnataka State: A Study in Post Reforms Situation

Talwar Sabanna

It is widely recognized that female work participation is changing rapidly in developed countries, while it is taking place at a slower pace in the less developed countries. As a consequence, the study of female work participation has stimulated considerable interest in the factors that influence it among researchers and policy makers, due to the economic and non-economic factors that dominate their decision-making, besides the need to make further utilization of female human resource for greater economic growth and development. Hence, in this chapter, an attempt has been made to explain the changing female workforce structure in Karnataka State.

For satisfying the basic need of food, shelter and clothing, work both domestic and non-domestic for money is essential. Domestic works such as cooking, washing clothes and utensils, taking care of the children and elders etc., do not bring 'money' into the household and, therefore, it is not perceived as "work." Since ages, women have performed these tasks but their work has never given the status of being 'employed.'

When the time to enter the field of employment comes, the males are better equipped than the females since, by and large, they have been given better skills, training and competence. Every male child is provided with some kind of training or skill, which helps him to get into workforce smoothly. On the contrary, girls are normally not brought up with the same intention. When suddenly the family feels compelled, she is 'pushed' into the workforce. Further, women's earnings remain significantly below those of men in spite of the increase in the female labour force. Differences in rates of pay and conditions of service between men and women persist till today. At almost all occupational levels women do indeed earn substantially less than men. Culture, tradition, social beliefs and economic conditions (i.e. low productivity level of women, etc.) combine to influence and generate an unfavourable occupational discrimination among female workers *vis-à-vis* male workers and to create pay differences.

Women constitute a major workforce in Karnataka State as in case of India. They work for long hours both at house and outside the home, but their work is unacknowledged or under reported in labour statistics. The work of women is usually invisible because it is mostly located in the domestic sphere and as a rule, household tasks defy quantification and monetary valuation. Eighty per cent of women labourers are employed in the unorganized sector that include agriculture, forestry, livestock, fisheries, khadi and village industries, handloom, handicrafts, sericulture, construction, domestic work and food industry.

There is a great deal of debate on the effects of liberalization on the poor and on workers. Positions seemed to have become polarized where those who support liberalization say that there has been a decrease in poverty and an increase in general well-being, and those who oppose it saying that in fact poverty has increased, employment opportunities and access to social services have declined.

We found that the liberalization has caused an increasing inequality in employment opportunities and incomes. Economic opportunities created by the liberalization are highly unequal. Those better endowed with more resources or better links internationally have been able to benefit. For women at the upper income, upper skill and the quality as well as opportunities for employment have improved. For most women workers, however, the quality of employment is poor, without opportunities either for skill development or moving up the ladder limited or with very low-income returns (Jhabvala Renan and Sinha Shalini, 2002).

It goes without saying that for coping with the new production, product-quality, marketing and networking norms, the quality of workforce acquires supreme significance. In other words, employment market too has to substantially reorient itself to new, and more stringent, recruitment standards; even for those aspiring to self-employ themselves, up to date knowledge of the trade and market networking are as much inescapable prerequisites as higher educational, training and skill accomplishments. Never before did the rural economy face such labour market challenges as during the nineties or would face in the coming years. The dualism in the labour market is getting further sharpened. A market for educated, trained and skilled job aspirants, typically characterized by new and upcoming production/marketing/management standards, significantly higher levels of productivity, wage rates and earnings, etc. is steadily expanding simultaneously with sluggishness as a steady decline in the job market for their less educated, semi or unskilled and untrained bethren. Employment prospects are thus getting brightened up for the more qualified while a squeezing scenario sets in for the untrained and the uneducated job seekers; differences in employment prospects get magnified between self-employment and wage-paid jobs, and still more significantly, between urban and rural areas (Chadha G.K.). Rural job aspirants, especially females among them, suffer far more severe setbacks, primarily because of their own educational and skill deficiencies.

Female Work Participation Rate

In Karnataka, of the total population of 52,733,958, the number of persons returned as workers is 23,521,533 or in other words, 44.6 per cent of the population of the state constitutes workers. Of these workers, 15,272,725 are males and 8,248,808 are females, accounting for 56.9 per cent and 31.9 per cent of the total male and female population in the state respectively. The rest of the population i.e., 29,212,425 or 55.4 per cent of the total population of the state constitutes non-workers.

The work participation rate since 1911 for the state is shown in Table 1. The work participation rate in the state has varied from one census to another. It has been argued that the 1961 Census had reported one of the highest WPRs; and the subsequent lower WPRs should not therefore, be rejected. This argument is not valid. The WPRs have declined between 1961 and 1971, because of the rising school-attendance ratios and the associated classification of children in the age group 5-14 as non-workers. The varying proportions of workers till 1971 are more or less attributable basically to the fluctuating concepts and definitions in recording the work rather than any socio-economic causes. From 1971 onwards one may observe that the overall work participation is steadily increasing.

The work participation rate of males during 1971-91 is more or less stable but went up from 54.1 per cent in 1991 to 56.9 per cent in 2001. Unlike in the case of males, the work participation rate in case of females is steadily increasing since 1971. It is remarkable that the work participation rate for females has almost doubled during the last four decades. In spite of this improvement, still there exists a wide gap between the work participation rates of males and females. The data presented in Table 1 can be looked at differently to attempt a preliminary assessment of the view that the technological advances in the past few years are likely to progressively reduce the employment opportunities for women and push them out of the labour market.

Main Workers and Marginal Workers

Out of total population of 52.7 million in the State, 19.3 million or 36.7 per cent are main workers and 4.2 million or 7.9 per cent are marginal workers and the rest 29.2 million or 55.4 per cent are non-workers (Census 2001). The Table 2 shows the distribution of population by workers and non-workers and their percentage in censuses during 1981, 1991, 2001. The workers are further classified into main workers and marginal workers.

As can be seen from the table the overall work participation rate has increased from 42.0 per cent in 1991 to 44.6 per cent in 2001. However, when we look at the percentages of the main workers and marginal workers it will be seen that the proportion of main workers has not registered an increase. In case of main workers, the proportion of which stood at 38.5 per cent in 1991, has slided down to 36.7 per cent in 2001. Thus, during last decade, as the above figures reveal, there has been considerable increase in number of persons reporting as marginal workers. The proportion of marginal workers among persons, males and females has increased from 3.5 per cent, 0.6 per cent and 6.7 per cent in 1991 to 7.9 per cent, 5.0 per cent and 11.0 per cent in 2001 respectively. Perhaps this may be due to a better coverage of the paid or unpaid work done by persons in farm and family enterprises in the 2001 Census.

Female Work Participation Rates—Rural and Urban Areas

As can be seen from Table 3 percentage of work participation rate both in rural and urban areas is steadily increasing since 1971. One may observe that female work participation rate both in rural and urban areas have recorded fairly high increase between 1971-

2001 the WPRs in rural areas is very impressive. Generally one would expect that the more participation rate in urban area would be higher than that of rural area. Contrary to this belief we see that the work participation rate in urban area is far lower than that in rural area. According to 2001 provisional figures 16.1 per cent of females in urban area are workers as against 39.9 per cent in rural area. This fact partly effects the difficulty of combining "work" with other household duties in urban areas than in villages where work on the family farm or in the family enterprise tends to be the predominant activity (Visaria Pravin, 1999). Further, some of this rural/urban discrepancy is due to the greater importance of subsistence production and the potential for women to work as unpaid family labour in the agrarian setting. The permeability that exists in the rural environment between work and non-work, and between the inside and the outside is less evident in the market-oriented urban economy.

The most dramatic change has been the increase in women's share in work participation rate of total agricultural employment. The female work participation rate in rural areas has moved from 18.9 per cent to 39.7 per cent between 1971 and 2001. This has been due to the combined effects of the introduction of HYV technologies (which appear to have lead to greater overall use of female than male labour) and the movement of men into non-farm employment.

It remains true that female agriculture labourers are among the poorest sections of our society. With the lowest wage levels and highest unemployment, with majority of them below the poverty line female casual labourers in rural areas show the highest incidence of poverty of any occupational category, male or female. Because of their relative lack of mobility or marketable skills (rural female workers are unskilled and illiterate), these women are the most vulnerable to seasonal fluctuations in labour demand. Their low levels of nutrition, frequent pregnancies keeps them out of the labour force even when jobs are available and limits their productivity.

This may mean that, indeed, fewer women are economically active in the cities because the barriers to be crossed to enter the urban labour force are not only conceptually more absolute (i.e. one works to earn cash or one does not), but that the need for mobility, bureaucratic know how, literacy, modern skills and the ability to line into non-traditional work situations may also be more acute in the fast paced, competitive urban labour market since women are at a disadvantage in all these areas, this may well constrain their labour force participation even though the greater need for cash and the relative lack of opportunity for alternative non-market household production may make female entry into the labour force desirable to poor household.

While this appears to be a positive sign indicating that women are moving into more highly skilled, formal sector jobs, it need to be interpreted with caution. Women tend to be concentrated in those processes and firons in each sub-sector where more traditional, labour intensive technologies are employed, and in industries where the proportion of women is high, the capital/labour ratio and the output/worker ratios are both well below the state average.

Employment Growth in Organized Sector

In Karnataka State employment in public sector grew rapidly in the 1970s. Between 1970-71 and 1980-81, the growth rate of employment was 4.22 per cent per annum. In the next decade, the growth rate of employment in public sector was relatively much lower at 2.81 per cent per annum. The growth rate in employment came down further in the 1990's (i.e. 0.73% per annum). This deceleration in employment growth in public sector enterprises in the post-reform period was, however, more than offset by a sharp increase in employment in the private sector enterprises, which led to acceleration in employment growth in organized sector.

Employment in organized public sector in Karnataka State has decreased steadily during the 1980's onwards. In sharp contrast, there has been a substantial increase in employment in the organized private sector during the 1980s onwards. Between 1980-81 and 1990-91, employment in public sector grew at the rate of 2.81 per cent per annum, in the next decade, 1990-91 to 1998-99, the growth rate was 0.73 per cent per annum. In the period 1980-81 and 1990-91 the growth rate of employment in private sector was 2.35 per cent per annum, which increased to 8.44 per cent per annum during the 1990-91 and 1998-99, well above the growth rate achieved of the population. Further it is seen from the table the private sector enterprising included for almost the entire increase in female employment in organized sector. The employment of male in private sector increased marginally.

Since a process of major economic reforms was initiated in 1991, the marked acceleration in employment growth in organized manufacturing in the 1990's may be thought to be a result of the economic reforms, there is some basis for taking such a view because, in certain ways, economic reforms are expected to have a favourable effect on the growth of employment in industries. The favourable effect may arise from greater labour market flexibility and increased trade orientation leading to changes in the structure of industries in favour of labour intensive industries and technique of production (Bishwanath Goldar).

Problems

The problems of women are multi-dimensional ranging from economic and social problems of female workers differ to a considerable extent depending upon level of education, kinds of jobs, social equity, places of work like rural or urban, and agricultural or non-agricultural etc. The level of women-employment is always the indices of the kind of socio-economic progress, which a community pursues. Therefore, the problem of the low rate of women labour participation is always viewed in the context of the overall problems of the social and economic progress. It is also essentially a problem in social equity between men and women.

A liberalized economy like ours has always to discriminate against the more socially backward and economically dependent and poorer sub-sectors of the community. The socially and educationally deprived and economically poor segments of population remain till today least benefited section of our society. Similarly, the women labour has also been subjected to the vagaries of the liberalized system. The women labour in our economy has been provided with proper share in work opportunities and continually remain being exploited. The economic problems of women labour range from raising unemployment, low wages, long duration of work hours, stagnant and deteriorating working conditions, sex-wise discrimination of wages between male and female workers, absence of job security, and the inadequate and irregularity implemented protective legislations like social security, minimum wages, social insurance etc.

Poverty, ignorance and ill treatment, insecurity of jobs and non-availability of benefits under social security measures etc., impose the inevitability of accepting low wages, unhealthy working conditions by these working women. Moreover, the trade unions have not been developed to protect and safeguard the interests of these workers. The factors responsible for low wages and insecurity of jobs etc., are also responsible for the absence of women trade unions. Social status, traditions and inhibitions are also responsible for slow growth of unionism among women workers.

Further, the condition of women workers in unorganized sector is matter of great concern. Ignorance, lack of skills, seasonal nature of employment, lack of minimum facilities at the work place, ill treatment and bondage are some commodities among unorganized women labour. Several studies on women workers in the unorganized sector revealed that exploitation is rampant in this sector. They are forced to work for low wages and in poor conditions with no security of work for future. They lack a single employer to whom they can negotiate. They get money at piece rate basis. They are mostly concentrated in home-based industries as casual workers.

One of the problems that effects women's participation in agriculture is the introduction of modern methods of cultivation, which is resulting in gradual displacement of women and shrinking of their activities. Lack of information and awareness of women about governmental and non-governmental schemes for loans or adopting modern technologies or mechanization in agriculture and other small-scale industries, affects their growth and development. Poor women workers are unable to access even small sums or loan from formal financial institutions. The gap between availability to technology in agriculture and its utilization by rural women should be narrowed.

Conclusion

The analysis has brought out the level and spread of women employment and the problems of women workers in Karnataka State and reveals that the labour market hinders the accumulation of job experience as far as women are concerned. Therefore, the share of women in employment compared to their male counterparts has been very small. Even the small amount of women labour force has been accorded discriminatory treatment by the set-up creating socio-economic problems. It is emphasized that as in the growth of an economy physical infrastructure investment is necessary so is the investment in social infrastructure. The investment in health, education and childcare centres not only create employment opportunities and build human capital but also release women for participating in the labour market. Health and education are the sectors, which are hardest hit in the liberalized economy resulting in an increase in the demand for women's labour time.

Table-1

Female Work Participation Rate in Karnataka State 1911-2001

(in Per cent)

Census Year	*Work Participation Rate*			
	Persons	*Males*	*Females*	*Male-Female Group*
1	2	3	4	3 – 4
1911	40.2	54.9	25.3	29.6
1921	36.8	49.0	24.1	24.9
1931	39.7	53.5	25.3	28.2
1951	34.1	49.6	18.1	31.5
1961	45.5	58.4	32.0	26.4
1971	36.1	54.6	16.8	37.8
1981	40.2	54.6	25.3	29.3
1991	42.0	54.1	29.4	24.7
2001	44.6	56.9	31.9	25.0

Source: Census of India (2001), 'Distribution of Workers and Non-Workers', Director of Census Operations, Karnataka, Bangalore, 2001.

Table-2

Percentage of Workers and Non-Workers and their Growth Rate in Karnataka

Category of Workers	*Persons/Males/Females*	*Proportion of Total Population*		
		1981	*1991*	*2001*
Total Workers	Persons	–	42.0	44.6
	Males	–	54.1	56.9
	Females	–	29.4	31.9
Main Workers	Persons	36.8	38.5	36.7
	Males	53.8	53.5	51.9
	Females	19.3	22.7	20.9
Marginal Workers	Persons	3.4	3.5	7.9
	Males	0.8	0.6	5.0
	Females	6.2	6.7	11.0

Contd...

Category of Workers	Persons/Males/Females	Proportion of Total Population		
		1981	1991	2001
Non-Workers	Persons	59.8	58.0	55.4
	Males	45.5	45.9	43.1
	Females	74.6	70.6	68.1

Source: Census of India (2001), 'Distribution of Workers and Non-Workers', Director of Census Operations, Karnataka, Bangalore, 2001.

Table-3
Employment in Karnataka State 1971-2001

Period	Rural			Urban		
	Male	Female	Persons	Male	Female	Persons
1971	56.7	18.9	38.1	48.4	9.8	29.9
1981	57.2	30.7	44.1	48.4	11.8	30.8
1991	56.0	36.6	46.5	49.8	12.9	32.0
2001	58.3	39.7	49.2	54.1	16.1	35.7
Annual Growth Rate						
1971 to 1981	0.09	6.24	1.57	0.00	2.04	0.30
1981 to 1991	-0.21	1.92	0.54	0.29	0.93	0.39
1991 to 2001	0.41	0.85	0.58	0.86	1.99	1.16

Source: Census of India (2001), 'Distribution of Workers and Non-Workers', Director of Census Operations, Karnataka, Bangalore, 2001.

Table-4
Employment in the Organized Sector in Karnataka State 1971-99

Years	Public Sector			Private Sector			Total		
	Male	Female	Total	Male	Female	Total	Male	Female	Total
1970-71	506.1	52.6	558.7	217.5	56.7	274.2	722.6	109.3	832.9
	(90.59)	(9.41)	(100)	(79.32)	(20.68)	(100)	(86.88)	(13.12)	(100)
1980-81	704.2	90.0	794.2	292.8	55.5	348.3	997.0	145.5	1142.5
	(88.67)	(11.33)	(100)	(84.07)	(15.93)	(100)	(87.26)	(12.74)	(100)
1990-91	857.3	160.0	1017.3	337.9	92.1	430.0	1195.2	252.1	1447.3
	(84.27)	(15.73)	(100)	(78.38)	(21.42)	(100)	(82.58)	(17.42)	(100)
1998-99	857.4	234.6	1092.0	446.5	311.5	757.0	1303.9	545.1	1849.0
	(78.52)	(21.48)	(100)	(58.98)	(41.02)	(100)	(70.52)	(29.48)	(100)

Contd...

Years	*Public Sector*			*Private Sector*			*Total*		
	Male	*Female*	*Total*	*Male*	*Female*	*Total*	*Male*	*Female*	*Total*
				Growth Rate					
1970-71	3.91	7.90	4.22	3.46	-0.21	2.70	3.78	3.31	3.72
1980-81 to 1990-91	2.17	8.64	2.81	1.54	6.59	2.35	1.99	7.33	2.67
1990-91 to 1998-99	0.01	5.18	0.73	3.21	26.35	8.44	1.01	12.91	3.08

Source: Economic Survey 1991-2000, Planning Science and Technology Department, Government of Karnataka.

Note: Figures in Brackets indicates percentage.

REFERENCES

Bhalla Sheila, "Social Changes in a Globalise Economic Environment: Issues of Income Disparity, Intensified Poverty, Employment and Worker Productivity in India", Institute for Human Development, New Delhi.

Biradar R.R. and Bagalkoti S.T., "Changing Facets of Employment in Rural India: Emerging Issues and Challenges", Indian Journal of Agricultural Economics, Vol. 56, No. 3, July-September 2001, pp. 538-551.

Census of India (2001), "Distribution of workers and non-workers", Director of Census Operations, Karnataka, Bangalore, 2001.

Chadha G.K., "Impact of Economic Reforms on Rural Employment : No Smooth Sailing Anticipated", Indian Journal of Agricultural Economics, Vol. 56, No. 3, July-September 2001, pp. 491-525.

Dev Mahendra S. and Mahajan Vijay, "Employment and Unemployment", Economic and Political Weekly, Vol. 38, Nos. 12 & 13, March 22-28/29 April 4, 2003, pp. 1252-1261.

Golder Biswanth, "Employment Growth in Organised Manufacturing in the 1990's", Institute of Economic Growth, Delhi.

Jhabvala Renana and Sinha Shalini, "Liberalisation and the Women Workers", Economic and Political Weekly, Vol. 37, No. 21, May 25-31, 2002, pp. 2037-2052.

Nanjundappa D.M. and Sreenivas M.A., "Employment and Unemployment in Karnataka State", in Employment Policy in Developing Country, Edited by Austin Robinson, Brahmananda P.R. and Deshpande L.K., The MacMillan Press Ltd., London.

Nirmala V., *et al.*, "Genderwise minimum wages, wage differentials and determinants", The Indian Journal of Labour Economics, Vol. 41, No. 2, 1998, pp. 339-349.

Shariff Abusaleh and Gumber Anil, "Employment and Wages in India: Pre and Post Reform Scenario", The Indian Journal of Labour Economics, Vol. 42, No. 2, 1999, pp. 195-216.

Visaria Pravin, "Level and Pattern of Female Employment, 1911-94", in "Gender and Employment in India", Edited by Papola T.S. and Sharma A.N., Vikas Publishing House Pvt. Ltd., New Delhi, 1994.

14

Determinants of Female Agricultural Wage: Evidences from Andhra Pradesh

S. Venkata Narayana Reddy and
K. Satya Narayana Reddy

Introduction

Agriculture, as a basic industry has been playing a prominent role in Indian economic development and its contribution occupies one-third share of national dividend. Also providing majority part of employment to the people, though industrial and tertiary sectors are growing significantly. But the contribution of agriculture to the national dividend varies from nation to nation depending upon their degree of economic development. At present stage of fairly high level of economic progress, the importance of agriculture gradually declines. Whatever, agriculture with its basic importance, has its own contribution to make the everlasting an action of economic development of Indian economy. To emphasize the role of agriculture in Indian economic development, it is obviously observed that, owing to limited development in agricultural sector, there is no rapid growth in non-agricultural sector.

Until the 1960's the terms 'economic development' and 'economic growth' are oftentimes used as synonymous words in economic literature. Economic development may be defined as "the possession of an economy, which is superiority and traditional of agriculture into dominant industrial and modern one". As quoted German economist and national projectionist, Frederick List "almost all of the developed economies moved from the savage stage of economic development to the take off stage" i.e., 'agricultural, manufacturing and commercial stage' of economic development through out the path of 'agricultural stage'.

It is very difficult task to define agricultural labour because of intricacy phenomena. Though it is difficult, may define agricultural labour as "the people who are getting greater part of their annual income by working on other lands" called agricultural labour. In agricultural sector, female labours are approximately equals with the size of male labours. Agricultural workers constitute the most disregard segment of Indian rural structure and large number of agricultural workers belongs to economically and socially suffered sections of rural structure. Their income is below their subsistence level and irregular employment. Most of the agricultural workers have no proper sanitary conditional residence and more of them are living under single roof along with cattle like goats and sheaves. Recently this condition is something eliminating by Indira Avas Yojana programme, which is adopted by Central Government. The functions performed by women labour differed from region to region and according to their social and economic status. Generally, female labours are engaged in hulking, transplanting of seeds, thinning, sowing, weeding, plant protection, grading, kitchen gardening, cleaning of grains, harvesting, feeding the cattle, irrigating fields, taking care of live stock, collection of flowers and vegetables etc., are exclusive examples. Especially female labours are engaged in coffee and tea plantations huge in size.

About the Anantapur District

Being one of the 23 districts of Andhra Pradesh, Anantapur district is founded the place in the Rayalaseema region of Andhra Pradesh. The district is formed in the year 1882. And derived its name after the headquarter town of Anantapur. According to 2001 census figures, the rural literacy rate in Anantapur district is 36.2, where as male and female literacy rates are 40.6 and 16.8 per cent respectively. It is most to be need to improve the rural literacy rate in the district. Especially female literacy rate.

The Anantapur district is the driest of all the drought prone districts of Andhra Pradesh. In the district it is clearly estimated that the drought visits at least thrice in a decade. The irrigation commission and central commissions has been identified the whole district as drought-prone. Due to converting the district into desert the people, especially agricultural labour and tiny-formers in the district founded that their lives are 'rigorous and not bearing' and they are migrating in searching gainful employment.

The Review of Literature

The literature available on the labour market in general and the rural labour market in particular is quite extensive.

The study of V.N. Misra, about 'Labour Market in Agriculture: A Study of Gujarat District', based on cross section analysis at a point of time 1960-61, found that the factors like per day wage rate in rupees, per capita income, crop pattern and percentage of irrigated area taken together were found to have a significant relationship with the demand. In the supply model, the factors per day wage rate in rupees, and percentage of rural workers in occupation other then agriculture to the rural labour force, considered in the model, were not found significantly influencing supply. In the wage determination model, between the two factors, namely the percentage of agricultural labourers to total working force (supply) and per hector hired labour (demand), the second one is found to be significant determinant of wages. Consequently, wage rate determination seems to be independent of the market conditions.

The study of Guy Standing and Glen Sheehan, 'Labour Force Participation in Sri Lanka', has recorded high level of women participation in estate areas of Sri Lanka. This study has revealed that there is positive relationship between education and participation, while fertility and urbanization have a negative impact on participation.

Michael Lipton, "Labour and Poverty", has emphasized that personal characteristics like caste, tribe and race, health and disability are seasonally affecting wage rates in India.

S.M. Pandey, in his study of wage determination in Indian agriculture found that demand factors play vital role, wherever the pressure of population is high, the supply factors play vital role, where the population pressure on land is less however, the demand factors become prominent.

D.N. Reddy's study on female work participation-facts, problems and policies in terms of quantitative as well as qualitative aspects based on 1971 Census data reveals that female work participation in India is low and female participation is influenced by socio-cultural and the level of income.

Objectives

The following are objectives of the present study.

1. To study the inter-Mandal variation in female agricultural work participation rate.
2. To study the major determinants of female agricultural wages.

Methodology

To study first objective, female labour work participation rate, the co-efficient of variation has been calculated, which reflect the variations in female labour work participation rate. The inequalities in employment status have been shown by the co-efficient of variation.

$$C.V. = \frac{\text{Standard Deviation}}{\text{Average}} \times 100$$

To find out the inter-mandal inequalities in employment status of rural female labour, the co-efficient of equality computed. The formula for co-efficient of equality is:

Co-efficient of equality for rural females =

$$\frac{\text{Percentage share of rural females in rural employment}}{\text{Percentage share of rural female in population}} \times 100$$

So many factors are influencing 2 the female agricultural wages. Some of the important variables are to be considered in the present study. They are given with regression formula.

Division-wise female agricultural wage determinants are analyzed with the help of multiple linear regression. The functional relationship is:

Y = f (X1, X2, X3, X4, X5, X6, X7)

Where,

Y = female agricultural wage rate

X_1 = availability of female agricultural labour per hector

X_2 = availability of male agricultural labour per hector

X_3 = land concentration ration

X_4 = cropping intensity

X_5 = percentage of agricultural labour households to the rural households

X_6 = percentage of irrigated area

X_7 = average size of operational holdings

Type of the Variable and Expected Relation

Variable	*Description of Variables*	*Type of Variables*	*Expected Relationship with Wage Rate*
Y	Female agricultural wage rate	Explained	–
X_1	Availability of female agriculture labour per hector	Explanatory	Negative
X_2	Availability of male agricultural labour per hector	"	Negative
X_3	Land concentration ration	"	Negative
X_4	Cropping intensity	"	Positive
X_5	The percentage of agricultural labour households to the rural households	"	Negative
X_6	Percentage of irrigated area	"	Positive
X_7	Average size of operational holding	"	Positive

The specification of the variables is given below:

Y = female agricultural wage rate

$$X_1 = \frac{\text{Total rural female agricultural labour}}{\text{Total cultivated area}}$$

$$X_2 = \frac{\text{Total rural male agricultural labour}}{\text{Total cultivated area}}$$

$$X_3 = \frac{\text{Total land of households}}{\text{Total members in family}}$$

$$X_4 = \frac{\text{Gross are sown}}{\text{Net area sown}} \times 100$$

$$X_5 = \frac{\text{Agricultural labour households}}{\text{Total rural households}} \times 100$$

$$X_6 = \frac{\text{Net area irrigated}}{\text{Net area sown}} \times 100$$

$$X_7 = \frac{\text{Total area of operational holdings}}{\text{Number of households}} \times 100$$

To test the significance of each independent variable, t-test statistic is adopted.

$$t = \frac{\hat{a}_i}{S.E\,(\hat{a}_i)} \longrightarrow t\,(n\text{-}k)$$

Where,

n = number of observations
k = number of variables
i = refers to the variable

The combined effect of all independent variables on dependent variable calculated by multiple correlation co-efficient (R^2)

$$R^2 = 1 - \frac{\text{å}ei^2}{\text{å}v^2}$$

For the significance of R^2, F test statistics is carried out.

$$F = \frac{R^2\,(k-1)}{(1-R)\,/\,(n-k)}$$

Where,

R^2 = multiple correlation co-efficient
k = total number of variables
n = total number of observations (sample size)

Both the linear and log-linear models are estimated. The proposed log-linear models is:

$$\text{Log } Y = a_0 + a_1 \log x_1 + a_2 \log x_2 + a_3 \log x_3 + a_4 \log x_4 + a_5 \log x_5 + a_6 \log x_6 + a_7 \log x_7$$

It is said that the log-linear model is the best fit, since, the estimated values are appropriate. Hence, the entire analysis of female agricultural wage determination is in relation to the results of log-linear model.

Data

The present study is fully depended on secondary data. The secondary data related to rural female agricultural work participation rate is drawn from the hand book of statistics 2001-02, issued by district statistical office, Anantapur; census of India 2001 (population census). The collected raw data is converted into convenient form for the study. The determinants of female agricultural labour wage rates also based on secondary data for the year 2001-02.

Analysis

Rural Female Work Participation Rate

Inter-mandal variation of RFWPR and co-efficient of equality in the revenue divisions i.e., Anantapur, Dharmavaram, and Penukonda divisions of Anantapur district are studied.

The RFWPR in Anantapur division is 37.87 per cent and ranges from 35.94 per cent for Raptadu mandal to 39.75 per cent for Uravakonda mandal. Four mandals having RFWPR between 35 and 37 per cent, remaining sixteen mandals having between 37 and 40 per cent out of 20 mandals of the division. The co-efficient of variation is 2.83, which indicates less inter-mandal variations in RFWPR. The co-efficient of equality for rural females in various mandals of Anantapur division also shows a similar consistent pattern as shown in the Table-1 (appendix). It is for Anantapur division is 77.69 and varies form 73.69 for Narpala mandal to 82.23 for Peddavadugur mandal. It is between 73 and 76 for seven mandals, for remaining mandal is above 76 and below 83 in the division. It leads to conclusion that in majority of the mandals, the real agricultural employment states of the rural females is more than 73 per cent. The value of co-efficient of variation for rural females is 3.00.

The RFWPR in Dharmavaram division is 38.99 per cent and it ranges from 37.24 per cent for Kanekal, Kambadur mandals to 41.38 per cent for C.K. Palli mandal (appendix, Table - 2). Thirteen mandals out of 17 mandals have RFWPR between 37 and 40 per cent and in remaining four mandals the RFWPR is above 40 per cent but below 42 per cent. The co-efficient of variation is 3.20, which indicates less inter-mandal differences in RFWPR. The co-efficient of equality for rural females in Dharmavaram division is 79.70. It ranges from 75.99 for Kanekal mandal to 84.39 for C.K. Palli mandal. Thirteen out of 17 mandals, it is below 80 but above 75. In the rest of four mandals it is between 80 and 85. The co-efficient of variation is 3.26. It reveals that there are less variations in the real agricultural employment status of rural females.

The RFWPR and co-efficient of equality for rural labour in Penukonda division shows Table-3 (appendix). The RFWPR in Penukonda division is 38.66 per cent and ranges from 35.98 per cent for Talupula mandal to 41.52 per cent for Gorantla mandal. Twenty one mandals out of 26 mandals have RFWPR below 40 per cent but above 35 per cent. Remaining of five mandals having above

40 per cent but below 42 per cent. The co-efficient of variation is 3.37, which shows less inter-mandal differences in RFWPR. The co-efficient of equality for rural females in Penukonda division is 78.96 and ranges from 73.51 for Talupula mandal to 84.99 for Gorantla mandal. In sixteen mandals it is between 70 and 80. In remaining ten mandals it is below 85 but above 80. It leads to the conclusion that in majority mandals of the division, the real agricultural employment status of the rural females is at high-level. The co-efficient of variation is 3.45.

The RFWPR in Anantapur district is 38.49 per cent and it ranges from 35.94 per cent for Raptadu mandal to 41.52 per cent for Gorantla mandal. Fifty-four out of 63 mandals in the district have the RFWPR between 35 and 40 per cent. In the remaining nine mandals, it is between 40 and 42 per cent. The co-efficient of variation is less order 3.38. The co-efficient equality for rural females in Anantapur district is 78.76 (appendix Tables 1, 2 and 3). It varies from 73.51 for Talupula mandal to 84.99 for Gorantla mandal. It is apparent from the Tables (appendix–1, 2 and 3) that, there are less variation in the real agricultural employment status of the rural females. In 4 mandals out of 63 mandals, the co-efficient is equality is below 75 but above 73. In 39 mandals have the co-efficient of equality between 75 and 80, in 20 mandals it is between 80 and 85. The value of co-efficient of variation is 3.42, is conforming that majority of mandals have the high level of the real agricultural employment status of rural females.

Rural Labour Work Participation Rate and Co-efficient of Equality for Rural Agricultural Female Labour-Anantapur District

Sn.	*Particulars*	*Female*							
		R.F.W.P.R.				*Co-efficient of Equality*			
		Avg.	*High*	*Low*	*C.V.*	*Avg.*	*High*	*Low*	*C.V.*
1.	Anantapur Division	37.87	39.75	35.94	2.83	77.69	82.23	73.69	300
2.	Dharmavaram Division	38.99	41.38	37.24	3.20	79.70	84.35	75.99	3.26
3.	Penukonda Division	38.66	41.52	35.98	3.37	78.96	84.99	73.51	3.45
4.	Anantapur Division	38.49	41.52	35.94	3.38	78.76	84.99	73.51	3.42

Above table shows the RFWPR and the co-efficient of equality for rural female agricultural workers in the three revenue divisions of Anantapur district and for the entire district. Among the three divisions, Penukonda division shows highest of variation (3.37) in RFWPR followed Dharmavaram and Anantapur divisions. It is noticed that entire district as a whole, recorded highest variation 3.38 than these three divisions. The co-efficient of variation is 3.38 in RFWPR. Penukonda division recorded highest variation in co-efficient of equality followed by Dharmavaram and Penukonda division is 3.45 where as the co-efficient of equality for entire district is less than Penukonda divisions co-efficient of equality. The co-efficient of the entire district is 3.42.

Determinants of Female Agricultural Wages

Anantapur Division

The estimated regression equation, i.e., 'female agricultural rate' is a function of seven selected variables of Anantapur division is:

$$Y = 0.9270 \quad \underset{(0.0449)}{-0.1440^{*} x_1} \quad \underset{(0.0210)}{-0.0773^{*} x_2} \quad \underset{(0.0958)}{-0.3332^{*} x_3} \; +$$

$$\underset{(0.0847)}{0.1986^{*} x_4} \quad \underset{(0.0410)}{+\,0.0987^{*} x_5} \quad \underset{(0.0323)}{+\,0.1511^{*} x_6} \quad \underset{(0.0408)}{+\,0.1284^{*} x_7}$$

$R2 = 0.7778 \quad F = 6.0002^{*}$

- Significant at 5 per cent probability level.
- Figures in the parentheses are the standard errors of the estimates.

The co-efficient of the 'availability of female (x) and male (x) agricultural labour per hector, and 'land concentration ratio'(x) are negative and significant with 'female agricultural wage rate'. It reveals that there is limited scope to increase the 'female agricultural wage rate' by increasing the x, x and x variables. The co-efficient of 'cropping intensity'(x) and 'percentage of agricultural labour households to the rural households' (x) are having positive and significant relation with 'female agricultural wage rate'. It reveals that the x and x variables increase the 'female agricultural wage rate' decreases. The co-efficient of the 'percentage of irrigated area' (x) and 'average size of operational holdings' (x) are positive and significant relation with 'female agricultural wage rate' and indicating there is very limited scope to increase the 'female agricultural wage rate' by increasing the x and x variables.

The value of multiple correlation (R) is the collective effect of all independent variables on dependent variable is 0.7778. It means 77.78 per cent of variation is observed in 'female agricultural wage rate'. F-value is 6.0002. It is also significant.

Dharmavaram Division

The estimated value of regression equation in Dharmavaram division is:

$$Y = 0.9524 \underset{(0.2100)}{-0.9301^{*} x_1} \underset{(0.0956)}{-0.8189^{*} x_2} \underset{(0.0802)}{-0.6604^{*} x_3} +$$

$$\underset{(0.0563)}{0.1842^{*} x_4} \underset{(0.0270)}{+0.0701^{*} x_5} \underset{(0.0140)}{+0.0795^{*} x_6} \underset{(0.0890)}{+0.2977^{*} x_7}$$

$R2 = 0.6118 \quad F = 4.1250^{*}$

- Significant at 5 per cent probability level.
- Figures in the parentheses are the standard errors of the estimates.

The co-efficient of the 'availability of female agricultural labour per hector' (x) and 'land concentration ratio'(x) are having negative and significant relation with 'female agricultural wage rate' and an increase in one unit of x and x variables will increase the (Y) variable by 0.93 and 0.66 units. The co-efficient of the 'availability of male agricultural labour per hector' (x), 'cropping intensity'(x) and 'percentage of agricultural labour households to the rural households'(x) are having positive and significant relation with 'female agricultural wage rate' and reveals that there is limited scope to increase the Y variable by increasing the x and x variables. The co-efficient of the 'percentage of irrigated area' (x) and 'average size of operational holdings' (x) are also having positive and significant relation with female agricultural wage rate (Y) and there is no scope to increase the female agricultural wage rate.

From the data related to the Dharmavaram division, the computed value of R is 0.6118. It means 61.18 per cent of variation is observed in 'female agricultural wage rate'. F-value is 4.1250 and is significant.

Penukonda Division

The estimated regression equation of female agricultural wage rate for Penukonda division is:

$$Y = 4.5487 \quad - \underset{(0.0600)}{0.3162^{*} x_1} \quad + \underset{(0.09397)}{0.2328^{*} x_2} \quad - \underset{(0.0824)}{0.4908^{*} x_3} \; -$$

$$\underset{(0.0897)}{0.7777^{*} x_4} \quad + \underset{(0.0450)}{0.2855^{*} x_5} \quad + \underset{(0.0392)}{0.2839^{*} x_6} \quad + \underset{(0.1591)}{0.2591^{*} x_7}$$

R2 = 0.3389 F = 4.5263*

- Significant at 5 per cent probability level.
- Figures in the parentheses are the standard errors of the estimates.

The co-efficients of the 'availability of female agricultural labour per hector' (x_1), 'land concentration ratio' (x_3) and 'cropping intensity' (x_4) are having negative and significant relation with 'female agricultural wage rate' (Y). It reveals that there is some scope to increase the female agricultural wage rate by raising the concerned variables. The co-efficient of the 'availability of male agricultural labour per hector' (x_2) is positively related to 'female agricultural wage rate'(Y). The co-efficient of the 'percentage of agricultural labour households to the rural labour hours holds' (x_5), and the 'percentage of irrigated area' (x_6) are having positive and significant relation with variable Y. It reveals that an increase in one unit of x_5 and x_6 variables will reduce the 'female agricultural wage rate' by 0.28 and 0.29 units respectively with significantly.

The value of multiple correlation (R^2) is 0.3389 per cent of variation is observed in 'female agricultural wage rate'(Y). From f-test statistic, this percentage is 4.5263 and is significant at 5 per cent probability level.

Anantapur District

The fitted regression equation for Anantapur division is:

$$Y = 3.9335 \quad - \underset{(0.0310)}{0.1175^{*} x_1} \quad + \underset{(0.0766)}{0.2317^{*} x_2} \quad - \underset{(0.0370)}{0.1489^{*} x_3} \; -$$

$$\underset{(0.0418)}{0.1703^{*} x_4} \quad + \underset{(0.0490)}{0.1919^{*} x_5} \quad + \underset{(0.0544)}{0.1822^{*} x_6} \quad + \underset{(0.0687)}{0.2837^{*} x_7}$$

R2 = 0.3963 F = 5.1588*

- Significant at 5 per cent probability level.
- Figures in the parentheses are the standard errors of the estimates.

The co-efficient of the 'availability of female agricultural labour per hector' (x_1), 'land concentration ratio' (x_3) cropping intensity' (x_4)

and 'percentage of agricultural labour households to rural households' (x_5) are having negative and significant relation with female agricultural wage rate. It reveals that there is some scope to increase the female agricultural wage rate by increasing the x_3, x_4, and x_5 variables in the district. The co-efficient of the 'availability of male agricultural labour per hector' (x_2), 'percentage of irrigated area' (x_6) and 'average size of operational holdings' (x_7) are having positive and significant relation with female agricultural wage rate. There is very limited scope to increase the female agricultural wage rate (Y) by increasing the x_6 and x_7 variables.

The value of multiple correlation (R^2) is 0.3963. It means 39.63 per cent of variation is observed in 'female agricultural wage rate'. F-value is also significant and is 5.1588.

Inter–Divisional Comparison

The co-efficient of 'availability of female agricultural labour per hector' (x_1) is negative and significant on all the three divisions as well as in the district as a whole. It express that an increase in x_1 variable will increase in 'female agricultural wage rate'. The co-efficient of 'availability of male agricultural labour per hector' (x_2) is positive and significant in all the divisions as well as in the district except in Anantapur division. The co-efficient of 'land concentration ratio' (x_3) , is negative and significant in all the three divisions as well as in the district. It is observed that there is some scope to increase the Y variable. The co-efficient of 'cropping intensity' (x_4) is positive and significant in Anantapur and Dharmavaram divisions. But it is negative and significant in Penukonda division and also in the district. It reveals that female agricultural wage rate may increase by increasing the x_4 variable in the district. The co-efficient of 'percentage of agricultural labour households to the rural households' (x_5) is positive and significant in all the three divisions except in the district as a whole. There is no scope to increase the female agricultural wage by increasing the x_5 variable. The co-efficient of the 'percentage of irrigated area' (x_6) is positive and significant relation with female agricultural wage rate in all the three divisions and in the entire district. The co-efficient of the 'average size of operational holdings' (x_7) is positive and significant in all the divisions and entire district except in Penukonda division. In this division it has negative and significant relation with 'female agricultural wage rate'. It reveals there is some scope to increase the Y variable by increasing x_7 variable.

Summary and Conclusion

In the Anantapur district female agricultural labour are playing a prominent role in agricultural operations. The RFWPR in the district is 38.5 per cent, where as the literacy rate for the female in the district is 16.8 per cent. The agricultural operations performed by female labour are varying from region to region and also among the social groups in the district. In the same way, the wage differences are also considerable. In the present study, determinant of female agricultural wages are analyzed by using the regression equation.

The highest average RFWPR is recorded in Dharmavarm division (38.99) followed by Penukonda (38.66) and Anantapur (37.87) divisions. In the case of district as a whole, 38.49 per cent of average is observed. The highest co-efficient of variation in RFWPR is recorded in Penukonda division (3.37) followed by Dharmavaram (3.20) and Anantapur (2.83) divisions. It in the entire district as a whole is 3.38 per cent. The co-efficient of equality for rural female is high in Dharmavaram division (79.74) followed by Penukonda (78.96) and Anantapur (77.67) divisions. The average of the district is 78.76. It is suggested that by reducing male work participation rate, by improving irrigation facilities may increase the RFWPR, consequently female wage rate may be increase.

In the view of Determinants of Female Agricultural Wages, in the case of Anantapur division, the variables – 'availability female and male agricultural labour for hector' and 'land concentration ratio' are having negatively significant relationship with 'female agricultural wage rate'. It reveals that there is very few scope to increase the 'female agricultural wage rate'. Similarly, the variables – 'cropping intensity', the 'percentage of irrigated area' and average size of operational holdings' are having positive and significant relation with 'female agricultural wage rate'. It reveals that there is no scope to increase the 'female agricultural wage rate' by increasing the x_4 x_5 x_6 and x_7 variables. Nearly 78 per cent of variation in 'female agricultural wage rate' is observed by these selected variables in the model.

In the case of Dharmavaram division, the variables – 'availability of female agricultural labour per hector', 'land concentration ratio' are shown negative and significant effect on 'female agricultural wage rate'. It is suggested that there is few scope to increase the 'female agricultural wage rate'. Similarly, positive and significant relation is observed between 'female agricultural wage rate' and each of the independent variables, 'availability of male agricultural labour per hector', 'cropping intensity' the 'percentage of agricultural labour household to the rural households', the 'percentage of irrigated area' and 'average size of operational holdings'. All the selected independent variables considered in equation, collectively, recorded significant variation of 61.18 per cent in 'female agricultural wage rate'.

In the case of Penukonda division the variables, 'availability of male agricultural labour per hector', the percentage of agricultural labour household to the rural households' the 'percentage of irrigated area' and 'average size of operational holdings' are positive and significant relation with 'female agricultural wage rate'. Similarly, the variables – 'availability of female agricultural labour per hector' and 'cropping intensity' are having negative and significant relation with 'female agricultural wage rate'. This is done due to over 'concentration of land'. All explanatory variables in the model explain nearly 33.9 per cent of variation in 'female agricultural wage rate', the percentage of irrigated area' and 'average size of operational holdings.

In the case of Anantapur district as whole, positive and significant relation is observed between in each of the variables, 'availability of male agricultural labour per hector', the 'percentage of irrigated area' and 'average size of operational holdings' and 'female agricultural wage rate'. Similarly the four independent variables, 'availability of female agricultural labour per hector', 'land concentration ratio', 'cropping intensity' and the 'percentage of agricultural labour household to the rural households' are having negative significant with 'female agricultural wage rate'. Every increase in these four variable will increase the 'female agricultural wage rate' by significantly the total effect of explanatory variables on explained variable, 'female agricultural wage rate' is 37.67 per cent.

REFERENCES

Ammaraju Nerurker, 'Segmentation of Labour Market in India with special reference to Women', The Indian Journal of Labour Economics, Vol. XXXII, Nos. 1 &2, April-July 1980, pp. 52-65.

Leela Gulathi, 'Female Work Participation: A Study of Inter-State Differences', Economic and Political Weekly, Vol. X, Nos. 1&2, January 11th, 1975, pp. 35-42.

Misra V.N. and S.B.L. Gupta, 'Productivity, Wages and its Determination in Gujarat Agriculture: An inter-district Analysis', Indian Journal of Agricultural Economics, Vol. XXXIX, No. 3, July-September, 1974, pp. 22-34.

Panday S.M. 'Determination of urban-rural worker participation rate in India: An Exploratory Analysis', Indian Journal of Industrial Relation, Vol. 9, No. 2, October 1973, pp. 209-255.

Reddy D.N. 'Female Work Participation in India – Facts, Problems and Policies', Indian Journal of Industrial Relations, Vol. 15, No. 2, October 1979, pp. 196-212.

Saxena P.K. 'Rural Female Work Participation Rate in Gujarat : An inter-District Analysis', Margin, 1989, March 1990, Vol. 22, No. 12, pp. 124-132.

R.S. Sidhu and S.S. Grewal, 'Factors affecting for Human Labour in Punjab Agriculture: An Econometric Analysis', Indian Journal of Agricultural Economics, Vol. 45, No. 2, April-June 1990, pp. 147, A 150.

B.D. Paramar, 'Wage Determination in Developing Economy: The Case of Gujarat Agriculture', The Indian Journal of Labour Economics, Vol. XXIII, No. 4, January 1981, pp. 231-240.

T.S. Papola and V.N. Misra, 'Labour Supply and Wage Determination in Rural Uttar Pradesh', Indian Journal of Agricultural Economics, Vol. XXXV, No. 1, January-March 1980, pp. 106-120.

APPENDIX

Table-1

RFWPR and Co-efficient of Equalities for Rural Female Anantapur Division (2001-02)

Sl. No.	*Name of Mandal*	*Rural Female Work Participation Rate*	*Female Co-efficient of Equality*
1.	Anantapur	37.14	75.60
2.	Raptadu	35.94	75.06
3.	Garladinne	36.94	75.05
4.	Atmakur	37.91	78.23
5.	Kudaire	38.29	78.84
6.	Singanamala	37.32	75.92
7.	BK Samudram	37.89	78.11
8.	Narpala	35.98	73.69
9.	Tadipatri	37.50	76.82
10.	Yadiki	39.59	81.01
11.	Peddapappur	38.03	78.53
12.	Putlur	36.70	74.97
13.	Yallanur	37.02	75.69
14.	Guntakal	38.22	78.45
15.	Gooty	38.47	79.63
16.	Pamidi	38.84	79.08
17.	Peddavadugur	39.68	82.23
18.	Uravakonda	39.75	81.82
19.	Vajrakarur	38.41	78.34
20.	Vidapanakal	37.67	76.65
	Average	**37.87**	**77.69**
	C.V.	**2.83**	**3.00**

Table–2
RLWPR and Co-efficient of Equalities for Rural Female Dharmavaram Division (2001-02)

Sl. No.	*Name of Mandal*	*Rural Female Work Participation Rate*	*Female Co-efficient of Equality*
1.	Dharmavaram	37.78	77.33
2.	Tadimarri	39.65	81.18
3.	Battalapalli	39.85	81.63
4.	CK Palli	41.38	84.36
5.	Kanaganapalli	39.01	79.58
6.	Ramagiri	38.71	80.18
7.	Kalyandurg	40.28	82.04
8.	Beluguppa	39.21	80.23
9.	Kambadur	37.24	76.41
10.	Kundurpi	40.38	82.89
11.	Brahmasamudhram	41.05	83.65
12.	Settur	38.74	79.05
13.	Rayadurg	38.00	77.18
14.	D. Hirehal	37.46	76.80
15.	Gummagatta	38.17	78.24
16.	Kanekal	37.24	75.99
17.	Bommanahal	38.63	78.23
	Average	**38.99**	**79.70**
	C.V.	**3.20**	**3.26**

15

Two-Way Flow of Family Support: A Study of Pensioners in Mumbai

Aparajita Chattopadhyay and T.K. Roy

Family is the bedrock of a good quality of life. None of the institutions is more important than family in moulding human behaviour, its expectations and adjustments. It is perhaps the foundation pillar, which in many ways form the world of older people as later life leads to a decline of active participation in other social institutions. Replacement of family care and love by formal caring is a wishful western thought-formal caring can never be a substitute for familiar bonding. The basic desire of every elderly is the urges of do something useful, someone to share the basic emotions with and someone to tell that 'I care for you'. If an aging individual is given a pleasant surrounding, a congenial companionship and a loving environment, many of the old age problems can be solved. However, the whole paradigm of social values is gradually transforming with modernization. It leads to a transition of familiarity to individuality even in a country like India, which is respected and adored for its family cohesion since long.

Pattern of support or receiving and providing assistance in old age is a part of continuing process of interaction among parents, children and friends. Care or support provision by family is complex and built upon pre-existing relations, contacts and reciprocity as pointed out by Phillips (1993). Trend data of Asian countries reveals a strong material support of children towards data of Asian countries reveals a strong material support of children towards aged parents in spite of declining co-residence (Mason, 1992). Thus, this chapter is devoted to explore a two-way relation of economic, household and emotional support.

Methodology

To begin the study, a non-conventional secondary data has been collected from Pay and Accounts office, Mumbai with the intention of analysing the death risk of pensioners (which is beyond the scope of this chapter) and to make out a sampling frame for the primary survey. The secondary data set (total sample 1014, teachers (Males = 859 and Civil Servants (Males) = 155) provides information about the pensioners of two occupational groups namely, school teachers and civil servants who retired during the period ranging 1980 to 1999. Out of these 1014 pensioners, 650 teachers and civil servants were surviving till the end of observation and thus they formed the sample frame for the primary survey. Two hundred and forty eight teachers were randomly chosen based on Taro Yamane formula. Out of 124 retired civil servants, only 79 pensioners gave interview. The missed out cases were either out of the station during the survey period (December to April) or rejected to give the interview mainly due to time constraint. The present chapter is based on the primary survey data.

Economic Support

Majority of the respondents is the main bearer of household expenses, the proportion of which is remarkably higher for retired civil servants as out of hundred where the figure is only 33 per cent for teachers, it goes up to 84 per cent in respect of the other group. The self-reliant civil servants neither depend on son nor share the expenditure partly with his spouse or other kin, with a few exceptions. While, converse to the well off class, almost half of the retired teachers either entirely depends on son or support son for daily expenses.

The reason for skewed dependency can be explained with some statistical figures. More than half of the retired civil servants are currently working against only 15 per cent of teacher. Majority of the teacher is having an income of 5000 rupees per month while cent per cent civil servants earn more than 12000 rupees monthly, as their pension itself is high. All and above, far less civil servants are staying with son and hence the question of sharing daily expenses with son is more or less irrelevant when the economic backbone of the elderly itself is strong. However, when he is co-residing with son, marginal difference between two occupational sections is observed in son's sole responsibility to run the household. But, once again, occupational contrast is prominent. Even if at least one son is with the retiree, one-third civil servants opined that he is the major bearer of economic expenditure against only one fifth of teachers. When nearly half of the latter group shares the financial burden with son, it is true not even for 10 per cent of civil servants. Therefore, it is easy to derive that better off elderly does not incline towards their offspring in terms of economic support even if they continue their stay with children while middle class educated aged shares the responsibility when he resides with his child. When the reverse flow is looked into in terms of economic help, it is very interesting to find that the economically better off civil servants render less material support to their children, kin or non-relatives except in two instances. They help needy students and social organizations more regularly than teachers. Quite a few retired civil servants have established endowment for needy students and for rehabilitation of victims of social evils - at regular interval, they sponsor poor pupil for higher studies, in India or abroad. Thus, many of the retired elderly of higher economic class are having the attitude of helping the needy.

Table–1

Who Provides Economic Support to Meet Houschold Expenses

Household Expenses Provided by	*Per cent Distribution Among*		
	Total	*Teacher*	*Civil Servant*
Irrespective of stay with son			
Respondent solely	47.6	33.2	83.5
Son solely	17.8	21.4	8.9
Respondent and son	18.2	24.5	2.5
Respondent and wife	5.8	6.6	3.8
Respondent wife and son	3.6	5.1	0.0
Respondent and others combine	3.6	5.1	0.0
Others solely (excluding son)	3.3	4.1	1.3
Total	**100.0 (275)**	**100.0 (196)**	**100.0 (79)**
Staying at least with one son****			
Respondent solely	25.5	18.0	65.4
Son solely	29.7	30.2	26.9
Respondent and son	38.8	44.6	7.7
Other combination with respondent/ Others (not son)	6.1	7.2	0.0
Total	**100.0 (165)**	**100.0 (139)**	**100.0 (26)**

Note: Combinations with respondent or others include first relations only, except a teacher; (..) Sample size; **** Significant at 1% level in chi square test.

Support in Household Chores

Coming to the aspect of household support, as shown in Table 2, wife is the prime contributor of daily housekeeping irrespective of occupational class, though for teachers, daughter in law and for the civilians, domestic servants too play significant role. Ninety eight per cent retired teachers against 90 per cent civil servants reported about daily household help rendered by his better half. But, wide occupational difference is observed in terms of help given by children who are staying in father's house. When more than four fifth of girls do household chores either regularly or occasionally in a teacher's domicile, only 15 per cent daughter of civil servants belongs to this category. The variation widens with regard to sons. The reciprocity of household help also differs in terms, 83 per cent retired teachers do perform household jobs or help others as against 60 per cent civil servants.

Emotional Support

At the horizon of waning family structure, departure of married child from father's nest, emigration of youths for academic or job pursuits, less geographical proximity of separated son – it is crucial to find out with whom the old shares his subtle emotions. Civil servants as a whole are having lesser number of relations with whom they can confide than teachers. Age is well associated with the number of confidants one has, as evident from figure 1. But, the relation of these two is intricate. To elucidate, the linear trend of mean number of very close confidants, with whom the elderly confides whenever he feels like, is remaining constant for teachers but the pace of decline is faster for the elderly civil servants.

At an older age, that is beyond 70, significant difference is mean number of very close confidants are seen where the civil servants are on the lower side (Table 3). When the reverse flow is unveiled with a query of who confides always (very closely) with the elderly, age again depicts a negative association more or less for both groups without any significant variation. But in terms of close confidants (with whom respondent shares his feelings or *vice-versa* not as intimately as the other group who are 'very close'), the linear trend of mean number declines steadily with age for teachers but remains constant for civil servants. Among those aged below 65, the average number of persons with whom a retired teacher can confide is four, which increases to six in the middle old age and then confines to three at late old age days. Contrary to this, when a retired civil servant is having around four close confidants before 65, it decreases to one during 65 to 69 ages and again goes up to five, which is even higher than what he used to have within first five years following retirement.

Table-2
Extent and Regularity of Support in Household Chores

Extent and Regularity of Support	*Occupation*	
	Teachers Percentage	*Civil Servants Percentage*
Wife:		
Percentage provides help***	98.9 (173)	84.1 (66)
Distribution by regularity***		
Daily	97.7 (173)	89.7 (66)
Sometimes	2.3 (173)	10.3 (66)
Daughter:		
Percentage provides help***	83.8 (37)	15.4 (10)@
Distribution by regularity***		
Daily	71.0 (37)	50.0 (10)
Sometimes	29.0 (37)	50.0 (10)
Servant:		
Provides help regularly***	69.2 (195)	100.0 (78)
Son:		
Percentage provides help***	57.9 (136)	7.7 (26)
Distribution by regularity***		
Daily	39.5 (136)	0.0 (26)
Sometimes	60.5 (136)	100.0 (26)
Daughter in Law:		
Percentage provides help***	96.3 (107)	52.6 (19)
Distribution by regularity***		
Daily	92.2	90.0
Sometimes	7.8	10.0

Note: *** Significant at 1% level in chi square tests;

(..) Sample Size; @ 1adopted daughter, ^I nephew considered as son.

Table-3
Number of Confidants of Respondent and Number of Persons Who Confide in Respondent by Age and Occupation

Degree of	*Age Groups*	*Below 65*		*65–69*		*70 and above Support*	
		Teachers	*Civil Servants*	*Teachers*	*Civil Servants*	*Teachers*	*Civil Servants*
Very close confidants of respondent	Mean Number	2.56	2.31	2.39	1.83	2.32	1.04
Close confidants of respondent	Mean Number	4.29	3.45	5.52	1.43	2.96	4.58
Persons who confides very closely in respondent	Mean Number	3.37	4.59	3.95	2.39	2.44	2.62
Persons who confides closely with respondent	Mean Number	5.42	3.52	9.35	4.43	5.17	10.85
	Sample Size	52	29	62	23	82	27

Note: Bold figures show significant difference in mean.

In the middle ages, the number of close confidants differs significantly between retirees of two occupations. Some probable reasons can be cited for the aforesaid variations:

1. With age why do the number of very intimate confidants decrease? Respondents perceive mainly spouse, a few friends and sometimes son or daughter as very close confidants. With time, an elderly starts loosing his near and dear one, which naturally affects the number of very close confidants. For instance, below the age of 65, only one civil servant is widower. While beyond 70, a quarter of civil servants and 15 per cent teachers have lost their better half. It also explains the steeper decline of very close confidants among civil servants.
2. Why does the occupational differential in having close confidants emerge in middle old ages and for what reasons do the age wise trend is reverse? Profession plays vital role in developing close relations. An elderly consider his friends,

colleagues' as well as first relatives as 'close' confidant. For a civil servant the actual disengagement from service occurs in mid to late 60's, which is not for a teacher who retires from active service at the age 58. When a civil servant is disentangled from work environment, he finds a sharp decline in the number of close ties. However, he gradually develops close association with kith and kin, with whom he could not develop close ties though he intended to do so in his active life, while sometimes he indulges himself in social service and establishes new ties. On the contrary, a teacher, even immediately following retirement can maintain close ties with students and colleagues for the nature of his profession. With further aging, as their health falls (over age 70, 63% civil servants perceive their health as good against 38% teachers), once again they loose close ties because of shrinking interaction. Hence, the first decline in the number of close ties among civil servants coincides with the true work place disengagement followed by a period when quantity of ties again goes up and ultimately drops due to negative health factors as happened for teachers.

An attempt has been made to find out the effect of some important background factors on the likelihood of not having any confidant in old age. Table 4 includes two separate models, of which model *(a)* and model *(b)* predicts the possibility of not having any very close and close confidants respectively *vis-à-vis* those having the relations. Retirees are equally likely to have or not to have any confidant irrespective of age or whether they have variation in their present perceived health. However, past occupation, type of family, present income, present work status and co-residence with child do matter the probability of having confident in significant manners. To elucidate, being a retired civil servant, the possibility of not having either very close or close confidant magnifies remarkably. The odds for not having very intimate confidant are four times among the former compared to the latter. Those who are better off economically (based on monthly income) are significantly less likely to remain devoid of close confidants, which embrace mainly friends and colleagues. Same is the case of those staying in a joint family than staying in a nuclear family. Even after controlling occupation, family type and income, the likelihood of not having a single very intimate relation with whom the elderly can share his joy and woe is more than three times higher for widowers and never married than currently married retirees. The same is true for those who are not employed anywhere in comparison with currently working aged.

Table-4
Variations in Not Having Very Close and Close Confidants: Results of Logistic Regression

Predictor Variables	*For Very Close Confidant (a)*		*For Very Close Confidant (a)*	
	Exp (B)	*SE*	*Exp (B)*	*SE*
Age				
Below 65 #	1.173	.558	.660	.369
65 to 69	.651	.589	.886	.378
Occupation				
Teacher #				
Civil Servant	4.326**	.576	3.301***	.411
Monthly Income				
Less than 12000 #				
More than 12000	1,249	.548	.479**	.355
Childhood Place of Residence				
Mumbai #				
Out of Mumbai	.615	.496	.991	.381
Marital Status				
Other than currently married	3.361**	.622	1.102	.511
Family Type				
Nuclear #				
Joint	1.239	.517	.581*	.343
Number of Children Staying with Respondent				
One	.307**	.540	3.070***	.391
Two	.325	.714	3.620***	.474
Three	.586	1.204	1.326	.807
More than three	1.247	1.019	.704	1.161
Consultation of Household Members with Respondent				
Never #				
Sometimes	.543	.872	1.074	.826
Daily	.160**	.835	1.338	.778

Contd...

Predictor Variables	*For Very Close Confidant (a)*		*For Very Close Confidant (a)*	
	Exp (B)	*SE*	*Exp (B)*	*SE*
Currently Working				
Yes #				
No	3.103**	.531	1.542	.350
Perceived Health				
Poor #				
Average	3.354	.766	1.368	.521
Good	1.686	.770	2.020	.505
Constant	.629	.531	.420	.468
R^2			.250	.129
Sample size			265	265

Dependent Variable

In model:

(*a*) 0 = having very close confidant, I = not having very close confidant. In model.

(*b*) 0 = having close confidant, 1 = not having close confidant # reference category; ***, **, * = Significant at 1%, 5% and 10% level.

Last but not the least, another important factor in predicting not having versus having confidant of an elderly is the presence of son or daughter in the household. As revealed in the Table 4, presence of a son or daughter at home augments the chance of having very close confidant as compared to those elderly who are not staying with or not having any child. Contrary to this very finding, model (b) shows that the presence of one or two children at home significantly increases the probability of not having any close confidant against those who are not staying with son or daughter. The odds of not having any close confidant are three to four times more for the former than the latter. It is not at all unusual that if a person can confide fully at home with children, there is no need to develop close tie (friends and colleagues). As mentioned previously, close confidants are mainly composed of friends and colleagues while wife and children are the prime relations with whom an aged can confide very closely. Presence of very good friend at home (wife, children) will naturally suppress an old man to develop warm ties with non-relatives.

Table-5
Composition and Reciprocity of Confidants by Occupation

	Occupation	
	Teachers in Percentage	*Civil Servants in Percentage*
Wife:		
As a confidant of respondent	93.1 (173)	86.4 (66)
*Respondent as a confidant of Wife ****	89.0 (173)	72.7 (66)
Daughter:		
As a confidant of respondent	32.7 (156)	34.0 (53)
*Respondent as a confidant of Daughter****	37.8 (156)	32.1 (53)
Son:		
As a confidant of respondent***	72.6 (164)	35.2 (54)
*Respondent as a confidant of Son****	75.0 (164)	35.2 (54)
Friends:		
As a confidant of respondent**	62.5 (192)	46.6 (73)
*Respondent as a confidant of Friends****	73.4 (192)	56.2 (73)

Note: ***, ** : Significant at 1% and 5% level in chi square tests; (..) sample size.

Critical look at the composition and closeness with confidants, as shown in Table 5, depicts that for majority of elderly teachers, wife followed by son and friends are considered as confidants. But, for a civil servant, friends, then offspring, follow wife in this regard. Close relation with wife at old age can happen for the added time of the retiree to spend at home and retrospection of long association with wife in the ups and downs of life. Less than 40 per cent civil servants are emotionally close with their offspring through proportion confiding with daughter is marginally higher than with son. Conversely, about three-fourth of teachers consider their son as a confidant out of which in 65 per cent cases, son is a very close friend and only one third opens out with their daughters – a striking disparity indeed. Another feature, interesting to note is, when the reciprocity of intimacy is looked into (that is, whether the relation is a confidant of respondent and the respondent is a confidant of the relation too), it is balanced with regard to offspring, stronger for friends and weaker for wife. Further analysis depicts that out of the hundred, who shares his emotions with wife, ninety-four teachers believe that wife too confide with him when it is true for eighty civil servants. The inconsistency in exchange of emotions with wife among civil servants can be attributed to the fact that with age, male's expectation from his better half increases, as the former spends more time at home than what he used to do in service life. But, a balanced interaction only exists if it is nurtured since the beginning.

Table-6
Reciprocity of Emotional Support Between Respondent and Children According to Place of Stay of Children

Relationship	*Relation and Confidant*	*Occupation*	
		Teachers in Percentage	*Civil Servants in Percentage*
Son	Staying with at least one son	(136)	(26)
	Son as respondent's confidant***	76.5	46.2
	Respondent as a confidant of son***	80.1	50.0
	Not staying with any son	(27)	(28)
	Son as respondent's confidant**	51.9	25.0
	Respondent as a confidant of son**	48.1	21.4
Daughter	Staying with at least one daughter	(37)	(10)
	Daughter as respondent's confidant*	70.3	40.0
	Respondent as a confidant of daughter**	81.1	50.0
	Not staying with any daughter	(119)	(43)
	Daughter as respondent's confidant	21.0	32.6
	Respondent as a confidant of daughter	24.4	27.9

Note: Percentage calculated among those who are having the relation and mentioned as having confidant. 3 teachers are having son but not having any confidant. 2 teachers and 3 civil servants are having daughters and not having any confidant. ***, **, * : Significant at 1% and 5% and 10% level in chi square tests; (..) : Sample size.

Living arrangement can play an intricate role in determining the emotional exchanges between father and child. For instance, as revealed in Table 6, when son or daughter is residing under the same roof with father, emotional attachment is more. Seventy per cent teachers who are co-residing with daughter consider them as their confidant. While only 21 per cent fathers confides with daughter when she is living separately. It is true for father-daughter confidant relation for civil servants too but the gap is not as wide as observed in case of teachers. Moreover, when son or daughter is not staying with father, the two-way emotional flow between father and daughter is much better over father-son attachment among civil servants. In brief, it may not be hard to opine that the level of emotional exchanges is lower for civil servants than teachers perhaps the former remains content in themselves more. Wife is the best friend in old age irrespective of occupational difference followed by son for a teacher and friend for a civil servant.

In search of the major determinants of a satisfied life, five nested regression models have been developed step by step and the change in unstandardized slope is observed (Table 6). Age has a significant role in determining the level of satisfaction. The 'young old' (age less than 65) is more satisfied than the 'old old' (age 70 and above). It is interesting, however, to note that when variables related to health factors are introduced in the model (model 3), age of the elderly looses its significance in influencing the level of satisfaction. In other words, the higher satisfaction among the 'young old' compared to 'old old' (observed in models 1 and 2) is largely because of the deteriorating health condition of the elderly with age. If the health condition remains stable, the process of aging does not lead to dampening their level of satisfaction.

Conclusion

As regards support system, it is easy to derive that better off civil servants depend less on others, especially on children for financial support, household chores and even for emotional confinement than teachers. The reciprocity of support is also less for the former group over the latter. Age is a significant determinant of the number of very close confidants (mainly family members) an elderly is having. With age, the number of very close confidants diminishes steadily and the proportional change is sharper among civil servants than teachers. The latter group is having significantly higher number of close relations (mainly friends, colleagues) over the former to confide at late sixties. However, the reverse situation arises beyond seventy. For an elderly teacher, wife followed by son and friends are considered as confidants by a majority, while for most of the civil servants, friends, then offspring in this respect, follow wife. If reciprocity of intimacy is looked into, it is balanced for offspring, weaker for spouse (especially for civil servants) and stronger for friends.

Today, developing nations are standing at a critical crossroad confronting the issues of aging that must be addressed if social and economic developments are to make fast progress (Binstock *et. al*). Myer's (1982) examination of the aging of population suggests distinctive features among developing nations that will tend to make their aging process different from those experienced earlier by today's developed nations. Unlike the West, the mechanism that enhanced the aging of population of the developing world is somewhat induced. Thus, the designs of aging policies of countries like India are not supposed to alter the basic process of population aging, but it should be directed to issues that arise from the aging of population.

The most important issue that emerges from the aging process is how best to provide economic and social support for the older persons. Family and state are the two important supports of the elderly. But demographic challenge to family care is a two-sided coin as opined by Giele (1982). New demands are being constantly generated from the heterogeneous elders on one hand and on the other, changing values and aspirations of younger generation and steady reduction of family size are raising questions about the vulnerability of family to perform its role to look after the aged mass. A good interaction between family members altogether is significant enough for a safe old age, but reduced family size, as an outcome of demographic revolution is indeed a matter of concern. Excessive reliance, either on family or state is not a positive symptom and therefore, it has always been suggested by the international organizations to combine the help from various sectors of society towards the elderly; that is, the family, the economy and the state. Implementation of a sound policy for the aged population is the need of the hour in the context of India to avoid the situation whereby events overtake history.

REFERENCES

Binstock, R.H. and Chow, W.S. (1982) 'Introductory Overview', in International Perspective on Aging: Population and Policy Challenges, Policy Document Studies, No. 7, United Nations Fund for Population Activities, pp. i-viii.

Giele, J.Z. (1982) 'Family and Social Network', pp. 40-74 in International Perspective on Aging: Population and Policy Challenges, Policy Document Studies, No. 7, United Nations Fund for Population Activities.

Mason, O.K. (1992) 'Family Change and Support of the Elderly in Asia: What Do We Know ?' East West Centre Reprints, Population Series No. 286, East-West Centre, Hawaii.

Myers, G.C. (1982) 'The Aging of Population', pp. 1-40, in International

Perspective on Aging: Population and Policy Challenges, Policy Document Studies, No. 7, United Nations Fund for Population Activities.

Phillips, D. (1993) 'Formal and Informal Support System: Accommodation and Services', Paper presented in the Indo-UK Workshop on Public Health Implications on Aging in India: ICMR, New Delhi.

Part–4
ENVIRONMENTAL MANAGEMENT

16

Natural Disasters and Strategies for Mitigation in India

U.B. Singh and A.K. Singh

The world 'disaster' owes its origin to Italian word 'disastro' meaning 'unlucky event'. According to Compact Oxford Reference Dictionary, 'disaster is a sudden accident or a natural catastrophe that causes great damage or loss of life'. It is 'a sudden misfortune: a string of personal disasters'. The Websters Dictionary defines it as 'a grave occurrence having ruinous results'. The World Health Organization defines disaster as 'any occurrence that causes damage, economic destruction, loss of human life and deterioration in health services on a scale sufficient to warrant an extraordinary response from outside the affected community or area'. Thus, disasters may be either natural, such as floods droughts, cyclones and earthquakes or human made such as nots, conflicts, refugee situations and others like fire, epidemics, industrial accidents and environmental fallouts.

Magnitude and Impacts

Globally, natural disasters account for nearly 80 per cent of all disasters affected people. The insurance industry estimates that natural disasters account for 85 per cent of insured catastrophic losses globally.[1] In 1996, 40 million disaster affected people depended on humanitarian assistance. About $30 billion were spent on humanitarian assistance in the first-half of 1990's. The average cost of natural disasters over the past 25 years amounted $87 billion a year.[2]

The South-Asian and African countries are the world's most vulnerable regions to both natural and human made disasters. These are worst affected regions. The increasing level of disasters and their impacts on human life have increased the vulnerability and marginalization of poor. India is one of the world's major theatres of disasters. The frequency of all categories of disasters is escalating, resulting in a multifold growth of injuries, disabilities, diseases, deaths, disrupting life supporting systems, deprivation of developmental benefits and economic burden of impoverished people.[3] In the decade of 1988-97, disasters in India affected 24.79 billion people are killed 5116 every year.[4] In year 1998 alone, disasters affected 34 million people in India and killed 9846 persons. Between 1985 and 1995, disasters caused an annual economic loss of about $1883.93 million.[5] The disaster situation in the country is found worsening year after year (Table 1).

The Central Water Commission has noted that 11.2 per cent of India is flood prone while in 1998, floods inundated 37 per cent of India. About 28 per cent of total cultivated area is drought prone.[6] The country's 7516 kms. coastline is continuously whipped by high velocity winds that pummel the east-coast states of Orissa and Andhra Pradesh annually, causing severe damage. Earthquakes rise the northern Himalayan region and the Deccan plateau in southern and Central India. It is estimated that 57 per cent of the country is earthquake prone.[7]

Table-1
Damage Caused by Natural Hazards in India

Year	*Number of People Affected (in Crores)*	*Number of Houses and Buildings Damaged*	*Amount of Property Damaged (Rs. Crore)*
1990	3.17	1019930	171.0
1991	3.477	1190109	190.0
1992	1.909	570969	205.0
1993	2.624	1529916	580.0
1994	2.353	1051223	183.0
1995	5.435	2088355	473.0
1996	5.499	237669	543.0
1997	4.438	1103549	NA
1998	5.217	1563405	NA
1999	5.017	3104064	NA
2000	4.162	2736355	1020.9

Source: Ministry of Agriculture, Government of India, Delhi.

Man-made disasters are equally havoc. The terrorist activities in north-east region and Jammu & Kashmir and the Godhra massacre and post-Godhra scenario in Gujarat have not been less fatal to the country. Even development induced displacement (about 40 million) has caused vulnerability and impoverishment to the poor. Thus, the country is, on the face of it, a dismal picture, with a mounting human cost and severe damage to resources. It requires multi-sectoral approach to manage the situation and mitigate the problems.

Droughts

Droughts with stretches of heat cracked and land, dried up wells and ponds, helpless farmers and hungry families create an atmosphere of doom and despair. Water scarcity is the most visible attribute of droughts. It is also noted that in the Himalayan foothills lime quarrying has destroyed the forests and desiccated the perennial mountain streams. Similarly, the mining of natural aquifers of maleolitic limestone for bourgeoning cement industries in Saurashtra has resulted in the ingress of saline desertification into the fertile ecosystem. In the westernghat watershed of Tungabhadra, iron ore mining has created drought by reducing base flows and increasing silt load on rivers. In Cherrapunji the mixed natural forests in upper catchments have been destroyed. The critical changes in agricultural practices, over exploitation of ground water, negligence of traditional water structures etc., have resulted in drought like situations. Today, the hydrological disequilibrium causes aridisation and scarcity in one region and water logging and floods in another, a fitting epitaph to iniquitous systems.[8]

About 19 per cent of India's total area, with 12 per cent of its population, is considered drought prone. India has faced droughts and famines even in ancient period, however, the frequency and toll has increased to the greater extent in 20th century. The country has faced major droughts in 1966-67, 1972-73, 1979-80, 1986-87 and 2001. In each instance, food production fell below the national average. There were large scale losses through starvation, depletion of assets and livestock, and high mortality. In 1987, over 267 districts and 166 million people were recorded drought affected. Even in 1996, 10 meterological sub-divisions received deficient rainfall from northeast monsoon, 67 districts had below normal rainfall from the northeast monsoon. The drought of 2001 in 11 states of India was one of the worst.[9] About 170 million people in one lakh villages of India (one sixth of the country) were hit badly (Table 2).

Table-2
Impact of Drought in India During 2001

State	*Total Districts*	*Affected Districts*	*Villages Affected (No.)*	*Population Affected (lakh)*	*Cattle Affected (lakh)*	*Crops Affected (lakh ha.)*
Chhattisgarh	16	25	10252	94	NA	11.36
Gujarat	25	22	11240	291	107	13.50
Madhya Pradesh	45	32	22490	127	877	39.52
Orissa	30	28	15000	119	399	11.00
Rajasthan	32	31	31000	330	399	89.47
Himachal Pradesh	12	12	NA	46	NA	0.88
Maharashtra	35	26	20000	455	2.5	45.09
Total	195	176	109962	1462	995.2	210.82

Source: Government of India, Ministry of Agriculture, Adapted from Down to Earth, June 15, 2001.

At present the three life support systems, i.e, land, water, and forests remain unintegrated administratively and management wise. Thus, the integrated approach of drought management is the need of hour.[10] India has more than a dozen programmes within a budget outlay of more than Rs. 11000 crore per year to fight drought and reduce rural poverty. The first drought management programme in India, the Rural Works Programme, was started in the year 1950. It's focus was employment generation. It was re-christened as the Drought Prone Area Programme (DPAP) in 1974, with the focus shifting to using employment generation for creation of works. About Rs. 2195 crore since 1974 have been spent under DPAP yet drought prone area has increased from million hectares in 2001. This is in addition to the 2.6 million hectares covered under the Desert Development Programme, which started as a programme to revive the ecology in hot and cold deserts.[11] Hanumantha Rao Committee (1994-95) observed that these two programmes failed grossly and recommended their implementation on watershed basis with people's participation to make the programmes sustainable.[12] It has been alleged that the programmes prioritize conservation structures. It may be noted that villages with community initiated water activities are showing brilliant innovation in planning the use of scarce water resources and land management.

Floods

Evidence indicates that in the first half of the 20th century, floods changed in character from relatively harmless 'inundations' to highly damaging 'disasters' and the authorities were still trying to come to terms with this new event.[13] The annual average area affected by floods between the devastating floods of 1953-54, which had inspired the formulation of First National Policy on Floods, to 1978, has been estimated around 76 lakhs hectares, of which 33 lakh hectares (43%) is accounted for by crop lands. The data for 1996 and 1997 indicate that there has been no decline in the trend. The focus has shifted away from the Gangetic belt with widespread damage to crops, houses, human and cattle lives. The worst affected states are Andhra Pradesh, Karnataka, Kerala and Tamil Nadu in the south, Maharashtra, Gujarat and Rajasthan in the west, Uttar Pradesh in the north, and Bihar and West Bengal in the east. Orissa and Assam, which are normally amongst the most flooded regions, appear to have been spread in recent past (Table 3).

Table-3
Flood Damage During 1981 to 1997 in India

Year	*Area Affected (Million Ha.)*	*Population Affected (Million)*	*Damage to Crops Value (Rs. Cr.)*	*Damage to Houses Value (Rs. Cr.)*	*Damage to No. of Houses*	*Human Lives Lost*	*Damage to Public Utilities (Rs. Cr.)*
1	*2*	*3*	*4*	*5*	*6*	*7*	*8*
1981	6.120	32.480	3.270	524.560	912557	1376	512.3
1982	8.870	56.010	5.000	589.400	2397365	1579	671.6
1983	0.020	61.030	3.290	1285.850	2393722	2378	873.4
1984	10.710	54.550	5.190	906.090	1763603	1661	818.1
1985	8.380	59.590	4.650	1425.370	2449878	1804	2050.0
1986	8.310	55.500	4.580	1231.58	2049277	1200	1982.5
1987	8.890	48.340	4.940	1154.640	2919318	1835	950.6
1988	16.290	59.550	10.150	2519.64	2276533	4252	1377.8
1989	8.060	34.150	3.010	956.740	782340	1718	1298.8
1990	8.069	40.259	3.179	695.610	1019930	1855	455.3
1991	6.169	33.844	2.511	573.795	1125254	1145	685.6
1992	2.092	19.090	1.427	654.918	56969	1367	1170.8

Contd...

1	2	3	4	5	6	7	8
1993	4.632	22.901	3.129	169.3	470951	930	48.1
1994	2.752	29.024	1.806	888.618	601379	1511	739.6
1995	6.111	38.831	3.359	351.552	1195714	2209	87.7
1996	7.420	38.383	3.365	404.287	406718	1306	861.6
1997	3.855	26.548	1.838	449.743	399334	929	971.6

Source: Central Water Commission, Ministry of Water Resources, Government of India.

The Central Government response may be either a policy response or an administrative one. The Centre's primary relief functions at the administrative level are forecasting, operation and publicity of warning systems, maintaining uninterrupted communication, providing transport for evacuation and movement of essential goods, ensuring the availability of essential commodities and medicines at reasonable prices, investment in infrastructure and mobilizing financial resources.[14] The relief functions consist of flood forecasts, military aid to civil authorities, contingency plans for the health, protection of crops, cattle, and human beings, inputs for the provision of drinking water, technical assistance in water management and coordination of activities of state and voluntary agencies.

CASE STUDY-1[15]

Flood in Eastern U.P. and People's Initiative

In 1998, the rainfall in eastern Uttar Pradesh was thrice the normal amount, unprecedented in the region's history. Some 1968 villages were affected in Gorakhpur, Deoria, Maharajganj and Kushinagar districts. Of the 1579 villages in Gorakhpur 1187 were marooned. The floods engulfed 235,882 ha. of land in these districts in eastern region of the state. At its peaks on 21st August the river Rapti topped 85.82 mts. Three days later road links to Lucknow and Varanasi were breached at several places. Gorakhpur town turned into an island, snapping water and electricity supplies for 5 days. The damage was so severe that the breaches were plugged and the traffic resumed only in October. The administration was ill prepared and additional boats had to be air lifted from Varanasi and Allahabad and the help of the armed forces sought to facilitate rescue and relief operations.

The impact of submergence was so severe that some areas remained waterlogged for between one to three months. The hardships faced by the residents of 104 villages in the Brahmapur and Rudrapur blocks of Gorakhpur and Deoria districts respectively is a case in point. These villages are located in a doab between Rapti and Gorra rivers. To protect the residents both rivers are embanked on either side. A road has been constructed right across bisecting these villages.

Various governments have repeatedly offered dams upstream around the India-Nepal border as the only long-term flood control solution. These multipurpose dams (Kamali and Mahakali) simultaneously serving the dual purposes of electricity generation and flood control, both these objectives have conflicting demands. The primary focus is on power and irrigation and flood control follow later.

Immediately following the disaster, a group of individuals concerned with the root causes of this calamity decided to facilitate the setting up of an Independent People's Commission on Floods in Eastern Uttar Pradesh, comprising experts and voluntary initiatives. The idea was to trace the genesis to floods, analyse their impacts on the lives of the poor, diagnose the rescue and relief operations carried out by various institutions and evaluate the appropriateness of techno centric flood measure.

Cyclones

India's coastline has been raked by cyclones for centuries. Indian sub-continents is the worst cyclone affected part of the globe, as a result of a low depth ocean bed topography and coastal configuration. During 1977 and 1996, cyclones in Andhra Pradesh accounted for 13563 human toll, 5.75 million livestock losses, 4.33 million houses damaged, 87.15 lakhs hectares crop damaged, and Rs. 565.499 lakh monetary losses (Table 4).

Table-4
Recent Major Cyclones in Indian Coast

State	*Time*	*Wind Speed (Km./h)*	*Sea Surge (m)*	*Damages Lives Lost*	*Houses Damaged (Lakh)*	*People Affected (Million)*
Andhra Pradesh	May 1990	240-250	5-6	928	13.86	7.7
Andhra Pradesh	Nov. 1996	140-150	2-2	1057	6.5	7*
Gujarat	June 1998	200	2-3	1250	2.57	NA
Orissa	Oct. 1999	270-350	6-7	10086	21.6	37.5

Note: *Denotes families.

Source: National Centre for Disaster Management, Indian Institute of Public Administration, Delhi.

We cannot prevent cyclones yet, but we can minimize the damage they cause. Measures such as a forestation, cyclone shelters, evacuation mechanism and increasing people's knowledge and skills will help in doing so.[16]

Earthquakes

Earthquakes unleash energies on the scale of nuclear explosions. They leave behind death, destruction and trauma of life that occupy victims.[17] It is already accepted that tectonic motion cannot be prevented, but the probability of the occurrence of earthquakes of different magnitudes can be estimated. Safety measures can then be under taken in advance. Damage control is a life saving and cost effective alternative to reconstruction.[18] Earthquakes in India have accounted for over 900 lives a year, 5 per cent of the world average of 18,000.[19] The number of deaths is not proportional to an earthquake's magnitude (Table 5). The impacts of earthquake depend on its magnitude, intensity, duration, ground movement frequency, geological and soil conditions, and the time of occurrence, plus factors like local population density and quality of structures.[20] The relief and rehabilitation efforts generally fail to provide adequate temporary shelter, rebuilding damaged agriculture fields, reporting of damaged infrastructure and mobilizing resources for development programmes. Thus, this is the need of the hour that interactions with the affected community and service providers should be more productive and people at large are educated for building their houses, which are earthquakes safe.

Table-5
Some Recent Major Earthquakes in India

Year	*Place*	*Magnitude*	*Maximum Intensity*	*Other Factors*
1991	Uttar Kashi	6.6	VIII	Lots of damage to life and property
1993	Latur	6.4	VIII	Heavy damage to life and property, about 8000 people killed
1997	Jabalpur	6.0	VIII	Lots of damage to property, about 39 people lives lost
1999	Chamoli	6.8	VIII	Lots of damage to property, about 100 people lost lives
2001	Bhuj	6.9	X	Huge devastation, about 20,000 people lost lives.

Source: National Centre for Disaster Management, Indian Institute of Public Administration, Delhi.

Landslides

Landslides are common geo-hazards especially in the hilly regions of the country. Steep slopes, unstable geology and heavy monsoon precipitation make the Himalayan region high hazard areas. Changes in land use pattern, application of scientific methods of cultivation, commercial exploitation of the forest covers and illegal felling of trees are some of important factors affecting the ecology of the Himalayan regions. Importantly, building structures use concrete slab constructions with little evidence of design and material considerations to reduce the material impact of earthquake. This type of growth creates the potential for an earthquake disaster of enormous proportions. Significantly, soil erosion is the common feature of the fragile environment. Natural erosion is a widespread phenomenon throughout the Himalayan region (Table 6). It is being accelerated by human interference. Thus, natural hazards such as floods, slope failures, snow avalanches, forest fires, and other biogeochemical processes commonly impose costs on people and property. In the Himalayan region as a whole the frequency and magnitude of these processes are increasing as a result of human induced environmental changes such as deforestations, increasing population, land use intensification, building of tourist infrastructure, and extension of the transportations system have increased exposure to risk from natural hazards.[21] The cost of restoration work and associated economic losses due to land slides in India has been estimated to be Rs. 2.00 crore.[22]

CASE STUDY-2[23]

Community Participation in Post-Earthquake Scenario

There are exceptional experiences of community participation in disaster mitigation and preparedness but post-disaster situations are many. Latur (Maharashtra) experience is one of them. The Latur earthquake of September 1993 showed there were two ways of dealing with the crisis: to build houses and give them to the people or support the people to rebuild their houses and their lives.

The World Bank and several donors founded the large scale state-led earthquake rehabilitation project. A major component, repairs and strengthening programme, which widened over two lakh families, remains one of the largest community based post disaster efforts in the country. As a part of the programme, in over 500 villages, the 'Swayam Sikshan Prayog' (self information centre) team mobilized women's group to work as 'samvad sahayak' (village assistant) in the reconstruction programme. Women came out and participated in the self-help house construction as labour. 'Community construction watch teams' ensured that problems such as delays in disbursement, access to materials coupons, uncooperative neighbours and corrupt engineers were tackled on the spot.

Village schools and college teachers volunteered for the 'Lok Jagar' (information campaign network of street plays etc.). 'Payawat' (creation of path) was the disaster mitigation training that synchronized the strengths of different stakeholders. Training was provided to 10 'contract persons' in each village. Women's groups mediated between different groups within the community to work for a common cause. In every cluster, women were encouraged to take part in melas (information fairs). Every village had a 'mahila mandal' (women club). They initiated social awareness programmes and health camps and mobilized money for community works. The administration used them in campaign for health immunization and literacy.

The World Bank and the State Government recognized participation and self-help as key concepts and accordingly committees were actually created at district and village levels. The absence of institutional mechanism to ensure or monitor participation kept these communities inactive in the initial stages. To ensure that the affected don't end up as helpless victims but as active partners in the process of recovery and change, their participation in the planning and implementation of the rehabilitation programme is imperative.

Table-6
Major Landslides in Uttaranchal

S.No.	*Location*	*Year*	*Life Claimed*
1.	Gudiya Tal	1868	73
2.	Nainital	1880	151
3.	Birehi River	1893	–
4.	Nainital	1898	27
5.	Alakananda	1970	70
6.	Khaila village	1977	–
7.	Bhagirathi	1978	25
8.	Mandakini	1979	50
9.	Neelkanth	1990	100
10.	Dewar Khadara	1991	25
11.	Piderghati	1991,1992,1993	59
12.	Ookhimath & Malpa	1998	326

Source: Satyendra, Disaster Management in the Hills, Concept Publis., Delhi 2003-10-15.

CASE STUDY-3

Governments Approach Towards Malpa Landslide of 1998

Malpa is a small village located in Pithoragarh district of Uttaranchal. It is a staging camp for the Kailash Mansarovar Yatra. In 1998, it had a population of 20 people living in five huts. The village was located on a nullah meeting the swift Kali River. It had two hotels, a transit camp of ITBP, a hut of Army and a number of huts to cater yatris.

On 17th August 1998, the 12th batch of yatries enroute to Mansarovar was asked to stay in view of some maintenance work on the track. At about 00.30 hours on 18th August a dust storm occurred which was followed soon after by a massive landslide. A major portion of hillslide fell destroying everything and buying the entire village under three to six metres. The slide cause the nullah to change course and wash away remaining houses. The debris forced Kali River also to change course, which washed the tract to village. It is estimated that 210 persons killed. The only 10 survivors were locals. The PWD guest house and ITBP transit camp had minor damage.

The District Magistrate sent Most Urgent Fax message to Army's HQ Central Command at Lucknow and Air Force's HQ at Allahabad for immediate assistance. He personally requested the Army's Brigade at Pithoragarh for all possible assistance. The UP Government announced ex-gratia grant of Rs. One lakh to the next of kin of those killed and Rs. 50,000 for those injured. Immediately, one JCO and five troops of Army moved on foot and reached Malpa by late evening. An officer with 25 troops belonging to ITBP along with a doctor reached the same time. Of the 10 survivors, nine escaped while the 10th was rescued from the hotel. Two columns of Kumaon Scouts led by an officer were dispatched at 11.00 a.m. on 18th August from Dharchula by road upto Tawaghat from where they moved on foot. They could not reach due to blocked track. One column of 65 troops from Charma was asked to be ready to be air lifted and another was kept ready. On 19th August six Army doctors reached Dharchula to receive casualties. Brigade Commander also moved there and took control of rescue operations. In the mean time attempts were made to open the track to Malpa from South. On 20th August one Army Column finally reached by helicopters, a full 60 hours after the incident. The Army sought assistance from civil operation next day. After 20th August relief work centred essentially around improvement of track to cater for the yatris returning from Mansarovar and extrication of bodies. The option of carrying out relief through Nepal was considered and ruled out due to procedural delay and long distances. The Army Engineers rapidly reconstructed the track, prepared the helipad and removed large boulders.

Between 24th and 29th August, 163 stranded yatris. Helicopters evacuated 14 KMVN personnel 8 policemen and 20 ITBP personnel and 10 injured from Malpa including 36 dead bodies. Surprisingly, Government officials visiting the site return by the same helicopter and expressed reservations in carrying the victims along with them.

There is growing realization that disasters are natural corollaries to inconsiderate development, unconscious able development activity, which paves the way for soil erosion and the creation of many landslides zones. The local and international organizations realize the need for a holistic programme of relief and rehabilitation targeting the livelihood, employment, health and minimum basic necessities of the most vulnerable and marginalized people. The Malpa incident (Case Study 3) highlights the governmental unpreparedness and apathy towards disasters. Malpa being the staging camp requires to be developed to cater the yatris and to meet any such eventuality. There should be created an organizational structure with basic rescue and relief equipments positioned at selected transit camp enroute of Kailash-Mansarovar Yatra, an annual ritual. Had the local community been mobilized and organized and the contingency plan adopted the loss to human lives would have been minimized.

Managing Disasters

Disaster management activity vertically comprises of three stages:

(A) Pre-Disaster Stage	*(B) Emergency*	*(C) Post-Disaster*
1. Preparedness ■ Hazard map preparation ■ Disaster Preparedness Plan ■ Land use Zone ■ Information, edu. and communication	1. Rescues 2. Immediate relief 3. Assessment survey	1. Social Rehabilitation ■ Education ■ Training ■ Rehabilitation of vulnerable sections ■ Health Services
2. Mitigation ■ Disaster resistant house construction ■ Population reduction in vulnerable areas ■ Refortification of old houses		2. Eco. Rehabilitation

Ironically, even if the community is associated in any disaster management process, scope is limited to post-disaster situation only, there is a need to involve the community in preventive measures, preparedness process, rescue and relief operations and rehabilitation activities. The governmental efforts should be to channelising the community potential, optimize the community resources, monitor the actions, guide the programmes and supplement the community efforts.

Global Strategy

Disaster management globally has been accepted as a necessity. As such, the United Nations earmarked the last decade of the past century (1990-2000) as International Decade for Natural Disaster Reduction. The world body targeted to achieve by all nations by the year 2000:

1. *Complete National Risk Programme*
   - Identify the natural hazards which pose the threat of disaster
   - Evaluate the geographic distribution of hazard threat and their frequency
   - Assess the vulnerability of the most important concentrations of the population, developments and resources.
2. *Implementation of Natural and Local Prevention and Preparedness Plans*
   - Adopt land use and construction practices that will reduce risk.
   - Adopt emergency response plans that identify hazards scenario essential efforts and responsible organizations.
   - Implement awareness programmes to educate people about risks and training programmes to improve the capabilities of the responsive persons.
   - Implement concrete measures to mitigate damages and increase resistance to hazard.
3. *Implement Global Regional, National and Local Warning Systems*
   - Implement systems for monitoring and predicting threatening phenomenon in time to reduce impacts.
   - Implement communication systems for deregulating warnings.
   - Educate decision makers about hazards and opinion for reducing disaster risks.

National Paradigm Shift

The challenges of disaster management include lack of efficient organization set up, lack of effective administration to deal with emergent issues. Apathetic attitude of bureaucracy and political leaders, lack of effective leadership and communication to deal with disaster issues, lack of coordination among the agencies engaged in rescue and relief, lack of positive interest among academic and management institutions, lack of utilization of multilateral technical assistance available through UN systems, lack of effective disaster preparedness, planning and mitigation strategies, lack of coordinated and concerted efforts for rehabilitation of disaster victims and providing relief to them etc.

The history of policy intervention in disaster management in India is long. But in recent years, many policy shifts have been observed. Earlier, the thrust was on crisis management and developing codes for providing relief and emergencies. Now the shift is on pre-disaster planning, risk assessment, hazard zonation, land use regulation, prevention, mitigation and preparedness. An integrated disaster preparedness and management approach began to reform the emerging policy paradigms and plans for action.[24] Anticipation planning for drought management has been stressed and implemented. The Central Water Commission has evolved a model bill for flood plain zoning but most of the State Governments have still not enacted the required laws, and imprudent use of river channels and flood plains continues resulting in heavy recurring flood relate losses.[25] To improve disaster management and enhance capabilities for mitigation of impacts, some measures have been initiated by Central Government which include intensive training programme, documentation of disasters and lessons to be learnt, dissemination of information, taking of long and medium term mitigation measures and integration of disaster management with overall development planning. Emphasis has been laid on public awareness, research and improving communication systems for effective disasters preparedness and management and the use of modern technologies.

Further, realizing the need to continue the momentum developed during the International Decade at national level, Government of India observed the decade of 1990-2000 as the National Decade for Disaster Reduction. It had underlined to implement sustainable development policies comprising of disaster prevention, mitigation, preparedness and relief. The Union Government has also started a number of important programmes including hazard mapping and vulnerability assessment of buildings, strengthening of information technologies, monitoring and impact assessment of natural hazards, human resources development, disaster warning system and setting up of high power committee on disaster management. Though every document emphasizes on seeking active involvement of people at every stage of planning, formulating and implementing the programmes, official apathy mars the spirit of this good intension. Often the officials lack requisite orientation and associating the community becomes a talk of the power gallery only.

Conclusion

The above analysis reveals that there is no holistic national risk programme in the country. The preventive stage i.e. pre-disaster stage covering preparedness and mitigation finds no place in national disaster scheme. The government machinery gears up once emergency arises as a result of disaster either natural or man-made. All efforts are kept concentrated during the emergency period. A lot of resources are put in during the period and once emergency is over our efforts are also lessened. There is however an apparent paradigm shift in disaster management practices in recent past but it needs to be community centred.

The policy shift in disaster management pre-supposes community empowerment and its involvement in disaster management exercise.Civil society should be involved and encouraged and empowered to be actively involved at every level. Community needs to be oriented to traditional preventive systems. A sustainable effort in this direction requires active involvement of civil society in mitigating disasters. It is better to mitigate disaster rather than manage the crisis. It is possible only through active involvement of community.

Even the post-disaster stages are not fully taken care of. The disaster management practices being implemented do not meet the local needs effectively. There are many short-comings and drawbacks in the existing disaster management policy and its implementation. There is no effective check on slab construction of housing structures, buildings, human intervention, deforestation, mining, etc. In the fragile environment there is a mismatch between the requirement of resources and resources available to the states for preparedness, mitigation, management and rehabilitation of disaster victims. Despite huge investment on disaster management, the frequency, magnitude and toll of disasters are gradually increasing with wide spread impacts. Lack of community participation in disaster relief and rehabilitation causes serious hindrance in disaster management. Civil societies may perform crucial role in disaster preparedness, mitigation, providing relief and rehabilitation of victims but they face problems, challenge, and constraints both on part of poor governance, community participation and resources.

Policy Recommendations

- There is a need to have a comprehensive national risk policy. An extensive survey should be made and a holistic programme should be formulated.
- There should be politico-administrative will for adopting sustainable development practices which ensure people centred, decentralized, development paradigms.
- There is an urgent need for a specialized facility to provide professional training, education and management skills to prepare competent, synergic and dedicated team for emergency services and providing relief to victims.
- Rehabilitation of disaster-affected population needs a revised approach with the focus on overall development of the region and providing financial support for rehabilitation.

REFERENCES

1. World Disasters Report, 1997.
2. Report of the Centre for Research into the Epidemiologist of Disasters (CRED), Brussels, 1999.
3. Parusuraman, S. & Unnikrishnan, P.V. (eds.) India Disasters Report (IDR), OUP, Delhi, 2000, 6.
4. World Disasters Report, 1999.
5. CRED, *op. cit.*
6. Annual Report of the National Centre for Disaster Management (NCDM), Delhi, 1999.
7. *Ibid.*
8. Sengupta, S., Droughts: Reaping Scarcity, in IDR, *op. cit.*
9. Malapert, R., Drought of Relief, Down to Earth, June 15, 2001, 30.
10. Saxena, N.C. as quoted in Down to Earth, *op. cit.*, 33.
11. Mahapatra, *op. cit.*, 35.
12. As quoted in *Ibid.*, 35.

13. Roy, D., Flood: A Small Matter of History, in IDR, *op. cit.*, 47.
14. *Ibid.*, 149.
15. Based on Lochand R., & Awasthi, S., Lessons from Eastern Uttar Pradesh, in IDR, *op. cit.*, 161-3.
16. IDR Team on Cyclones: Trapped in a Spin Cycle in IDR, *op. cit.*, 181.
17. Chopra, R., Earthquake: Reconfiguring Life and Landscape, in IDR, *op. cit.*, 201.
18. *Ibid.*
19. Arya, A.S., Action Plan for Earthquakes, in V.K. Sharma (ed.), Disaster Mitigation, IIPA, Delhi, 1994.
20. Strahler, A.N., and Strahler, A.H., Environmental Geoscience, Hamilton, San Abarbara, 1973.
21. Pandey, B.W., Geoenvironmental Hazards in Himalaya, Mittal, Delhi, 2002.
22. Thakur, V.C., Landslide Hazard Management & Control in India, ICIMOD, Nepal, 1996.
23. Based on Gopalan, P., Community Participation in Latur, in IDR, *op. cit.*, 210-3.
24. Dhar, T.N., Disaster Management : Policies and Imperatives, in Training Document, DPA, Lucknow University, 2002 (Mimeo).
25. *Ibid.*

17

People Participation in Environmental Conservation: A Case Study from Tamil Nadu

A. Subbiah

There has been a growing awareness of global environment concerns such ozone depletion, the greenhouse effect, climate change and biological diversity. There is a direct relationship between environment and the economic development of the country. The growth of heavy industries is creating many environmental problems. The chemical industries are producing dangerous chemical effluents. The industries near rivers are sending dangerous effluents into the rivers. This leads to air and water pollution. Cancer, liver damage, neurological impairment and many other health problems are their harmful effects. Using pesticides and chemical fertilizers in extensive cultivation of crops, creates environmental problems. But bio-fertilizers, bio-pesticides and over all bio-energy resources have economic and environmental benefits. The exhaust emission from automobiles is a major source of air pollution in towns. Improving combustion chamber design can reduce much of the unburnt carbon in the exhaust. The poor who constitute a majority of our country have practically no access to covered toilets. They use open places as toilets, which produce harmful effects.

This chapter is based on my Minor Research Project sanctioned by the University Grant Commission entitled "General Public Awareness of Environmental Pollution and Involvement in Environmental Conservation—A Case Study of Virudhunagar District (TAMIL NADU)." As a part of this study a survey was conducted to assess the involvement of general public in environmental conversation in Virudhunagar District. For the purpose of the survey 450 persons of Virudhunagar District were selected. There was a proportionate selection of rural, semi-urban and urban people (i.e.150 persons from rural, semi-urban and urban areas). The primary data were collected from the respondents of different age, sex, income and literacy groups. For the purpose of primary data collection, an interview schedule for the respondents was prepared. The interview schedule was used to ascertain the awareness of the respondents about the environmental pollution and to know the involvement of respondents in environmental conservation. This chapter deals with involvement of general public in environmental conservation in Virudhunagar District (Tamil Nadu).

Involvement of People

The intensive and extensive cultivation and the consequent necessity of applying pesticides and insecticides, chemical fertilizers and the like create many types of disharmony. Soil erosion, reduction of fertility, devastation of earthworms is the serious reasons behind the danger. Even though most of the respondents (farmers) in the district are aware that extensive use of chemical fertilizers and pesticides create environmental problems, they still apply chemical fertilizers and pesticides instead of using bio-fertilizers and bio-pesticides. By the personal observation of the investigator, it is found out that involvement in this regard is poor in the district. Involvement of general public involvement in environmental conservation with regard to the use of covered toilets is poor in the district. Out of the 450 respondents surveyed only 270 have used covered toilets (Rural 52, Semi-urban 85 and urban 133) and the remaining use open places as toilets.

Now the government, through municipalities and Panchayats are providing subsidized loans to construct covered toilets. In the district, even the persons who are having covered toilets in their houses use open places as toilets in rural and semi-urban areas. In the urban areas, some of the parents allow their children to use the open places, which are very near to their residential areas as toilets, even though they have covered toilets in their houses. This creates many environmental problems.

Garbage collection is the job of municipalities and Panchayats. The municipalities in Tamil Nadu including Virudhunagar District are now experimenting with collecting the garbage, from door to door in two large bags. One bag for plastic items, which are non-biodegradable items and another one for other garbage, which are biodegradable. The collected garbage is disposed off separately at the disposal points. This is a very good method of garbage collection done by most of the municipalities in Tamil Nadu including the municipalities in Virudhunagar District.

The people should come forward to help the municipal employees in collecting the garbage. The involvement of general public is essential to keep their area clean. Environment is every body's concern. The involvement of majority of the people is poor in this regard. In some places the municipal employees took the trouble of knocking on the doors of some of the people who had forgotten to keep the garbage out.

Ban on use of plastic bags has not been successful in the district. In big hotel the Government of Tamil Nadu bans use of plastic bags for packing foodstuff. But this is not effectively implemented in the district. In some hotels (where the plastic bags are banned), most of the customers insist the hotel employees to pack the foodstuff in plastic bags. People's involvement is very essential for not using plastic bags for packing the food articles. By the personal observation of the investigator, it is found that involvement of public in this matter is poor in the district.

There are a number of hotels near the National Highway (N.H.) No. 7, which passes through Sattur and Virudhunagar Taluks of the district. There are no proper drainage facilities in most of the hotels situated near N.H. 7 in the district. A large number of plastic carry bags with other waste find a permanent resting place near the hotels. That cause many environmental problems including air pollution.

The owners of the big hotels in the district, as an environmental conservation activity, should come forward to shift from poly bags to paper and cloth bags. By the personal observation of the investigator, it is found that their involvement in shifting the poly bags to paper bags or cloth bags is poor in the district.

Most of the extension areas of towns and villages in the district have no proper drainage facilities. In some places the sewage passes very near to drinking water pipelines, which causes water pollution. The people who are residing near the riverbanks are sending sewage into the river. The sewage passes near to drinking water pumping stations in some places that will result water pollution. The people residing near the riverbanks and the municipal authorities should come forward to do proper drainage facilities for sewage. They should not allow the sewage to join the rivers that affect the quality of the drinking water.

The district receives a scanty rainfall, with an annual average rainfall of only 985.7mm. The bulk of rainfall is received during the northeast monsoon season from October to December. In these months, people can involve in tree planting (especially drought prone trees) activities near their residential area. But the involvement in this regard is not encouraging.

Biogas provides a clean and efficient fuel for domestic purposes. It saves consumption of wood, charcoal, kerosene and diesel. It saves the labour of women and children in rural areas who normally spend considerable time and energy to cover long distances daily to collect fuel. It would eliminate the practice of indiscriminate felling of trees and consequently prevent soil erosion. Biogas can also be used for lighting purposes.

Biogas plants are the effective means of the sanitary disposal of human excreta. By putting all human and animal excreta into a biogas plant, the problem of waste disposal is solved at the family level itself. During decomposition in biogas plant, most of the diseases causing organisms are killed. Thus biogas plants improve sanitation. The involvement of general public in using biogas is poor in the district. Out of total 450 respondents, no one use biogas.

Conclusion

There is an urgent need to create public awareness for environmental conservation. In schools and colleges, Environmental education should be introduced as a compulsory subject. Now All India Council for Technical Education (AICTE) and University Grant Commission (UGC) insist the universities to introduce environmental education as a compulsory subject for all undergraduate courses. As directed by the AICTE and UGC, most of the universities of our country introduced environmental education as a compulsory subject for all undergraduate courses. Appropriate steps must be taken by the government to introduce environmental education subject as a compulsory subject in schools. This will create awareness among the younger generation of our country about environmental pollution problems and induce them in environmental conservation activities.

Regular awareness campaigns should be conducted by voluntary organization and by appropriate government agencies to create awareness among the general public about the environment pollution problems and induce them in environmental conservation activities. This helps us to protect our natural resources and to get pure air and clean water.

18

Surface Irrigation and its Determinants: A Study in Andhra Pradesh

P. Venkata Ramana Reddy and K. Satya Narayana Reddy

The world's largest civilizations have developed on the banks of rivers. Along with HYV Seeds and Fertilizers, water forms another important input of the package of new technology. Development of irrigation has conferred immense benefits to the rural to the Indian Rural Economy. Sustainable usage of natural resources is essential to realize the sustainable agricultural growth and development to cater the diversified food needs of the growing population in the third world countries in general and India in particularly. There are three categories of irrigation namely major, medium and minor projects. Projects with culturable command area of more than 10,000 hectares each are classified as major projects. The projects with culturable command area between 2000 to10000 hectares are classified as medium irrigation projects. The schemes involving culturable command are of less than area 2000 hectors, are classified as minor irrigation schemes. Major, medium, and minor irrigation systems are come under surface flow irrigation.

Surface water comprises of rivers, lakes tanks, reservoirs and canals. There has been a recorded evidence that Indian agriculture gamble with monsoon with series failure of crops resulting serious droughts and famines. It is also true in Kurnool District. Surface irrigation in Kurnool District has been fluctuating with great uncertainty over the long period of time. The present study deals with the determinants of surface flow irrigation, growth and instability of surface flow irrigation in Kurnool District.

Objectives

1. To study the growth and instability in irrigated area under different surface sources of irrigation.

2. To analyse and mate the determinants of the surface flow irrigation in Kurnool District.

Hypothesis

1. Surface flow irrigation has been greatly fluctuating.
2. Total surface source is declining over the period and hence there has been a corresponding decline in its gross irrigated area.

Methodology

The present study is based on empirical data mainly on secondary data, which is collected from various records of irrigation departments and published material of different government departments of Andhra Pradesh and Kurnool District. Data is analysed with the help of appropriate statistical techniques and presented to explain the different dimensions of irrigation facilities. The data of irrigation sources is available for all the 54 mandals in the Kurnool District.

To fulfill the first objective of the study, the simple averages and percentages over the totals were calculated and analysed accordingly. It is proposed to estimate the exponential equation of the form

$$Y = aX^b \qquad \text{-------} \; (1)$$

Where Y = area under Canals/Tanks/Other Sources
X = Time period.
a, b are the constants to be determined.

The compound growth rate was calculated by the formula (b-1) × 100

To estimate instability of surface source irrigation, co-efficient of variation was calculated.

$$C.V. = \frac{\sigma}{Y} \times 100 \qquad \text{-------} \; (2)$$

To estimate the net effect of each type of irrigation on total irrigated area a multiple regression analysis was carried out. The regression equation of the form is

$$Y = f(X_1, X2, X3, X4) \qquad \text{-------} \; (3)$$

Where Y = Total irrigation area
X_1 = Rainfall (mm)
X_2 = Irrigated area under surface sources

X_3 = Irrigated area under ground water sources
X_4 = Irrigated area under other sources.

To fulfill the scored objective, it is established a relation between total surface of irrigation and the canal, tank, other surface sources of irrigation. The proposed function is

$$Y = f(X_1, X2, X3, X4) \qquad \text{-------} (4)$$

Where Y = Total surface source irrigation
X_1 = Canal Irrigation
X_2 = Tank Irrigation
X_3 = Other surface sources irrigation.

Both the linear and log-linear equations were estimated for the functions (3 & 4). It is determined that the log-linear estimation yields better results. The analysis is based on the log-linear model.

The Irrigation Commission Report (1903) emphasized the need for proper management of water resources for irrigation to mitigate drought and famines. Similarly, the irrigation commission report (1972) Stressed upon the conjunctive use of water resources especially in drought prone area. Further the report stressed on the significance of minor irrigation sources which include tank irrigation, well irrigation, streams, nallas, spring channels etc. K.L. Rao, (1975) in his book "India's Water Wealth" tried to quantity water resources in India. He also tried to analyse various aspects of water used and the demand for water towards the end of the century Asit K. Biswas in his book "Water Management for Arid Lands in Developing Countries" analyzed different aspects of water resources. Johnson division UP in (1983) brought out act a book titled "Groundwater and Wells." It is an in-depth study covering various economic and technical aspects of underground water resources. V.K. Sharma in his research study 1985 on "Water Resources Planning and Management" referred to a wide spectrum of water resources use of economic development of nation. As it K.B. is was in his research work (1993) on water for sustainable development in his twenty first century. B.D. Dhawan (1993) in his book India's water resource development for irrigation opened that no technology or invention ment for the society. Prof. K. Rama Krishna Reddy (1995) in his book "Irrigation and Agriculture Development in India" stressed the importance of irrigation for agriculture development. In the light of the above studies it is proposed to study the surface irrigation developments and its determinants in Kurnool District.

There are two completed major irrigation projects in the district are K.C. Canal and Tungabhadra Project low level canal and four ongoing major irrigation projects serving the irrigation facility. Zureru and Sanjeevaiah Sagar (formally known as Gajuladinne Project) are two medium irrigation project in the district. Apart from some more minor irrigation schemes are serving irrigation facilities.

Gross Area Irrigated – Source Wise

(Area in Hectares)

Year	*Canals*	*Tanks*	*Other Surface Sources*	*Total Surface Irrigation*	*Total Gross Irrigation*
1994-95	80538	10927	532	91997	177045
1995-96	85962	12241	1760	99963	176834
1996-97	86421	17427	1447	105295	176834
1997-98	78046	12761	1395	92202	192899
1998-99	91404	17146	1852	110402	228257
1999-00	80236	12778	1751	94765	204389
2000-01	82465	18384	1622	102511	220951
2001-02	71080	12864	1044	84808	206610
2002-03	36449	12201	713	49363	166467
2003-04	40490	7362	580	48432	15394
C.V.	24.81	23.76	38.29	23.58	11.52

Source: Chief Planning Officer, Kurnool.

From the above table, the co-efficient of area under canal irrigation is 24.81 per cent. It is noticed that the instability in canal irrigation is 24.81 per cent. Similarly 23.76 per cent of variation in tank irrigated area and 38.29 per cent of instability in other surface sources of irrigation was recorded. The highest instability in surface irrigation was recorded under other sources of surface irrigation. The variation in total surface source of irrigation is 23.58 per cent. Almost, on average, nearly 29 per cent of variation was recorded in all types of surface irrigated area.

The above table tells us percentage of surface irrigation with gross irrigated area. During the year 1994-95, total surface source irrigation is 51.97 per cent. The canal irrigation is the major source with 45.50 per cent. But it has decreased to 26.30 per cent in 2003-04. By observing the tank irrigation, it has been fluctuations in the study period. The table reveals that the percentage of surface irrigated area in to total irrigated area is decreasing. It has been loosing its share from the total gross integrated area.

Per cent of Source Wise Surface Irrigation with Gross Irrigated Area in Kurnool District

Year	*Canals*	*Tanks*	*Other Surface Sources*	*Total Surface Irrigation*	*Total Gross Irrigation*
1994-95	80538 (45.50)	10927 (6.17)	532 (0.31)	51.97	177015
1995-96	85.962 (43.55)	12157 (6.61)	1760 (0.89)	50.60	197411
1996-97	86421 (40.90)	17427 (8.24)	1447 (0.68)	49.82	192901
1997-98	78046 (40.46)	12761 (6.62)	1395 (0.72)	47.81	192901
1998-99	91404 (40.04)	17146 (7.51)	1852 (0.81)	48.36	228257
1999-00	80236 (39.26)	12778 (6.25)	1751 (0.86)	46.37	204389
2000-01	82465 (37.33)	18384 (8.32)	1622 (0.73)	46.38	220916
2001-02	71080 (34.45)	12684 (6.14)	1044 (0.51)	41.05	206623
2002-03	36449 (21.90)	12201 (7.33)	713 (0.43)	29.66	166467
2003-04	40490 (26.30)	7362 (4.78)	580 (0.38)	31.46	153941

Source: Chief Planning Officer, Kurnool.

Source Wise Compound Growth Rates

Surface irrigation is the important source of irrigation in agriculture. The compound growth rate of surface irrigation i.e. canals, tanks and other sources will be analysed by estimating the exponential function.

Canals

Canals irrigation occupies first plays among surface irrigation sources. The fitted exponential of canal irrigation for the period 1994-95 to 2003-04 is:

$$Y = (62860) \times \frac{1.9247}{(0.6548)} \quad CGR = 92.47^{*}$$

In the above exponential equation, the estimated value of b, i.e. the co-efficient of X is 1.9247. The compound growth rate of canal irrigation is 92.47. It is noticed that the average annual growth in canal irrigation over the previous year is 92.47 hectares and it is significant at 5 per cent probability level.

Tanks

The percentage of X, i.e. the value of b is less than one (0.8104). It indicates negative growth. The compound growth rate of tank irrigation is – 18.96. It expresses that the average annual decrease in tank irrigation is 18.96 hectares.

$$Y = (33.1517) \times \frac{0.8104}{(0.9646)} \quad CGR = 18.9564$$

Other Sources

Other Sources of surface irrigation are nallas, spring channels etc. The percentage of surface irrigation is less than one in each year over the last ten years. It is negligible in Kurnool District. The exponential equation of the form is

$$X = (3.3709) \times \frac{1.0427}{(0.5371)} \quad CGR = 4.2746$$

The co-efficient of X is 1.042. From this value it is noticed that the average annual increase in other sources of surface irrigation is 1.0427. The compound growth rate of other sources of irrigation is 4.2746. This positive growth rate indicates that the average annual increase in other surface source irrigation over the previous year is 4.27 hectares. It is not significant growth rate in Kurnool District.

Total Surface Source Irrigation

The percentage of total surface irrigation in Kurnool District is continuously decreasing from 51.97 per cent to 31.46 per cent during the period 1994-95 to 2003-04. To calculate the compound growth rate of total surface irrigation the exponential equation for the last ten years is

$$X = (1023) \times \frac{1.2751}{(0.7353)} \quad CGR = -72.4941$$

The value of compound growth rate is negative with 72.50. It expresses that there is a decrease in total surface irrigation. The average annual decrease is 72.5 hectares over the previous year in Kurnool District.

To find out the combined effect of selected independent variables i.e. rainfall, surface irrigation, ground water irrigation and other sources on total irrigated area. The multiple regression analysis was adopted, the estimated equation is

$$Y = 3.4930 + 0.0148 \times 1 + 0.3752 \times 2 + 0.3333 \times 3 + 0.0548 \times 4$$

$$(0.0233) \quad (0.0257) \quad (0.0152) \quad (0.0346)$$

$R^2 = 0.9919$ $F = 413.6603^{*}$

The collective effect of all independent variables on the dependent variable (combined effect R^2) is 0.9910. It explained that 99.1 per cent of variation in total irrigated area by all selected independent variables. From F-test statistic, it is observed that the collective effective of independent variable is significant at 5 per cent probability level. It is observed that the three variables surface sources, ground water sources and other sources of irrigation shows positive and significant effect on total irrigated area.

To establish the relationship between total surface source irrigation and canal, tank, and other sources of irrigation, a log-linear model function was used. i.e.,

$$Y = C_O X_1^{C1} X_2^{C2} X_3^{C}$$

The logarithmic form of equation is

$$Y = 0.6138 + 0.8421 \times 1 + 0.1375 \times 2 + 0.0066 \times 3$$

$$(0.0078) \quad (0.0089) \quad (0.0037)$$

$R^2 = 0.9991$ $F = 57118.03^{*}$

It is noticed that the collective effective of all independent variable i.e. canal, tank and other sources of irrigation to the total surface irrigation (R2) is 0.9991. It explained that 99.91 per cent of variation in total surface irrigated area by all selected independent variables. From F-test statistic, it is observed the collective effect of independent variable is significant at 5 per cent probability level. The values of estimated co-efficient indicate that every unit increase in each of the independent variables will increase the dependent variable by 0.8412, 0.1375 and 0.0066 units respectively.

From the above analysis, it can be inferred that the area under surface source irrigation has been decreasing in Kurnool District due to the uncertain and scanty rainfall since surface irrigation sources have direct functional relationship with rainfall. The canal irrigated area is highly influencing in the total surface irrigation followed by tank irrigation. Other sources of irrigation is positive but not at significant. The co-efficient of variation in total surface source irrigation is 23.5 per cent. The percentage of surface sources, canal. Tanks and other sources irrigated area is decreasing, through this decrease, it is inferred that the total surface irrigation is declined from 51.97 per cent to 31.46 per cent.

Through the compound growth rates, the canal irrigated area compound growth rate is 92.47 hectares over the previous year. It is noticed that the negative growth rate was identified in the tank irrigated area. The annual average decline in the tank irrigation over the previous year is 18.96 hectares. Total surface source irrigated area has been declining with 72.49 hectares over the previous year.

Through the multiple regression analysis it is identified that the effect of each independent variable was 84.12 per cent, 13.75 per cent and 0.66 per cent on the dependent variable surface source of irrigation.

From our study, it is suggested that, to raise the surface sources of irrigation in Kurnool District, proper harvesting of rainfall is an important one. Construction of reservoirs, tanks, canals, check-dams etc. are also raise the irrigated area through surface flow of irrigation. By enhancing the surface sources of irrigation the ground water level may be increased.

REFERENCES

Asit. K. Biswas: "Water Management for Arid Lands Developing Countries" Oxford University Press, 1980.

Charan A.S.: "Irrigation Development in India: Problems and Prospects" Vishuham, Vik 5, 1979.

Dawan, B.D.: "Irrigation in India's Agricultural Development", Sage Publication, New Delhi 1986.

Iqbal Ali Gold: "Irrigation and Agricultural Realities and Challenge under Mallikarjun. G. Under Cool Water Resources: Seminar 26-27 March 2005, S.K.U. Anantapur.

Johnson Division Uopinc : "Groundwater and Wells" Johnson Division Minnesota USA-1983.

Lakshminarayana Reddy. K., "Economic of Rural Drinking Water University Book House Pvt. Ltd., Jaipur - 1997.

Ramakrishna Reddy. K., "Irrigation and Agriculture Development in India" Ashish Publishing House, New Delhi-1995.

Sharma V.K., "Water Resources Planning and Management" Himalaya Publishing House, Bombay-1985.

Satyanarayana G., "Water Resource Management in A.P." UGC Seminar is S.K.U. March, 2005.

Part–5
WOMEN EMPOWERMENT

19

Problems of Women Entrepreneurship in India

D. Pulla Rao

Women community though equal to men in population, is subject to a lot of deprivations even, in this modern sophisticated world. Women are still treated as the second rated citizen or subordinate to men in all major fields of life i.e., social, economic and political. Though various efforts are being made to improve the status of women, women folk could not make maximum use of them and hence remained backward. In almost all countries, the governments are providing special provisions for women's development and efforts are being made to extract maximum use of women's talent. It has been clear for decades that women in many parts of the world make key contributions in areas of development such as agriculture, health, education, water resources management etc.

In India, the shift from "welfare" to "development" of women took place in the Sixth Five-Year Plan (1980-85). The Eighth Five-Year Plan (1992-97) promised to ensure that the benefits of development from different sectors do not bypass women. The Rashtriya Mahila Kosh was set up in 1993 to meet the credit needs of the poor and the asset less women. The Ninth Five-Year Plan (1997-02) made two significant changes in the strategy of planning for women. Firstly, "empowerment of women" became a primary objective and secondly, the plan attempted "convergence of existing services" available in both women-specific and women related sectors. The Tenth Five-Year Plan (2002-07) has made a major commitment towards "empowering women as the agent of socio-economic change and development". Based on the recommendation of National Policy for Empowerment of Women, the Tenth Five-Year

Plan suggests a three-fold strategy for empowering women, through social empowerment, economic empowerment and gender justice.

The Concept of Entrepreneurship

Entrepreneurship is the creative and innovative response to the environment, which can take place in variety of fields of social endeavour-business, industry, agriculture, education, social work and the like and it is the potent limiting factor in economic development. It is an act of assuming risk of business ownership. In fact, it is the mental urge to take risk in the face of uncertainties and an initiation and capacity of seeing things in a way afterwards proves to be true. And it is an individual set-up of managing things in a proper manner. It is multidimensional encompassing financial, managerial and functional aspects.

Empowerment of Women

In India, females' head only 10 per cent of the total households and the ownership of land and other properties are mainly in the name of the male members of the family. Hence, women have hardly any ownership of resources and autonomy to take decision. However, the participation of women in income generating activities of the family has been increasing over time. Female work participation not only increases their family income but also brings economic independence among women in the household. This helps them to participate more effectively in intra-household decision-making and have better access to information. Moreover, where women are economically active, female children are perceived as potential wage earners and they receive a higher share of household resources than where women are economically unproductive. But female work participation alone cannot ensure true economic empowerment as the ownership of resources may still lie in the hands of the male members. Thus, female work participation rate is a necessary condition but is not a sufficient condition for economic empowerment of women. Economic empowerment of women is possible only when women have full autonomy to spend their income and also control resources. Entrepreneurship development among women can be considered a possible approach to economic empowerment of women. A woman as an entrepreneur is economically more powerful than as a mere worker because ownership not only confers control over assets (and liabilities) but also gives her the freedom to take decisions. This will also uplift her social status significantly. Through entrepreneurship development a woman will not only generate income for herself but also will generate employment for other women in the locality. This will act as an employment in the women sector.

Women Entrepreneur

In India, very few women entrepreneurs are in the big enterprises. They are mainly concentrated in the Small Scale Sectors (SSIs). In the SSI sector the participation of women can be classified into three types: Women as the owners of enterprises, Women as managers of enterprises, and Women as employees. With regard to ownership an SSI managed by one or more women entrepreneurs in propriety concerns or in which she/they individually or jointly have a share capital of not less than 51 per cent as Partners/Shareholders/ Directors of Private Limited Company/Member of Cooperative Society is called a women enterprise. The share of the units managed by women in terms of employment was 7.14. The employment generated per Rs. one lakh investment is the units managed by women was 2.49. Women in India are still less likely to start a new business than men, although the gap seems to be declining. The share of female entrepreneurs (10%) is still significantly low when compared to their work participation rate (25.7%). Hence, it is very important to know the impediment to growth of women entrepreneurship.

Women Entrepreneurship: Indian Scenario

Traditionally, it was believed that women are physically and mentally weak and, hence, they are not fit for hard, hazardous and risky tasks. But with the increasing empowerment of women in the world, now no job, profession or enterprise is such which women cannot undertake. Contrary to it, it can be observed that in oriental societies the women are born-risk seekers. They grow up with the feeling of management of risk and adjustment/adaptation with the changing environment. Women entre-preneurship is the process where women take lead and organise a business or industry and provide employment opportunities to others. Though women entrepreneurship is a recent phenomenon in India, which came into prominence in late 1970's, now we see that more and more women are venturing as entrepreneurs in all kinds of business and economic activities and service sector. Though at the initial stage women entrepreneurship developed only at urban areas, lately it has extended its wings to rural and semi-urban areas too.

Women industries mainly fall into informal sector where less than 10 persons with or without power and less than 20 persons without power are engaged and they will be of labour intensive and rely on indigenous resources, family ownership and only small scale skills are sufficient. Though earlier women concentrated much on traditional activities, due to the spread of education, favourable government policies towards development of women entrepreneurship, women have changed their attitudes and diverted towards non-traditional activities too. They show favourable response to changing situations and get adjusted to them and have improved their position. The Government and Non-Government Organizations are giving more prominence to promote self-employment among women and build women entrepreneurship. Special financial assistance is provided and training programmes are organized for women to start their ventures.

Work Force Participation Rate (WFPR) in India

The Work Force Participation Rate (WFPR), also called Labour Force Participation Rate (LFPR) is the percentage of working population to total population of a country. It is an important factor which affects production, saving and capital formation. It helps in analysing the occupational structure of a country and thus its level of employment. WFPR depends up on the age and sex structure of the population, age of marriage, average size of family, education, health, attitude to work, availability of work, etc. The work force participation rates in India for the Census years 1901 to 2001 are shown in Table-1. WFPR in the pre-independence period from 1901-31 was higher than in the post-independence period from 1951-91, except for the Census year 1961. It is due to the change in the use of different definition of the 'work force' in the censuses. In the pre-independence census, main workers were lumped with unpaid family workers. But in the 1951 Census, unpaid family workers were excluded from the main workers. That is why the WFPR in 1951 was 39.1 per cent as compared to more than 43 per cent in the pre-independence years (1901-31). Again in 1961, WFPR increased to 43 per cent because persons whose main activity was not economic were included in the main workers. WFPR declined to 34.2 per cent in 1971 because persons engaged in part time activities were excluded from the category of the main workers. But since the Census of 1981, WFPR had risen to 36.7 per cent in1981 to 37.7 per cent in 1991 and to 39.3

per cent in 2001. This has been due to the adoption of a rigorous of "worker" in terms of main workers and marginal workers.

In the case of WFPR by sex, it had been much higher for males as compared to females. This is because of the social status of women. They are generally not allowed to undertake productive work outside home. But since 1971, their work participation rate has been on the increase. It rose from 14.2 per cent in 1971 to 25.7 per cent in 2001. This is due to increasing literacy and declining birth rate. Now more and more women are entering the industrial and service sectors. With urbanisation and expansion of dairy and poultry farming, fisheries, horticulture, etc., more women are participating in such activities. On the other hand, the work participation rate for men declined from 52.7 per cent in 1971 to 51.9 per cent in 2001. This again shows that more women are taking the place of men in productive activities.

Table-1
Gender-Wise Work Force Participation Rate in India: 1901-2001

(In Percentage)

Year	*Females*	*Males*	*Persons*
1901	31.1	61.1	46.6
1911	33.7	61.9	48.1
1921	32.7	60.5	46.9
1931	27.6	58.3	43.3
1951	23.3	54.0	39.1
1961	28.0	57.1	43.0
1971	14.2	52.7	34.2
1981	19.7	52.6	36.7
1991	22.7	51.6	37.7
2001	25.7	51.9	39.3

Source: Census Reports for various years.

Employment of Women

Women contribute greatly to the economy. They are pioneers in various professions. Women are working in different sectors of the economy as agricultural labourers, road construction workers, domestic helpers, petty crafts women, self-employed women, doctors, engineers, lecturers and white collared executives. Employment of women is an index of their status in society. According to census data the work participation rate of women is steadily arising from 14.22 per cent in 1971 to 19.67 per cent in 1981. The rise in work participation of women has been even steeper from 37.81 lakhs in 1991 to 47.74 lakhs in 1998. Table- 2 shows male and female work force in public and private sectors.

The UN Statistics on women indicate that a majority of the female work force is involved in unpaid family work. Only a few of them work as employees, very few were self-employed or employers. An overall representation of women in the labour force still remains low. It reflects a higher capacity of the population. Globalisation and liberalization and privatization have adverse effect on women employment. They are loosing employment due to technological changes, substitution of women labour and deskilling of women's work.

Table-2
Employment of Women in Organized Public and Private Sectors: 1971-2001

Year	*Public Sector*		*Private Sector*		*Total*	
	Male	*Female*	*Male*	*Female*	*Male*	*Female*
1971	98.70	8.60	56.80	10.80	155.50	19.30
1981	139.80	14.90	61.00	12.90	200.50	27.93
1991	167.10	23.40	62.40	14.30	229.50	37.81
1997	168.66	27.28	67.77	19.09	236.08	46.37
1999	166.04	52.11	66.80	20.18	232.84	48.29
2000	164.57	28.57	65.80	20.66	230.37	49.23
2001	162.79	28.59	65.62	20.90	228.40	49.49

Source: Ministry of Labour, (DGE&T).

Major Areas of Women Entrepreneurship

Agriculture, Horticulture, Sericulture, Dairying and Animal Husbandry, Fisheries, Home based Industries like Handicrafts, Beedi Industry, Agarbati making, Tailoring and Garment Industry, Pottery and Blacksmithy Industry, Doll making, Fancy items, Bee keeping, Jewellery, Beauty Parlour, Printing, Textiles, Electronics, Chemicals, Food processing, nursery and Baby crèche centres, Stationary etc. Thus women entrepreneurs can take a lead in both unorganized and organized sectors.

Major Problems of Women Entrepreneur

In India women entrepreneurship is facing so many problems. The major problems are:

- *Family Discouragement:* As women in India have to work amidst social taboos, restrictions etc., they are not supported much to undertake entrepreneurship by their family members.
- *Social Barriers:* Women entrepreneurs in India are always seen with suspicious eyes, particularly in rural areas, they face more social barriers.
- *Caste and Religion:* Though India is a secular country, in practice, castes and religious systems dominate with one another and it hinders women entrepreneurs.
- *Lack of Self-Confidence and Risk Bearing Capacity:* Women lack self-confidence and always feel that they may not be successful and hence hesitate to take risks.
- *Psychological Factors:* Always woman feel that she is 'women' and less efficient than man and hesitates to take risks. She has to play a dual role if she is employed or engaged in work. She has to strive hard to balance her family life with care and hence feels better to be housewife.
- *Lack of Practical Knowledge:* Though women may be educated and have qualified knowledge, she lacks practical knowledge and hence hesitates to establish her own venture.
- *Problem of Finance:* Women entrepreneurs lack property in their own name and hence banks and financial institutions may hesitate to finance women based projects.
- *Problem of Marketing:* As generally women entrepreneurs will have small-scale business they have to strive hard to sell their products in the modern competitive world. Their marketing knowledge will be less and lack marketing skills as compared to men.
- *Problems of Middlemen:* Women entrepreneurs have to face the problems of middlemen more, as they generally depend, more on them. Their margin of profit will be more and hence cause for higher selling price, which affects consumer's attraction towards women's products.

- *Lack of Information:* Women entrepreneurs lack knowledge of availability of raw materials, financial facilities and government help and subsidy etc.; they lack knowledge of advanced technology also and hence cannot widen their markets.

Hence, it becomes necessary for the society and government to find remedies for the problems of women entrepreneurship. Already the Central and State Governments and Non-Governments Organizations have taken so many steps to solve the problems of women entrepreneurs, yet they have to provide special incentives and subsidy. As entrepreneurship opportunities will be more in small and medium scale industries, the sector should be given prominence and proper marketing strategy of such products should be planned and implemented, which will give scope for women entrepreneurs. If Indian women's talent will be utilized properly, one day India will become an ideal country to others.

REFERENCES

Birley, S. (1989): "Female Entrepreneurs: Are they Really any Different", Journal of Small Business Management, 27 (1), pp. 32-37.

Garg, R.B.L. (2004): "Women Entrepreneurs: Problems and Prospects", Social Welfare, 50 (12), March, pp. 16-18.

Khurana, I.R. (1988): "Strategy for Rural Development", Khadi Gram Udyog, 34 (8), pp. 335-344.

Mohiuddin, A. (1987): "Entrepreneurship in Rural Women", Kurukshetra, 35 (12), pp. 22-25.

Nelson, R.E. (1985): Entrepreneurship and Self-Employment Training, Asian Development Bank, Manila.

Rao, S.K. (1976): Entrepreneur Development in India – Is Achievement Training the Answer, Laghu Udyog, 4. pp. 9-12.

Sinha, Poonam. (2003): "Women Entrepreneurship in the North-East India: Motivation, Social Support and Constraints", Indian Journal of Industrial Relations, 28 (4), April, pp. 425-41.

Sundaram, I. Satya. (2004): "Encouraging Women's Entrepreneurship", Social Welfare, 50 (12), March, pp. 15-19.

Vidyu Lata. (1990): Developing Rural Women, Discovery Publishing House, New Delhi.

Vitz, M.D. (1987): Women Entrepreneurs in India, Mittal Publications, New Delhi.

20

Empowering Tribal Women: Experience of Andhra Pradesh

L. Reddappa

Admittedly, women have been playing a vital role in the family, more so the economically and socially backward women. They used to have more responsibilities in domestic and agricultural activities. More specifically, there is no substitute for women in certain activities of domestic and agriculture. Their ability to save and invest in their families is well documented. As the family's nutritional gatekeeper, women fight hunger and malnutrition. However, their role in decision-making in the family matters like purchase of assets, provide education, perform marriage and payment of dowry to their girl child, adoption of family planning methods; and purchase of household items has been limited. Their voices are missing on key issues and important decisions not only at the family level, but also at higher levels – society, community, institution, organization, state and nation. The social conventions and stigmas of the past in the society have made them to restrict their movement either to kitchen or to work in the field of agriculture. More specifically, it is a custom in the society even now that the assets management and financial matters are to be considered as male prerogative, with the exception of few cases where the women have education and employment, and have fixed assets of their own, particularly in urban areas.

Empowering of women can be viewed as sensitisation of gender issues; awareness creation about their rights and entitlements; building capacities of the women in the involvement of decision-making process; improvement of their leadership qualities and organising abilities to solve their problems and achieve their needs on their own. Apart from these, building capacities of the women through imparting training to improve their technical skills and entrepreneurial abilities; creation of basic infrastructure facilities; and improve their access to credit for creating income generating assets to achieve economic independence. It is obvious that the former would create social empowerment and latter would create economic empowerment. Both are required for alround development of women on par with men. The reservation policy adopted to the women in education, employment, legislation and judiciary of the country at all levels has achieved social and economic empowerment to a certain extent vertically in all sections of the society, more so in the hierarchy of the privileged sections. However, the women in rural areas, particularly the poor neither have involvement in the process of decision-making at family and higher levels nor have economic independence due to illiteracy, poverty, lack of assets and required skills for generating income. Thus, the need of women empowerment has received the attention of the policy-makers, planners, academicians and administrators, feminists, etc. for all-round development of the nation.

Although concerted efforts have been made for women empowerment in tribal areas, they could not achieve expected results due to illiteracy, poor health facilities and malnutrition, unemployment and under-employment, lack of alternative sources of employment, poverty, and also lack of income generating assets of their own and poor access to social and economic infrastructure, and other services. The individual beneficiary oriented programmes implemented to them are lacking integrated approach for the development of the community as a whole covering both its economic and social needs through building their own capacities of the community for optimum utilisation of resources. The welfare programmes have changed the direction from their own traditional path and increased the dependency of the tribals on the government. This in turn has destroyed the traditional tribal values of their self-reliance and communal spirit. It reflects that the interventions of the government have neither brought about adequate changes for their economic empowerment nor continue their own self-reliant economic life. The missing link in the very approach of their development is community participation, which is vital to their empowerment.

The empowerment process is classified into six stages– awareness building, skill and capacity assessment, capacity building and skill development, participation and gender control in decision-making, action for change and evaluation. Realising this, the government departments and development institutions in the country have taken initiatives for involvement and participation of rural women in the process of decision-making and also to achieve their economic independence. Provision of reservations to women in the Panchyati Raj Institutions and local self-government is a positive sign in the process of women empowerment in rural areas. Imparting training programmes for entrepreneurship development and provision of access to credit are the other important initiatives in the direction of women empowerment. More specifically, the programmes like DWCRA of IRDP and ICDS of World Bank, Women Self-Help Groups (SHGs) etc. have been implementing for the exclusive benefit of women societies/groups in Andhra Pradesh.

Empowerment of Women in Tribal Areas

The women self-help groups in tribal areas of the state have not popularised on par with the plain areas due to their poor saving and investment habits, lack of regular incomes, and also lack of interaction with the people in plain areas and with government officials, who are implementing the programmes of women SHGs. At the same time, there were instances of misutilisation of the government support (matching grants) by the middlemen/women in the earlier years. All these factors pushed them to the back in the formation of women SHGs in tribal areas. No doubt, each tribe is sociologically united and come together to perform ceremonies, poojas and festivals. However, they are poor in solving their community needs like drinking water, rural and village roads, health facilities and school buildings, irrigation and creation of other community assets through government support programmes. This may be perhaps due to lack of leadership qualities and organising abilities to make use of the government support. The tribals were non-participant observers 'or spectators in their own development programmes for the past several years, because these works were entrusted mostly to the private contractors for creation/execution of the works.

Of late, realising this, Andhra Pradesh Participatory Development Project (APPTDP) was initiated in tribal areas, which was focussed on capacity building of the Community Based Organizations (CBOs) like VTDAs, SHGs and individual tribals in the creation/execution of the individual and community assets on their own instead of private contractors. To achieve community participation among the tribals, Community Development Coordinators (CDCs) were appointed to work closely with the community. The CDCs have worked with the CBOs, particularly SHGs in mobilising their savings and contribution of their labour. They also extended guidance and cooperation in taking up of all soil conservation works with close monitoring of the women SHGs. There was a mass movement in the formation of women SHGs in tribal areas, because the groups can generate income through wage employment in the programmes of soil conservation, minor irrigation, horticulture schemes, etc. besides creation of income generating assets. The women SHGs were improved their level of income, savings and also created valuable community and individual assets with the support of the government.

APPTDP was under implementation for a period of 8 years, between 1994-95 and 2002-03. In the present study an attempt is made to analyse the empowerment of women SHGs based on the eight indicators as prescribed by the Hashemi, *et. al* in their study on rural credit programmes and women empowerment in Bangladesh. The eight empowerment indicators are: *(a)* mobility, *(b)* economic security, *(c)* ability to make larger purchases, *(d)* relative freedom from domination within the family, *(e)* political and legal awareness, and *(f)* involvement in political campaigning and protest. The study has been carried out based on the primary data/information collected from 94 women Self-Help Groups (SHGs) in 30 villages spread over in 6 Mandals, which are top in the order of highest tribal population in Adilabad district of Andhra Pradesh.

Socio-Economic Background of Tribals in Adilabad District

Major tribes living in Adilabad district of Andhra Pradesh are Gonds, Kolams, Pardhans, Nayakpodes, Thotis, Manne and Banjaras. All the tribal sub-castes have a symbiotic relationship with each other, with the exception of Lambadas/Banjaras. The Gonds are the numerically predominant and sociologically significant group. The Kolam, a primitive tribe is also significant in the size of tribal population after Gonds. Their food habits, working patterns and abilities to work in agriculture and allied activities are also different from the people in plain areas. Generally, the Gonds and Kolams managed to live with less intake of food and more of alcoholic drinks, which has made them to keep on rest for longer hours. Their ability to work in the field of agriculture is relatively poor and the productivity of their labour is much less compared to the non-tribals. The other tribes are thinly populated in certain pockets of the district. They are also depending on agriculture as their primary occupation. Majority of the tribals in the district could not speak even Telugu, which hampers their interaction with the non-tribals and also with the government machinery working for their welfare. The other significant tribal group in Adilabad district are lambadas. They are progressive in outlook and depend on agriculture and allied activities. In recent years, they are adopting modern methods of cultivation on par with the other farming communities of the state. They are now competeting for almost all the occupations including government service, legislations and judiciary of the country by virtue of the tribal reservations.

The group meetings are being conducted once in 15 days (25%) and once in a month (70%) by 95 per cent of the groups and the remaining 5 per cent of the groups are irregular in conducting their meetings. The attendance for the group meetings has been 98 per cent, which is quite encouraging. The collection of the monthly contributions are mostly done by the President/Secretary (60%), member of the groups (25%) and Village Liaison Workers and others (15%). It was observed from the study that all the group leaders have undergone training to improve their organising abilities and leadership qualities; to run the group activity with true team spirit; and to solve their common/community problems. They expressed that the training was most useful to achieve their community needs without the involvement of private contractors and outsiders.

The APPTDP has made them to purchase tent house material on account of the savings available with them. Now, all the members of SHGs are happy to perform social functions by using these tent house material, which is available at their disposal on cheaper rates of rent. The recent received on the tent house material would be the income of the community or SHGs. Under the programme of community participation, the SHGs were also given with television sets, tent house, mike sets, Harmonium and Tabla on payment of 50 per cent self-contribution. All these small incentives have made the women groups active in the mobility of the community.

Now, they are meeting with the officials more frequently without any hesitation and also enquiring about the beneficiary oriented programmes of the government. They are identifying not only their individual needs but also their community needs like road facility, bus facility, and drinking water facility. They had solved their community needs with teamwork, involvement of their physical labour and also participation in terms of financial self-contribution. Now, the level of confidence and true spirit of team work has developed among them. They are under transition to achieve self-reliance without depending on the private contractors.

Economic Security

Under the programme of APPTDP all works relating to minor irrigation, soil conservation works and horticulture activities have been entrusted to women Self-Help Groups (SHGs) on nomination basis. These works have generated substantial incomes to the women SHGs through wage employment, which has certainly increased food security. Now, there was mass movement in the tribal villages to take up more such works to earn more income through wage employment, because they hardly get any employment from private sources with reasonable wage. For instance, the existing wage rate to work in the agriculture sector has been varied from Rs. 20 to Rs. 50 per day depending on the type of work, season and area, which may be available for 30 to 60 days in the entire season. It shows that the wage employment is more crucial for sustenance of the family and also for small investments intended to purchase agricultural inputs. Hence, soil conservation works were taken up to achieve twin objectives, provision of livelihood and stabilising agriculture for sustainable development through wage employment.

The groups have been formed with common interest to prosper on government support, because each member of the family can earn an income of Rs. 100 to Rs. 150 per day in working together as a wage labour in different soil conservation activities. All the group members have a binding to save 50 per cent of their total wage income generated from the soil conservation works as implemented by the government. It was observed from the study that the groups in tribal areas have neither received matching grant nor revolving fund from the government in recent years as received other social groups other than the tribals, because the average age of the groups in tribal areas is much less than that of the groups in plain areas. However, they have generated savings of their own with team work. Now, majority of the groups (49%) have a cumulative saving of more than Rs. 40,000 (See Table -1).

Table-1
Savings Available with the SHGs

S.No.	*Range of Savings (in Rs.)*	*Number of Groups*	*Percentage*
1.	Nil	6	6.4
2.	Up to 5,000	8	8.5
3.	5,001-10,000	16	17.0
4.	10,001-20,000	5	5.3
5.	20,001-40,000	14	13.8
6.	40,001-1,00,000	36	38.3
7.	1,00,001 and above	10	10.6
	Total	94	100.0

The amount saved by the groups have been using as a common fund for creating community facilities and income generating assets of their own. Such groups are 71 per cent. The remaining 29 per cent of the groups have been sharing the common fund and utilising according to their needs and priorities. About 64 per cent of the groups expressed that the concept of the group activity is most useful and the remaining 36 per cent expressed that the group activity is useful and useful to certain extent. On the whole, the group activity is running with good cooperation and team spirit in 83 per cent of the groups; about 15 per cent of the SHGs are running with problems and the remaining SHGs (2%) were given up their thrift activity.

The soil conservation works have provided great impetus in growth of the income. This in turn has a positive impact in ensuring food security, enriching their nutrition levels of the women and children, minimising the health problems, increasing the expenditure on education. Now, they are realising the importance of education to their children.

Ability to Make Larger Purchases

- Purchased Tractors with a self-contribution of Rs. 1 lakh each in 2 study villages by the women SHGs.
- Purchased Thresher/Huller with a self-contribution of Rs. 11,000 each in 8 study villages for the purpose of their crop harvesting.
- Purchased Flour Mill/Girni with a self-contribution of Rs. 13,900 each in 5 study villages.
- Purchased two Autos and one Jeep with a self-contribution of Rs. 30,000 to Rs. 60,000 each in 3 villages.

- Paid self-contribution and made efforts for getting protected water supply in 4 villages by the women SHGs.
- Generate power (electricity) supply with Pongima Oil in 2 villages.
- Constructed their own houses with the support of Group Sávings in 3 villages through housing scheme without depending on private contractor.
- Purchased pair of plough bullocks by the members of the SHGs in majority of the study villages.
- The women SHGs pursued/lobbied for getting sanction of cement roads in their villages, bus facility and protected water supply in half of the study villages.
- All these community assets are in use and the self-management of the asset has been considerably better in all the villages. However, the repayment has not been prompt in the case of all the community assets, particularly in the case of tractors. This requires guidance and training for optimum utilisation of the assets in the generation of income and self-management of the assets.

Relative Freedom from Domination within Family

- The amount available in their group savings account has been utilising by the group members to meet their demands like purchase of agricultural inputs, education for their children, health of their family members, and also for social functions.
- The groups have improved their capability in identifying their community needs and priorities, and distribution of their group savings as a loan to the members for meeting their needs like health problems, agricultural credit, children education, marriage and other social functions depending on the availability of group savings.
- It was observed from the study that they were lethargic, and shabby prior to the implementation of soil conservation works. Now, there was lot of change in their dress pattern, keeping their house and environment clean. There was a decline in the rate of hospitalization and occurrence of deaths as against prior to the implementation of Soil Conservation works through women SHGs.
- It was a convention that all the family members were used to spend lot of time to attend marriages and also important

festivals. Now their appearance and dress pattern explicitly improved and their attendance to the marriages has been minimised to one or two persons instead of the entire family as per the earlier practice. This may be perhaps due to their binding to the other group members in completing the soil conservation works.

- The amount of saving available with the SHGs was more than Rs. 50,000 in majority of the cases. In some of the groups, the total amount saved by them was more than Rs. 2 lakhs, which is mostly using for the purchase of community assets like tractors, jeeps, autos; and the agricultural equipments like threshers/hullars and seed drills to generate income for the group. The group savings were also used to purchase individual assets like Plough Bullocks as per the requirement of the group members. Now, they are firm to given up their lending activity from the traditional moneylenders.

Political and Legal Awareness

They are under the process of transition to achieve self-reliance without depending on private contractors of non-tribals. It will take some more time to take up big works (more than the worth of Rs. 10 lakhs) like laying of black top roads, construction of culverts and bridges, big M.I. Tanks, etc. besides the works involved with technical and engineering expertise. This may be perhaps due to non-involvement of the tribals in their own developmental activities for the past several years. However, after implementation of soil conservation works, the women self-help groups have achieved self-reliance at least to solve their community problems with their team effort.

The maintenance of the accounts and minutes of the meetings are written by the Village Liaison Workers (55%), VTDA Presidents (25%) and members of the educated persons (20%). It shows that they have not achieved self-reliance with regard to the self-management of the accounts. The transaction of bank account is mostly taken up by the President/Secretary (85%) and the remaining (15%) are doing by the group members. Added to this, there was no leadership change among the groups due to lack of leadership qualities and education for the other members of the groups. In spite of this, the members of the SHGs are happy with the acting leaders of their group. According to them, the group leaders have additional work without any monetary benefit. The group leaders have been reliable to them and putting their sincere efforts to strengthen the groups in all respects.

The empowerment achieved by the women SHGs are shown with a clear example from a village, Mahagoan of Narnoor Mandal that the contractor has created a small kunta with a cost of Rs. 2 lakhs under food for work programme without listening to the objections of the SHGs. As a consequence of which, they had strictly warned the VTDA President for non-payment of the amount to the contractor without any notice of the women SHGs, because the payment for the work has to be made to the contractor rooted through VTDA of the village. This matter is still pending for the past several months and it will not be settled, unless the contractor agree to pay at least 20 per cent of the project cost to the women groups. The contractor did not get any amount from the VTDA, in spite his sincere efforts, which shows the level of empowerment achieved by the groups.

It was observed from the study that the participatory methodology of APPTDP has improved leadership qualities among the tribals in 44 per cent of the cases. To achieve desired results to the community at large, team spirit is required among the beneficiaries/stakeholders. Otherwise, it would be difficult to achieve desired results to the community. The true spirit of teamwork has improved in 62 per cent of the beneficiaries. Involvement and decision-making by mobilising the stakeholders and resources have in 37 per cent of the cases. Lobbying for getting sanction has improved in 46 per cent of the cases. Involvement in identification of their community needs improved in 50 per cent of the cases. Ability to solve their community needs have improved in 39 per cent of the cases. Participation with self-contribution has improved in 24 per cent of the cases.

Imparting training to the VTDAs, SHGs and other CBOs and individuals is one of the most important aspects in the capacity building of the tribals. Training was imparted mainly to the leaders of the SHGs and also individual tribals to strengthen their abilities, particularly group activities to improve the teamwork, accounts maintenance, writing minutes of the meeting, etc. Apart from these, training was also imparted to the tribals on modern methods of cultivation to achieve better results in agriculture. It was observed that 93 per cent of the ITDA/SHGs have received training under the programme of APPTDP. The beneficiaries expressed that they have achieved creditworthiness/credit facilities after APPTDP in 53 per cent of the beneficiaries and it was followed by improvement in community and individual assets/facilities (15% of the beneficiaries). Skill up-gradation was one of the important factors in 14 per cent of the beneficiaries. Leadership qualities, sharing of benefits with cooperation were expressed by about 10 per cent of the beneficiaries.

Conclusion

Self -Help Groups in recent years are emerging to be a strong reckoned force to save small amounts so as to mobilise funds for their common benefit through participatory approach. The soil conservation works have created a working environment as well as inducement to save money among the members of the women SHGs. It was observed from the study that the women SHGs have achieved considerable improvement in their participation in identification of their community needs and priorities, lobbying for getting sanction of financial support from the government, involvement of their physical labour and financial contribution in the asset creation, utilisation and self-management of the assets. Hence, the capacity of the women SHGs are to be strengthened further in the villages where the quantum of savings are less in their group account in terms of the generation of employment and income to the SHGs through implementation of various infrastructure development programmes without any involvement of private contractors.

The status and role of the women in the decision-making process in the family, community and village level have improved after formation of the Self-Help Groups. The spirit of the team work has improved among them. In recent years, the political parties are also announced some sops in their election manifestos and also election campaigns to gain their vote bank. These are the positive signs for their empowerment. Now, they are under the process of transition to achieve financial self-reliance to solve their credit needs instead of depending on private moneylenders at high rates of interest. However, they are to be imparted appropriate training programmes to improve their skills to take up viable income generating activities suitable to the local conditions.

REFERENCES

World Bank, "World Development Report-2003, Sustainable Development in a Dynamic World—Transforming Institution, Growth and Quality of Life, Oxford University Press, New York.

Donatus de Silva and Naella Denby (1989), "Banking the Unbankable—Bringing Credit to the Poor, Horizon India Books, New Delhi.

Mishra, B.N. and Das. D. (2000), "Women Empowerment—Perspective of Development: On Orissa in the edited book of Kalpana Sinha on "Empowerment of Women in South India", AMDISA, Hyderabad, p. 103.

IFAD (1994), Appraisal Report—Andhra Pradesh Participatory Tribal Development Project, Vol. I, Asia Division—Project Management Department.

Ibid.

Alex Counts (1996), "Give us Credit", Times Books, Random House, New York, pp. 309-312.

Hashemi, S.M., *et. al* (1996), "Rural Credit Programmes and Women Empowerment in Bangladesh, World Developmental, Vol. 24, No. 4, pp. 635-653.

21

Globalization and Women Empowerment

D. Uma Devi and P. Adinarayana Reddy

Women constitute half of the population and half of them are illiterates. However, they perform two thirds of the work, but receives only one tenth of the total income. Their working day is longer than that of men from 15-19 hours a day. They contribute both to the productivity and reproductive spheres. Even though they are contributing for the national development, they are suffering from chronic malnutrition, hygiene in the home and ignorance heightens their conditions. Added to this their illiteracy, they are disadvantage segment, constrained many respects like limited access to crucial inputs like credit, low wages, suppressed, ill-treated, marginalized and accept inequality between men and women as the natural order and meekly submit. They were deprived and often become victims of a male violence, rape and other atrocities in the male dominated society. Recognizing the role of literacy in the process of development in the globalized society, the National Policy on Education framed the following parameters for the women empowerment.

- To enhance self-esteem and self-confidence among women
- Building a positive image of women by recognizing their contribution to the society, polity and the economy
- Developing ability to think critically
- Fostering a decision-making and action through collective processes
- Enable women to make informed choices in areas like education, employment and health, especially reproductive health
- Ensuring equal participation in developmental processes

- Providing information, knowledge and skill for economic independence and
- Enhancing access to legal literacy and information relating to their rights and entitlements in society with a view to enhance their participation on an equal footing in all the area.

The goal of literacy for all is the key requisite for the economic development, social and political re-structuring of society which is still remaining as inaccessible mirage for the girls and women. It has the potentiality to develop the abilities, skills, attitudes, power to take decisions, to be self-reliant; able to fight against exploitation which enable them to participate in all spheres of life leading to empowerment and with the passage time and regular utility of literacy skills strengthens the empowerment process. Empowerment among women is a continuous process and passes through various stages like, understanding the situation in different angles, recognizing the social barriers and norms affecting and changing the situation in favour of them through individual and collective action to met their demands and rightful share.

Globalization

India is rich in managerial skills, technical man power and abundant of natural resources have not been efficiently utilized. India with the plenty of skilled manpower and other natural resources is in a good position to benefit from globalization. According to Eduardo Aninet (2002), "Globalization is a process through which an increasingly free flow of ideas, people, goods, services and capital leads to the integration of economies and societies has brought raising prosperity to the countries that have participated."

Indian economy is now on the path of global integration, accelerating growth, improving productivity, innovation and international competitiveness. Growth of the infrastructure sector is the prerequisite for the sustainable growth and development of the economy. The basic infrastructure services like, energy, transportation, telecommunication, water, education, health etc., plays a crucial role in supporting economic growth and development. The kind of infrastructure put in place also determines whether growth does all that it can to reduce poverty. As most of the poor are in the rural areas, the growth of farm productivity and non-farm rural employment is linked closely to the infrastructure provision. To counteract increasing urban rural divergences, decentralized development through improvement in agriculture and agro industries and creation of socio-economic structures in rural areas are necessary. The state has to provide various utility services like road construction, irrigation system and environment management etc., to help the farmers and the people living in the rural areas.

Impact of Globalization on Women Empowerment

Today the world faces globalization of production and trade, more intense fundamental beliefs in all religions, reduced national budgets and intense ethnic rivalries. On the other hand, more extended definitions of democracy have been envisaged and applied, pluralistic political systems are emerging and individuals and groups in mass movements are asserting themselves as legitimate social factors.

As half of the population is women, the process of globalization has adversely affected them as second citizens. In Indian society, particularly in the rural areas, gender plays a dominant role in determining the education, status, training and all spheres of life of the women. Moreover, the benefits of the growing global economy have been unevenly distributed leading to wider economic disparities, the feminization of the poverty, increased gender inequality through deteriorating working conditions and unsafe working conditions and unsafe working environment especially in the informal economy and rural areas.

Even the planning commission admits that the employment growth rate has fallen 2 per cent per annum in 1980 to 0.98 per cent in 2000. Employment growth in the organized sector has slipped down from 2.4 per cent in 1987-93 to 0.45 per cent in 1994-2000 and that of the public sector came down from 0.10 per cent to 0.03 per cent. In rural sector, the unemployment growth was 0.4 per cent during 1994-2000 as against 2.10 per cent in 1987-93.

So far, as the impact of globalization is concerned, there is a clear indication of unemployment growth and poor living conditions in India. In the process of globalization rich become rich and poor become more poor. As the major share of total unorganized workforce is from women, agricultural and allied sector workers, as a result of the globalization, many of them lost their jobs due to the closure of the uneconomic units besides shrinkage in public sector employment entailing drastic reduction in expenditure in different government activities. Increased competition amongst the domestic industrial units and foreign units forced restructuring of many units, which invariably involved labour restructuring with shrinkage of employment. This particularly affected the women due to lack of technical know-how, low or nil education, low income, low wages etc., which show severe impact on their living standards.

In this context, various trends in the world pose special challenges to women. The emergence of an increasingly knowledge-intensive society and the growth in information and communication technologies require that women acquire appropriate education and vocational training to function in the contemporary society. In the light of the above context, some strategies may be adopted and tested for achieving the women empowerment. They are:

Strategies

Changes in the economic environment include the shifting nature of the formal sector in light of global economy, which can provide opportunities for women and men both to balance the family, social and economic responsibilities. The same applies to the growth in inflexibility in the economy, which can provide opportunities for women and men better to balance the family, social and economic responsibilities.

Environmental degradation has affected the women, particularly in the rural areas in adverse ways. Many of the women in rural and remote areas who were dependent on nature for their daily subsistence are finding it increasingly difficult to survive with the resources at their disposal and the demands on their time and energy. Hence, effective eco-management steps to be taken while framing the policies. The call for gender-sensitive approach should be emphasized to enable the women and men to recognize and revalue women's experiences, skills and contributions to the economy and social life; to share domestic and caring responsibilities; to participate in the society as conscious, active and responsible citizen; to enjoy gender relations based on equality and solidarity and to value tolerance, diversity and peaceful resolution of conflict.

Policies should be strengthened to make access to the quality education and vocational skills for the women. Educational policies should identify the need for legislation, administrative actions, educational inputs, the media participation and partnerships and resources. Extensive researches must be encouraged and promoted to identify the field level problems and to develop appropriate strategies to over come the problems. New strategies and approaches should be framed based on the needs of the women who need empowerment.

Conclusion

The empowerment of the women should not be stopped at initial stage. All the people from all the sections of the society should be awared, involved in the programmes, which are meant for empowering the women, and they should be trained in appropriate way to reach the goal. Then only it may not remain as dream and will be a fact.

22

Empowering Women through Group Approach: Some Issues

D. Sunder Raj and M. Venkataramana

Women comprise a half of the population and often their contribution to development in the society is undermined. Gender bias still manifests in many civilised societies of the world. Women are marginalized over years at various stages right from the fetus to the funeral. Being agreed that women are the part and parcel of the humankind, are branded as second sex and are kept aside from reaching the front stage. For women, opportunities are not equal with men, responsibilities are more and they have to overcome greater odds with less support from their families. Women's role in development cannot be overlooked. However in recent times, gender has been increasingly viewed as a principle underlying the distribution of resources in the household as well as in the society. Economic progress in any country whether developed or underdeveloped could be achieved through social development. Empowering women contributes to social development. The process of economic development would be incomplete and lopsided unless women are fully involved in it. According to Gurumoorthy (2000), emancipation of women is an essential prerequisite for economic development and social progress of the nation.

Women empowerment is a global issue, which has gained momentum in recent decades. India, besides ratification of international conventions, there are provisions in the Constitution and several Acts have been passed by the government to ensure women empowerment. It, however, appears that on this front the situation on ground is far from satisfactory. Women as an independent target group, account for 495.74 million, as per the

2001 census. No country can achieve its potential without adequately investing in and developing the capabilities of women. In the interest of long-term development it is necessary to facilitate their empowerment.

Empowerment in its simplest form means redistribution of power that challenges the male dominance. This does not, however, mean that the empowerment process adopts an antagonists' approach. It is only to enable women to supplement and coordinate with men. Improvement in economic status is a more visible indicator of women empowerment. This naturally gets reflected in improved social, political and cultural status of women. Self-confidence and self-esteem of women proceed simultaneously with their empowerment (Venkataramana, *et. al.*, 2006). Women organizing into groups is not a new approach and well visualized from the period of freedom movement in our country. Mahila Mandals are organized to create awareness among women and break their shackles in the process of their development. After independence and till now the government is trying to improve the status of women through various programmes. Political empowerment of women is essential but political empowerment will not succeed in the absence of economic empowerment.

Economic independence is an essential requisite for the empowerment of women. Formation of SHGs for economic independence of women is one way of economic empowerment of women. Self-Help Groups (SHGs) or the Thrift and Credit Groups are mostly informal groups whose members pool savings and re-lend within the group on rotational or need basis. Self-help groups are organized in the selected villages for economic and social development of the rural poor particularly women. This group approach is a viable alternative to achieve the objectives of rural development and to get community participation in all rural development programmes. In all stages of economic and social activities involvement of women becomes essential.

The credit needs of the rural poor are determined by a compiled socio-economic milieu where dependence of the rural poor on money-lenders still continue in many areas, especially for meeting the emergent needs. Under the circumstances, it is difficult for a non-formal agency to adopt project-lending approach as usually followed by banks and where the dividing line between credit for consumption and productive purposes is blurred. Despite rapid pace of expansion of financial system encompassing spheres of social and mass banking, the credit supply to the poor, in the form of SHG could emerge as promising partner to the formal credit system (Kumaran, 1997). Self-help groups are now gaining acceptance as an alternative system credit delivery, for meeting the credit needs especially to the people who are the poorest of poor.

Development of SHGs in India reveals that the existing formal financial institutions have failed to provide finances to landless marginalized and disadvantaged groups. SHGs encourage savings and promote income generating activities through small loans. The experiences available in the country and elsewhere suggest that SHGs are sustainable, have explicability, stimulate savings, and in the process help borrowers to come out of vicious circle of poverty (V.M. Rao, 2002). Self-help groups are now gaining acceptance as an alternative system credit delivery, for meeting the credit needs especially to the people who are the poorest of poor generally comprising small/marginal farmers, landless agricultural labourers, rural artisans, women folk and other micro entrepreneurs.

The primary challenge facing women today is to increase their participation and become actively involved in the process of decision (Chandra 1997). Gender discrimination is a universal phenomenon. Both inside and outside the house, women are excluded from positions of power. They are denied the opportunities to participate in decision-making process. Participation has two dimensions-quantitative and qualitative. Participation in terms of numbers has no meaning. Today there is a need for change from quantitative to qualitative. Active participation in social, economic and political spheres would help in enhancing process of decision-making empowerment and it will also give women the desired self respect and social dignity and these of course, are the prerequisites of empowerment. Very rightly Karl (1995) expressed that, "increased participation of women in decision-making at all levels will help to "adjust" the goals pursued through development."

Participation is the one important point where women take decisions along with men equally. To reach this level, mobilization is necessary. By organizing themselves and working collectively, women will be empowered and gain increased representation which would lead to increase empowerment and ultimately greater control.

Participation of women in SHGs makes a significant impact on their empowerment, both in social and economic aspects. Participation helps, women come out in open to articulate, discuss and solve their problems. It also helps in bringing awareness among rural women about savings, education, health, environment, cleanliness, family welfare, social forestry, etc. and make them self-reliant.

Development programmes of different types (employment provision, income generation, awareness creation etc.), have been designed and implemented aiming at enhancing the socio-economic condition of the downtrodden. Many programmes do not succeed as every one accepts, is that people are not given a role to play in identifying analyzing and prioritizing their needs and finding ways and means to solve their problems. People's voice is often ignored. Participatory approach must be introduced at all stages, if we are really concerned with peoples' empowerment. As this approach brings the people to the focus in the project activities, the result would certainly be fruitful and rewarding for the people as well as for the implementing agency (Tamilmani, 2002).

The Copenhagen Declaration on Social Development and as well as the Beijing Declaration of Fourth World Conference on women both of 1995 recognised the need to enhance the participation and leadership roles of women in political, civil, economic, social and cultural life and in the development process. The informal groups of women significantly improve women's participation both from economic and social aspects. There is a greater potential for the group approach in future while conceptualising and implementing any programme for the poor, particularly women.

The multi-dimensional process of empowerment requires awareness, access to education and training, participation in decision-making and politics and the mobilization of women for economic self-reliance. The micro-credit movement in India is gathering momentum as women at the grassroots organize themselves into SHGs (Sudha Rani *et. al.*, 2002). Empowerment serve as a powerful instrument for women to achieve upward social and economic mobility and achieve power and status in society. It is a source of mobility, equality and emancipation, both at the individual and at the societal level. Gender development constitutes an important part of development in this context. It is important in this respect to bring women into the mainstream of development so that society benefits from the women empowerment. Attempts to empower women, with the formation of local women's collectives intended to foster new opportunities for women to gain economic and political power are ultimately expected to become self-sustaining, self-governing and self-reliant.

Women empowerment is synonymous with the achievement of equality and equal mindness in society. Women's empowerment will result in traditional female values being more respected in the society. The empowerment of women through SHGs would lead to benefits not only to the individual woman and women groups but also for the family and community as a whole through collective action for development. They assume the role of decision makers in major and deciding aspects of the family and village. According to Suguna (2001), "empowerment is a process of awareness and capacity building leading to greater participation to greater decision-making power and control and transformation action." The empowerment is not essentially political alone in fact; political empowerment will not succeed in the absence of economic empowerment. The micro finance through SHG has transferred the real economic power in the hands of women and has considerably reduced their dependence on men. This helps in empowering women and building their confidence level.

Poverty alleviation has been the primary concern of development planners since long. Poverty alleviation efforts mainly through state driven credit intervention produced only sub-optional results. The new people centered paradigm has broadened the scope of anti-poverty policies and gave a special role to credit, particularly micro finance in the overall poverty eradication process. It is a recognized fact, today that the relationship between finance and poverty is a complex one. Beside, a few experiments under South Asia poverty alleviation programme implemented under aegis of UNDP have demonstrated the credit could play a role in financing the provision to basic needs, especially in the areas of low-cost housing, water supply and sanitation and health services. In other words, the process of empowerment envisages allowing people to create necessary conditions to mitigate socio-economic exclusion more effectively.

Empowerment of poor, particularly approach and social mobilization are the possible process for eradicating poverty. Poverty can be effectively eradicated only when the poor start contributing to the growth process through their active involvement. Voluntary organization, community-based self-help groups and local governmental organizations have a substantial role to play (Sivasubramanian, 1999). Women are critical actors in the process of moving their families out of poverty. According to Agarwal, Deepti (2001), women need to be viewed not as beneficiaries but as active participants in the process of development and change. The group approach to poverty alleviation implies strengthening of collective self-help capacities at the local level to enable the poor to plan, manage and monitor their access to assets more in line with their needs and views. Empowerment of women can be effectively achieve if poor women could organize into groups—for community participation as well as for assertion of their rights in various services related to their economic and social well-being. Simultaneously micro-credit and SHGs are also key elements for the empowerment of the rural women and help them to improve their living conditions and acquire small capital assets. A systematic strategy seeking to change societal attitudes for women, improve women's self-perception, create an enabling policy, institutional and legal environment and faster economic empowerment through mobilization, thrift, easy credit, up gradation of services and improved income generation opportunities are essential for emancipation of women. Satya Sundaram (2001), opines organizing the poor is crucial for their upliftment. They do not have crucial inputs like credit, it is here, the empowerment of women assumes importance. SHGs have emerged, in order to help the rural poor particularly women, in securing inputs like credit and other services.

According to Dodkey (1999), "SHGs have been found an effective and economic means of ensuring access of credit to the poor and vulnerable sections of the society, as the translations cost is much less and because of the constant and effective supervision the loan is properly utilized and repayments are prompt and excellent." It is here the importance of the women and potentiality are exhibited, where a few women together are rewriting the fate of themselves and their families. The group approach has emboldened women financially and mentally by improving the quality of life and their social status. The impact of women participation on social front could be assessed mainly in terms of improvement in literacy level, health, quality of life and standard of living.

Conclusion

The Group Approach leading to women empowerment, which would simultaneously lead to the benefits, not only to the individual woman and women groups but also for the family and community as a whole through collective action for development. They assume the role of decision makers in major and deciding aspects of the family and village. Women empowerment is synonymous with the achievement of equality and equal mindness in society. Women's empowerment will result in traditional female values being more respected in the society.

The possible out come through group approach (community based Self-Help Groups) at individual level are self-employment/ assured wage employment through they year, sustainable livelihoods, improved health and education, enhanced social dignity and better status of women/girl child etc. And at the community level self-managed and self-reliant, inclusive role in Gram Panchayats, all children are in schools and social equality etc. The informal groups of women significantly improve women's participation both from economic and social aspects.

REFERENCES

Agarwal, Deepti, (2001), "Empowerment of Rural Women in India", *Social Welfare*, Vol. 48, No. 4.

B. Tamilmani, (2002) "People-centred Development Projects through PRA", *Kurukshetra*, Vol. 50, No. 3, January.

Chandra, (1997), "Women and Empowerment" *Indian Journal of Public Administration*, Vol. XLIII, No. 3.

Doodkey, M.D., (1999) "Sustaining Rural Women", *Social Welfare*, Vol. 45, No. 12.

Dr. K. Sudha Rani, Uma Devi & Surendra; (2002), "SHGs, Micro-Credit and Empowerment", *Social Welfare*, Vol. 48, No. 11, February.

Geetanath V., (2001), "SHGs doing Wonders for Women", *The Hindu*, April 3.

Gurumoorthy, T.T., (2000), "Self-Help Groups Empower Rural Women", *Kurukshetra*, Vol. 48, No. 5.

Karl, Marilee, (1995), *"Women and Empowerment Participation and Decision-making"*, Zed Books Ltd., London and New Jersey.

Kumaran, K.P., (1997), "Self-Help Groups: An Alternative to Institutional Credit to the Poor: A Case Study in Andhra Pradesh", *Journal of Rural Development*, Vol. 16, No. 3.

Lalitha, N. & B.S. Nagarajan; (2002) "Self-Help Groups in Rural Development", *Dominant Publishers & Distributors*, New Delhi.

Laxmi R., (2000), "Micro Finance: The New Development Paradigm for Poor Rural Women", *Kurukshetra*, Vol. 48, No. 13.

Satya Sundaran, I., (2001), "Self-Help Groups: Challenges and Opportunities", *Social Welfare*, Vol. 48, No. 4.

Sivasubramanian, M.N., (1999), "Credit Based Poverty Alleviation Programme: Innovative Approach", *Kurukshetra*, Vol. 48, No. 2.

Suguna, B. (2001), "Women's Empowerment: Concept and Framework", *Social Welfare*, Vol. 48, No. 9.

V. M. Rao, (2002), "Women Self-Help Groups: Profiles from Andhra Pradesh & Karnataka", *Kurukshetra*, Vol. 50, No. 6, April.

Venkataramana, M. & D. Sunder Raj, "Empowerment of Rural Women: Issues and Concerns", article communicated to edited book, 2006.

Part–6
DEVELOPMENT POLICIES AND ISSUES

23

Child Development in India: Some Economic Implications

P.N. Pandey

Children belong to a generation of young ones, which is sociologically, a dependent class. A class that is dependent on family, community and society at large. Socialization and education are the initial processes in the physic-mental development of this generation. Education is an interaction process, an experience exercised by the adult generation on those that are not yet ready for social life. Its object is to arouse and to develop in the child a certain number of physical, mental, emotional and intellectual capacities that are demanded of him by both the political society as a whole and the social milieu for which he is specifically destined (Durkheim: 1959, p. 61). In common parlance the development of the child involves the totality of environment i.e., the entire social milieu and education - both informal at the family and community level and the formal at school, play a significant role in building and preparing the generation of children. The education in the development of children, sociologically speaking, deals with the following central objectives:

- *(i)* The objective of self-realization
- *(ii)* The objective of relationship (role perception)
- *(iii)* The objective of economic efficiency, and
- *(iv)* The objective of civic responsibility.

The point, which is under focus, is education that is a concomitant of the child development in a society or section of society. As regards the development of generation of young ones, the advent of Independence in 1947 ushered a new era with respect to the education of female and that of the downtrodden people, the Scheduled Castes and Tribes (Five Year Plan Documents: 1961-66,

1969-74, 1992-97, 1997-02). The Central and State Governments have, no doubt, taken serious steps to educate the children of scheduled castes and scheduled tribes and thereby to improve their socio-economic and cultural conditions along similar lines as in case of the children of the upper castes by providing democratic facilities, special provisions, protective discrimination and amenities through the state legislations and Five Year Plans. (Lynch: 1969, 2-19, 20-128).

But still a desired portion of result is not achieved as yet. Its main cause is the bulk of illiteracy, ignorance, lack of conscious awareness, indebtedness, social and economic deprivations among the landless farm labourers, village peasantry, and masses of the weaker sections. As a result of which mortality, morbidity, insanity, and miserable sub-human conditions continue as destiny of the poor children and their natural guardians. This has certainly awakened national concern not only in India but in all the third world countries viz. Latin America, Africa and Asia. Poverty, illiteracy and gigantic population growth set the clock of development in its reverse gear. According to a survey nearly 50 per cent of the total amount received from World Bank, International Monetary Fund, Inter Continental Bank and other funding agencies are invested in these countries of the third world in controlling the population, meeting the necessity of war against poverty and feeding, clothing, health, recreation, schooling and hygiene of the unwanted growth of children. This is economically speaking a non-productive investment (Hayter: 1971, 151-52, Bauer: 1972; 49-68).

The Main Issues

The main issues, which I have tried to raise in this chapter, are as follows:

1. Why the development of children in the developing societies in general and in India in particular is not in keeping with the national expectation?
2. Are the illiteracy, ignorance, indebtedness and the relative socio-economic deprivations concomitants to the detrimental conditions of development and abuse of children in India?
3. Can a socially dependent class improve its lot by mere constitutional sanctions of rights? If not, what would be then, the imperative for it?
4. Do the age-ridden superstitions and patrilical superiority on lines of gender difference creates differential access to the

development of male and female children in the same social order?

Basic Postulates

The basic postulates on the basis of which I have proceeded in this chapter are as follows:

1. A child is an indicative of a generation of dependent class and the dependent class has little potentials to implement its rights in its own interest. This has to be handled properly by family, community and society. Therefore, the more the conducive conditions of a family, community and society, the greater there shall be probability of physical, mental and social development of the child.
2. The higher the growth of education, the greater there shall be qualitative improvement on lines of child development.
3. The greater the socio-economic deprivations in a society, the more there will exist the debilitating conditions of health, hygiene, morbidity and carelessness leading at length to increasing poverty, dependency, forced child labour and inevitably recurring orientation to employ children at an early age for profiteering movies and pecuniary gains.

The Present Scenario

If we have a global view of demography we find that by the 21st century has emerged with six billions world population. Presently 16.6 per cent of the world population is in India, which inhabits 2.24 per cent of the globe. Out of the total population of above one hundred crore of our country, the child population comprising in age group of 5 to 16 years, constitutes around 36 per cent. This is a significant segment of our population.

The percentage of literary in the total population is 65.38 per cent (India: 2003). The male literacy is 74 per cent and female literacy 55 per cent. This means according to a general assessment that nearly 50 per cent of the total child population still remains out of touch of the schools. Such children are either in employed in agricultural activities along with their parents and custodians or they carry on some forced employment or they are aimlessly associated with their family without education or employment.

The problems of development of children in our country is mainly a problem of the two classes, specially:

(*a*) The bottom class i.e. the poor landless farm labourers, from the scheduled castes and scheduled tribes, who work in unorganized private sectors as agricultural farm labourers, stone grinders, producers of building materials as concrete, lime, bricks, tendu leaves workers (Tendu patti workers) and workers in the tea gardens.

A study of carpet industries of Bhadohi, Khamaria, Gopiganj & Sant Kabeer Nagar District and Mirzapur and Varanasi Regions conducted by the sociologists of Banaras Hindu University confirms that small children between the age group of 7 to 16 years are employed in large number to carry on a number of activities in the carpet industry. Such child workers are neither forced workers nor bonded rather they are persuaded by their own natural custodians to carry on work in the carpet industry. This is also beneficial for the entrepreneurs and proprietors as they have to pay a comparatively lesser amount of money to children as compared with their adult counterparts for the same quality and nature of jobs (Singh: 1989). This is really an outcome of illiteracy, ignorance and socio-economic deprivations. As long as economic scarcity and deprivations continue in a sizable portion of our population, the deprived people, as economic asset will use the children in their very premature age. The stigma can be removed by social awareness and demunition of deprivations. It is not feasible to go by the dictates of Rug-mark of germancy or Harlans Act (1994) neither of the U.S. nor even by the NH Charter on child labour under Human Rights Commission.

(*b*) The children happen to be problematic in upper and upper middle class where parents and guardians do not devote their time to their children. This is generally a case where husband and wife both are employed and bear the strain of their professions. The economically affluent class of the upper stratum too has problems. The people of this section try to appoint guardians, tutors and in most cases they put their wards and children in the hostels.

During the last two decades the government at the Central and the State levels have taken serious steps through Five Year Plans and special constitutional provisions to ensure the process of development and improvement in the living conditions of the poor people, farmless labourers and other weaker sections. A number of programmes, policies and projects have been implemented to accelerate the process of socio-economic uplift and development. The Scheduled Caste Development Corporation, the Jawahar Rozgar, the reorganization of Panchayat, rural youth employment, the decentralization of health and medical service centres, rural health programmes, the community health education, adult and continuing education, the village health workers at the village level, the child development project at the district levels and numerous such other programmes have been implemented to improve the lot of children and the poor illiterate people (10th Five Year Plan Document).

My postulate here is that child development is a part of the wider perspective of socio-economic development. An optimum situation of child health care, child development and prevention from abuses of minority age group children are possible only when social and economic development continues to be effective to minimise the deprivations and scarcity, and bid good bye to illiteracy and elevate those who live in a sub-human conditions in remote rural settings and also in the slums and jhugi hutments or in squaltered settlement in the mega-cities like Lucknow, Kanpur, Varanasi, Allahabad, Agra, Aligarh and such others have also grown with a huge population of child workers.

Further, it is essential to avoid and stop the practice of unwanted children and illegitimate parenthood. Such a child becomes the hostile son of the soil. One can see a flood of growth of such children roaming in the cities and towns, on railway stations, bus-stops and other public places. They sometime become the orphans of government. Then there are children of prostitutes and professional call girls who become the problematic children. In the absence of proper education, schooling, health and medical care either they die premature or become imbecile, physically or mentally handicap or they become juvenile delinquents in the urban areas.

As regards legal and constitutional safeguards, a child in the womb of mother gets his/her rights according to law but mere accord of rights is not enough unless it is implemented in his or her interest and this is the task, a major concern of the family, community and the state. I have already hypothesized that a child is an indicative of a generation of dependent class and the dependent class has little potentials to implement its rights in its own interest.

This has to be handled properly by parents, community and society. A child may be father of the man in a poetic Wordsworthian tone but not "The Man" in his very premature shape of personality. Thus any development concerning child's physical, mental, intellectual and social growth of potentialities must first improve the social climate in which and through which the child has to emerge in adulthood. The Constitution of India, no doubt, provides a strong safeguard to ensure the healthy growth and improvement of children. Article 45 requires the state to make provision within 10 years, for free and compulsory education for all children until they complete the age of 14 years. The object is to abolish illiteracy from the country. It gives a grimy picture of employed children: A number of laws, Fundamental Rights, Directive Principles, International Covenants are violated. Violation of Prohibition of Child Labour Act 1986, and Bonded Labour 1976 are common features.

Employment of children in factory and mines below age of 14 years and also in agriculture below the age of 15 years is prohibited. Article 39 guarantees for equal pay for equal work irrespective of male or female. Article 42 provides for just and humane conditions of work. Article 46 deals with promotion of educational and economic interest of weaker sections and Compulsory Education for Children upto age of 14 years, Education for all and Mid-day Meal for Primary School Children (ICDS) was launched in 1975-76 as a centrally sponsored scheme of Union Ministry of Social & Women's Welfare provides a lot of packages to children upto 6 years and nursing and expectant mothers—Immunization, Health Checkup, Referral Services, Supplementary Nutrition, Informal Pre-School Education, Nutrition and Health Education and Functional Literacy for Adult Women during 1984-85 Rs. 36 crore were allocated in the Central Government Budget for the purpose. Presently, the project is aided by the World Bank and is passing through 3rd phase. But unfortunately, the outcome of the investments is not very encouraging. It is due to lack of aftercare and follow of surveys in this direction. The reluctance & lack of dedication of bureaucracy at the district and block levels are also the major concerns, which hinder the proper implementations of the programmes. Several states in the country have already passed Juvenile Vagrancy Acts, the Juvenile Smoking Acts and a number of such other provisions. The age of marriage has been already defined as 18 years for girls and 21 years of age for boys.

But attitudinal, sentimental, psychic and superstitions practices still continue leading to violation of the rules. Gender differences, unequal wages in the unorganized sectors still continue. Among the illiterate families the practice of child marriage and differential attitude and practices in regard to providing food, nutrition, health, hygiene, recreational and enjoyment facilities still continue. In the poor, illiterate families specially among the landless farm workers, scheduled castes and tribes, the male children are regarded as family asset and are forced to contribute in the family income while the labour and dignity of the female children are exploited and they are considered as objects who will move to law's houses in future.

In such a state of affairs there is a major concern of the government, the statesmen, the intellectuals, the social scientists, the planners of government and the enlightened gentry to awaken mass consciousness against such evils. In this direction the role of mass media specially radio and television programmes are really commendable so far their documentary programmes regarding marriage problems, health, hygiene and nutritious foods, prenatal and antenatal care, use of precautionary medicines for children such as triple antison, polio drops, anti dyptheria drugs, tetnus toxide, etc. are concerned. Unfortunately, most of the television serials and episodes commercially propagated do not leave healthy impressions. Some of them are quite demoralizing. Such programme should be banned.

Suggestive Measures

Some measures in regard to healthy improvement of children may be suggested which are sociologically relevant as follows:

1. Involvement of government agencies and voluntary organizations in the community, specially in the areas of weaker sections, minorities and landless poor people.
2. Block level and village level visiting team of expertized hands should be effective under the care and control of officers entrusted with rural development and child development projects.
3. Social and economic deprivation must be minimized and aids and assistance given to underfed, underclothed and shelterless people must be ensured with strict measures. In this direction a quarterly or biannual survey by a team composed of community social workers, enlightened citizens

and technical experts from higher educational institutions should be ensured.

4. The doctors at the community health centres, rural sub-centres should be advised to make a schedule for their visit at least once a fortnight and instruct people abut sex-behaviour, health practices, hazards of population growth and unwanted issues rather than confirming themselves within premises of the hospitals and dispensing with the patients and medicines. These and many such approaches would be effective means to remove the drawbacks of the society at the regional level and may ensure better prospects for the development of healthy generation of children in the country.

REFERENCES AND NOTES

Durkheim, Emile (1959), Education and Sociology, The Free Press, Glaencoe, Illionois, p. 61.

Five Year Plan Documents: Specially Eighth and Ninth Five Year Plans (1992-97 and 1997-2002), Planning Commission, Government of India Publication, New Delhi.

(Lynch, O. 1969). The Politics of Untouchability: Social Mobility and Social Change in a City of India, California University Press, New York, London, pp. 3-19, 20-128.

Hayter, Teresa (1971), Aid as Imperilism, Harmed Swarth, pp. 151-52.

Bauer, P.T. (1972), Dissent on Development, Cambridge, Mars pp. 49-68.

India 2003 Year Book, A Government of India Publication, New Delhi.

Singh, A.S. (1989), Child Labour in Carpet Industry: A Sociological Study, A Ph.D. Thesis in Sociology, Dept. of Sociology, Banaras Hindu University, Varanasi.

Bose, A.B. (2003), The State of Children in India, Manohar Publisher, New Delhi.

Daniel Paul (2003), Children and Social Policy, Palgrav/Macmillan, U.K.

Bergmann Barvara R. (2003), America's Child Care Problem, Palgrav/Macmillan, U.K.

Five Year Plan: Sixth and Seventh Plans (1980-85 and 1985-90), A Government of India Publication, New Delhi, 9th and 10th Five Year Plan Documents, Government of India Publication, New Delhi.

Constitution of India: Government of India Publication, New Delhi, vide J.N. Pandey: Constitutional Law of India, Central Law Agency, Allahabad, thirteenth edition, 1983.

24

Modernization and Development

P.P. Satyanarayana Rao

Till very recently, development was defined only in economic terms and measured in terms of Gross National Product. Even after fifty years of Independence, the increased growth rates have only made the rich richer and the poor poorer. It was when the elaborate programme of planned development had failed to register impressive gains that the need was felt to look for new strategies of development and to take a fresh view of the concept of development. As a result, development came to be defined in terms of Gross National Welfare as much as Gross National Product. Development now needs to defined in terms of people and the extent to which the basic needs of the people for food, housing, portable water, health, hygienic conditions and education are being met.

The new nations had been striving with all intensity of purpose to achieve economic development that would enable them to get out of the rut of backwardness. Economic studies on development problems of under-developed countries acknowledge that a close relationship exists between the effectiveness of development policies in the economic field and prevailing attitudes and institutions. "Development is not governed in any country by economic forces alone and the more backward the country the more, this is true. The key development lies in the men's minds, in the institutions in which their thinking finds expressions and in the play of opportunity on ideas and institutions."[1]

Since, development cannot be achieved without involving the people. Involving the people in the development process implies dealing with generation of men and women – alteration of the way of life of these people in development direction. If there is a leg between the developmental efforts on the one hand and the attitudes and mental preparedness of the people on the other, it will result in the stalling of these programmes. The realization of nation's aspirations involves changes in the knowledge, skills, and interests and values of the people as a whole for National Development.

It is clear that the most powerful thrusts of the planner can be stalled without the involvement of masses. Involving the masses in the development process implies the mobilization of a generation of men and women. This means the development requires the very transformation or modernization of the nature of man...a transformation that is both a means to the development goal and, at the same time, one of the greatest ends itself of the development process. The problem becomes one of the correcting the lag between the developmental efforts and the attitudinal and mental preparedness of the people. It requires in the words of Rostow, "the building of a new generation of men and women trained appropriately and motivated to operate a modern society."[2]

Unless the change is accomplished, the social and economic revolution necessary to make India a modern and progressive country is being postponed. While the development of physical resources is a means to an end, development of human resources is an end in itself, and without it, even the adequate development of physical resources is not possible. Modernization of man seems to be the only solution to the problem because the modern man not only facilitates development but also ensures sustained development. The modernization of man thus becomes at once the means of development and the goal of development also.

Modernization stands for rational approach to all aspects of human life. The term modernization is often used as a synonym for economic growth, since modernization calls for directed change in the system of attitudes, beliefs, and values and also in the institutional complex. While economic development is certainly one of the goals of modernization, it has another goals like social and political development. Therefore, modernization is a means, the end of which is National Development and as such, it is a process, which involves change in the social, political and economic system.

Black[3] defines modernization as a process by which historically evolved institutions are adapted to the rapidly changing functions that reflect the unprecedented increase in man's knowledge permitting control over his environment that accompanied the scientific revolution. This means that modernization refers to the dynamic form that the age-old process of innovation has assumed as a result of the explosive proliferation of knowledge in recent centuries. It owes its special significance both to its dynamic character and to the universality of its impact on human affairs. It sterns initially from an attitude, a belief that society can and should be transformed, that change is desirable. Modernization should begin upon tradition and issue forth from it. It is an additive process and not a substitutive process in developmental direction. Modernization is a process of becoming modern—the process of change in values, attitudes and behaviour that is required for participation in a modern/modernizing society.

Eisenstadt[4] characterizes modernization as a process of transformation involving both social mobilization and social differentiation. Social mobilization stands for a psychosocial, qualitative transformation and is the process whereby commitments to traditional economic, political and social roles are loosened and the individual is made susceptible to new values, new socialization patterns and new commitments. Social differentiation refers to the structural aspects of modernization and denotes a high degree of specialization and differentiation of individual activities and institutional structures, which are characterized by the specificity of roles and allocation of roles on the basis of achievement criteria.

Inkels[5] in an effort to provide an empirical basis for defining modern man conducted a survey of people in six nations and concludes that the modern man is characterized by certain traits. He is change oriented, less suspicious of novelty, he is more present and future oriented rather than backward looking and bound to tradition. He casts off fatalistic attitudes prevalent in the more traditional societies and acquires a faith that he can dominate his environment. He also tends to hold opinions over a range of issues reaching beyond local matters. In the modernization context, it is a liberal instrument for development of human resources that involve changes in the knowledge, skills, values and attitudes of the people.

Modernization parallels at the individual level, what development represents at the national level. It is a process of individual change in ways of perceiving, expressing and valuing and refers to the acquisition of a set of values, attitudes and ways of behaviour, which better fit men for life in modern societies. Especially, the rural and tribal poor are found to be conservative and resistant to change because their cognitive orientations are conditioned by the past when such attitudes and values were effective in daily living and as these cognitive orientations change very slowly in comparison with the rapidly modernizing world around them, they are found to be out of tune with reality. This is the reason why they behave in ways that seem irrational or ignorant to those better attuned to reality. Therefore, modernization acts as an accelerating agent in bringing change in their cognitive orientation and adaptation making them more modernized in their attitudes and behaviour at individual level being looked upon as a means for National Development. According to Lerner[6] the basic challenge of modernization is the infusion of a, "rationalist and positivist spirit."

Effective functioning of a modern society requires that citizens have certain qualities, attitudes, values, habits and disposition. It requires of its citizens a readiness for new experience and an acceptance of innovation, a concern with public issues at the community and national levels, a sense of efficacy that encourages and supports various developmental programmes of social change. Inkeles[7] study of modernity has identified the modern man as innovative. Knowledgeable and opinionated, future oriented, committed to planning and believing in the calculability and controllability of events by means of Science and Technology. Further, modern man sees his roles in social process as efficacious; he is tolerant of difference, a believer in distributive justice and holds the dignity of man in high value.

Modernization is usually studies at two different levels of analysis. The first level of analysis in the study of modernization gives emphasis to patterns of social organization, the second level emphasizes the cultural and ideational. Whereas the first approach stress ways of organizing and doing, the second assigns primacy to ways of thinking and feeling. The former approach is concerned with the institution and, as such, is more sociological. The late, being concerned more with the individual, is more social-psychological. Contemporary writers have envisioned psychosocial modernity as a determinant of social and economic development. If not sufficient, modernity is defined as at least a necessary condition for these societal goals.

From the studies of Lerner, Smith and Inkeles[8], Armer and Youtz[9], Peshkin and Cohen[10] and Armer have be derived the themes of Mastery (efficacy and activism), Empathy, Mobility, High Participation, (Individualism), Innovativeness, Achievement Orientation, Future Orientation, Growth of Opinion, Faith in Science and Technology receptivity to change Aspirations which constitute the indices of modernity. The variety of scales (indices) of modernity (at individual level) has been developed to measure the set of attitudes and behaviour that characterizes the modern man in development process. The modern man develop through improved access to knowledge skills and changes in attitudes and perspectives.

The result, the modern man is change-oriented, less suspicious of novelty, more present and future oriented rather than bound to tradition; he casts off fatalistic attitudes and acquires a faith that he can dominate his environment; he also tends to hold opinions over a range of issues reaching beyond local matters. Modernization is not an end in itself but a means, in one case, for economic and political development and in the other for social and cultural transformation. Modernization promotes other aspects of development including social equality, social and political consciousness and better quality of life. It enables the individual to gain knowledge about himself, his environment, the society in which he lives thereby enables him to lead a meaningful and richer life by participating more effectively in the development process. Thus modernization seems to be very closely linked with development.

REFERENCES

1. Cairncross, A.K., International Trade and Economic Development, *Economics*, Vol. XXVIII, No. 109, February 1961, p. 250.
2. Rostow, W.W., *The Stages of Economic Growth*, Cambridge University Press, 1960.
3. Black, C.E., *The Dynamics of Modernization: A Study in Comparative History*, Harpert Row, New York, 1966.
4. Eisenstadt, S.N., *Modernization: Protest and Change*, Prentice Hall of India Private Ltd., New Delhi, 1969, pp. 2-3.
5. Inkeles, Alex., *Making Men Modern: On the Causes and Consequences of Individual Change in Six Developing Countries* (paper presented in the Annual Meeting of the AAAS, Dallas, 1968).
6. Lerner, Daniel, *The Passing of Traditional Society: Modernizing in the Middle East*, The Free Press of Glencoe, 1964, p. 45.

7. Inkeles, Alex, Making Men Modern: On the Causes and Consequences of Individual Change in Six Developing Countries, *American Journal of Sociology,* Vol. 75, September 1969, pp. 208-225.
8. Smith, M.D. and Alex Inkeles, "Becoming Modern": Individual Change in Six Development Countries, Harward University Press, Massachusetts, 1974.
9. Armer Michael and Robert Youtz, "Formal Education and Individual Modernity in an African Society", *American Journal of Sociology,* Vol. 76, pp. 604-626.
10. Peshkin Alan and Ronald Cohen, The Values of Modernization, *The Journal of Development Areas,* Vol.2, No. 1, 1967, pp. 7-22.

25

Social Development and Governance in India: Indicators and Challenges

J.S. Gunavathy

Economic development and social development are vital for human well-being and a nation's growth. Both should go hand in hand for a balanced growth, which is determined by governmental policies, natural resources, human resources, and so forth. According to Gore (2001), "the concept of social development is inclusive of economic development but differs from it in the sense that it emphasizes the development of the totality of society in its economic, political, social and cultural aspects" (p. 20). Thus the term may be used to denote the process of planned change designed to promote human welfare in conjunction with economic development.

Paiva (1977) highlights the pre-requisites of social development as "the political will i.e., the government of a country committed to the concept of social development, the existence of an ideology which serves as a driving force towards the accomplishment of the goal of social development (which requires leadership, a national policy and plan) and the involvement of the people and co-operation of all segments of the population despite their diversity of background and interest" (pp. 332-333).

The Canadian International Development Agency (2002) defines governance as the way in which governments use their power to manage the social and economic resources of a country. "Good governance" is characterized as the use of power that is efficient, direct, fair, clear, and responsible by the various branches of government. The United Nations Development Programme, UNDP (2002) states that without good governance, development efforts are weakened, if not completely destined for failure. Governance, thus, influences social development. This in turn implies that the challenges to governance impact the nature, quality, and pace of social development.

The primary objective of the article is to discuss the link between social development and governance in India. In this regard, the article discusses the concepts of social development, governance, and good governance. It presents data on select indicators of social development and governance followed by the challenges to governance based on the findings. The article then discusses the impact of national and local governance on social development in the Indian context. Finally it discusses ways to manage these challenges and facilitate social development in India.

Literature Review

Social Development

Ahuja (2001) states that social development is "the process of planned institutional change to bring about better adjustment between human needs and aspirations on the one hand and social policies and programmes on the other. It is declaring war on poverty, illiteracy, ignorance, inequality, irrationality and oppression prevalent in society. It aims not merely at the uplift of the weak, the under-privileged and the disadvantaged people but also at improving the quality of life of all citizens" (p. 437).

The Government of India (1987) defines social development as "a comprehensive term, which implies major structural changes – political, economic and cultural, which are introduced as part of deliberate action to transform society" (Encyclopedia of Social Work, 1987, Vol. 3, pp. 57-58). The World Bank (2001) defines social development as "development that is equitable, socially inclusive and therefore sustainable. It promotes local, national and global institutions that are responsive, accountable and inclusive and it empowers poor and vulnerable people to participate effectively in development processes" (See the World Bank's *Useful World Bank Links*, http://1nweb18.worldbank.org/ESSD/sdvext.nsf/64ByDocName/UsefulLinks).

The scope for social development is wide and varied. It includes programmes for universal literacy or primary education programmes; preventive health programmes as well as programmes for the control and treatment of diseases such as malaria and tuberculosis that affect large segments of the population; subsidized housing programmes for the rural and urban poor; family planning and population control programmes, without which faster rates of economic development are not possible, social services programmes that ensure access to the services so that the targeted populations benefit from the programmes; and programmes to preserve the ecological balance in the physical environment (Government of India, 1987). Thus social development includes economic development, human capital, quality of life, and so forth.

Indicators of Social Development

There are no standard indicators of social development. Ahuja (2001) identifies the important indicators of social development as: *(i)* change in levels of living, *(ii)* elimination of poverty, *(iii)* expansion in education, *(iv)* increase in level of employment, *(v)* social justice, that is, equal distribution of opportunities, *(vi)* uplift of the weaker groups, *(vii)* providing security against exigencies of life, *(viii)* improvement in social welfare amenities, *(ix)* reducing disparities – regional, sectoral and social, *(x)* protection and improvement of health, *(xi)* safeguarding environment, and *(xii)* popular participation in expansion programmes involving both qualitative and structural changes (p. 438).

The Statistics Division of the United Nations Development of Economic and Social Affairs (2004) presents a list of social indicators based on the outcomes of proceedings of various conferences on children, population and development, social development, and women. They include: *(i)* child bearing, *(ii)* education, *(iii)* health, *(iv)* housing, *(v)* human settlements, *(vi)* illiteracy, *(vii)* income and economic activity, *(viii)* population, *(ix)* unemployment, *(x)* water supply and sanitation, and *(xi)* youth and elderly population.

Governance

The UNDP (2002) defines governance as the "exercise of political, economic and administrative authority in the management of a country's affairs at all levels of society" (see the UNDP' s *Glossary of key terms*, http://magnet.unp.org/policy/glossary.htm). The United Nations Economic and Social Commission for Asia and the Pacific, UNESCAP (2002) states that the concept of governance is not new. It is as old as human civilization. Simply put, governance means the process of decision-making, and the process by which decisions are implemented (or not implemented). Governance can be studied in the corporate, international, national, local contexts.

The Department for International Development's guidance sheets on sustainable livelihoods (2001) defines governance as:

The form and quality of government system-structure, power, effectiveness, efficiency, rights and representation. Key governance concerns include:

(i) Is political power exercised fairly? If not, who is disadvantaged?
(ii) How efficient and accessible are local service providers?
(iii) Are government organisations honest, efficient, effective and accessible?
(iv) Are basic human rights protected and enforced through the rule of law?
(v) Do informal/traditional justice systems discriminate against certain groups? (See Department for International Development's Sustainable Livelihoods Guidance Sheets, http://www.livelihoods.org/info/guidance_sheets_ pdfs/ sect8glo.pdf).

Subjective and Objective Indicators of Governance

The Human Development Report (HDR) of 2002 identifies subjective and objective indicators of governance. The subjective indicators of governance include *(i)* Polity Score, *(ii)* Civil Liberties, *(iii)* Political Rights, *(iv)* Freedom of Press, *(v)* Voice and Accountability, *(vi)* Political Stability and Lack of Violence, *(vii)* Law and Order, *(viii)* Rules of Law, *(ix)* Government Effectiveness, *(x)* Corruption Perception Index and *(xi)* Graft (corruption). The objective indicators of governance are *(i)* Participation, *(ii)* Civil Society and *(iii)* Ratification of Rights Instruments. The details of the same and the scores obtained by India against them are portrayed in Table 1 and Table 2.

Table–1
Subjective Indicators of Governance and Respective Scores of India

Indicator	*Concept Measured*	*Range*	*Score*
Polity Score	Competitiveness of Chief Executive recruitment Openness of Chief Executive recruitment Constraints of Chief Executive Regulation of Participation Regulation of executive recruitment Competitiveness of participation	-10 to 10 (Less democratic to most democratic)	9

Contd...

Indicator	*Concept Measured*	*Range*	*Score*
Civil Liberties	Freedom of expression & belief Freedom of association & organizational rights Rule of law & human rights Personal autonomy and economic rights	1.0-2.5: free 3.0-5.0: partly-free 6.0-7.0 : not Free	3
Political Rights	Free & fair elections for offices with real power Freedom of political organization Significant opposition Freedom from domination by powerful groups Autonomy or political inclusion or minority Groups	1.0-2.5: free 3.0-5.0: partly-free 6.0–7.0: not Free	2
Freedom of Press	Media objectivity Freedom of expression	0-30: free 31-60: partly-free 61–100: not Free	42
Voice & Accountability	Free & fair election Freedom of the press Civil liberties Political rights Military in politics Change in government Transparency Business is kept informed of developments in law and policies Business can express its concerns over Changes in laws and policies	-2.5 to 2.5 Higher is better	0.66
Political Stability and Lack of Violence	Perceptions of the likelihood of destabilization (ethnic tensions, armed conflict, social unrest, terrorist threat, internal conflict, fractionalization of the political spectrum, constitutional changes, military coups etc.)	-2.5 to 2.5 Higher is better	-0.05
Law & Order	Legal impartiality Popular observance of the law	0 to 6 Higher is better	4.0
Rule of Law	Black markets Enforceability of private and government contracts	-2.5 to 2.5 Higher is better	0.23

Contd...

Indicator	*Concept Measured*	*Range*	*Score*
	Corruption in banking Crime & theft as obstacles to business Losses from & costs of crime Unpredictability of the judiciary		
Government Effectiveness	Bureaucratic quality Transaction of costs Quality of public health care Government stability	-2.5 to 2.5 Higher is better	-0.17
Corruption Perception Index	Official corruption as perceived by Business people, academics and risk Analysts	0 to 10 Higher is better	2.7
Graft (Corruption)	Corruption among public officials Corruption as an obstacle to business Frequency of "irregular payments" to officials and judiciary Perception of corruption in civil service, Business interest payment	-2.5 to 2.5 Higher is better	-0.39

(*Source:* Human Development Report, 2002, p. 37, pp. 40-41).

Table–2
Objective Indicators of Governance and Respective Scores of India

Indicators	*Concept Measured*	*Score*
Participation	Latest election for lower or single house-	
	Year	1999
	—Voter turn	
	Year women received right to vote	60
	Seats in parliament held by women	1950
	(as per cent of total)	8.9
Civil Society	Trade Union membership (as per cent	5*
	of non-agricultural labour force), 1995	1718
	NGOs as on 2000	
Ratification of Rights Instruments	International convention on Civil and	Yes
	Political rights	Yes
	Freedom of association & collective bargaining, 1987	

1. Data refers to a date other than specified.

(*Source:* Human Development Report, 2002, p. 36, pp. 42-43).

Good Governance

The Office of the High Commissioner of Human Rights (1996) states that "governance" refers to the means by which public institutions administer public affairs and public resources, and ensure that the human rights of all its citizens are respected. "Good governance" aims to do the same in a manner free of corruption or abuse and with respect for the rule of law. According to UNESCAP (2002), good governance has eight major characteristics. It is participatory, consensus-oriented, accountable, transparent, responsive, effective and efficient, equitable and inclusive and it follows the rule of law" (see UNESCAP's, What is Good Governance, http://www.unescap.org/huset//gg/governance.htm). Good governance ensures that corruption is curtailed, the views of minorities and other vulnerable groups of society are taken into consideration in the decision-making processes, and that the present and future needs of society are catered to.

Impact of Governance on Social Development

Primarily, social development is the onus of the government. The government seeks to generate social development through various programmes and policies routed through different economic, social, political, and educational institutions. These institutions play a significant role in social development. Society is changing at an incredible pace because of factors like capitalist ideologies, globalization, economic reforms, and pluralism. Ideologies like "survival of the fittest" and "market economy" continue to co-exist with concepts like social inclusion and concern for the marginalized. In this regard, political institutions play a vital and indispensable role in creating social development. The government and its implementing administrative bodies have an impact on the society at large. For example, if illiteracy is a social problem, the government has the all-prevailing authority to devise policies and programmes to tackle the situation. These programmes and policies may be either reactive or proactive in approach. The various civil society factors contribute at different stages of the programme, from policy formulation to programme implementation and evaluation. "Good governance is key to effective economic and social development. Conversely, poor governance constrains and distorts the general process of development and has a discernable negative impact on the poorer and more vulnerable sections of society" (see Asian Development Bank's,

Assessing Community Perspectives on Governance in the Pacific, http://www.adb.org/Documents/TARs/REG/tar_oth36192.pdf).

Findings and Discussion

The social development indicators presented and discussed in the ensuing section are based on the census data of the Government of India over two most recent census periods namely, 1991 and 2001. This article focuses on the following social development indicators: *(i)* population attributes, *(ii)* health, *(iii)* human settlements, *(iv)* literacy, *(v)* income and economic activity, *(vi)* Poverty and employment, and *(vii)* human development. These attributes have been adapted from the social indicators stipulated by the UNDP. The measures of governance are those published in the *Human Development Reports* of 2002.

Social Development Indicators

Population Attributes

India, the second most populous country in the world, has no more than 2.5 per cent of global land but is home to one-sixth of the world's population. India crossed the one billion mark in May 2000 (Government of India, 2000). The birth rate fell from 29 births per 1000 in 1991 to 25 births per 1000 in 2001 (Government of India, 2001).

The decadal population growth was 21.34 per cent between 1991 and 2001 compared to 23.86 per cent between 1981 and 1991. Population growth has, thus, marginally decreased compared to the previous decade (Government of India, 2001). According to Dutt (2001):

> "There is no doubt that India's population has been growing consistently. The growth rate was very high between 1951 and 1981, rising from 1.96 per cent per annum during 1961 to 2.22 per cent in 1981. Thereafter, the growth rate, though still high, has shown signs of decline. In 1981-91, the annual average rate of growth came down to 2.14 per cent and during 1991-2001 it fell further to 1.93 per cent. In absolute terms, in 1991-2001, India added nearly 180.6 million persons, which was larger than the addition during the 1981-91 decade of 163.1 million" (p. 5).

The sex ratio is defined as the number of females per thousand males in the population. The ratio is an important indicator when measuring the extent of equality between males and females at a given point of time. The sex ratio of the nation was 927 in 1991 and slightly increased to 933 in 2001 (Government of India, 2001). The sex ratio has slightly improved, but inter-state disparities do exist. Sharma (2004) remarks that:

> "The adult sex ratio in India has been declining for several decades. That itself was reason for concern. But the sharp decline in the child sex ratio in the last decade from 945 to 927 is a devastating indictment of our society. Sex detection and sex-selective abortions are today spreading like infectious diseases, from the rich to the poor, from the upper castes to the Scheduled Castes (SC) and even to the Scheduled Tribes (ST). No one wants girls any more. Eliminate them now instead of dealing with the problems of raising a girl, goes the thinking behind the deadly actions... The districts with the worst child sex ratio were all in Punjab and Haryana, two of India's wealthiest states", (p. 1).

It is disheartening to note that some of the wealthiest states of the country like Punjab and Haryana have an adverse sex ratio. Reasons for the unfavourable sex ratio include neglect of the girl child, sex-selective abortions, preference for sons, and the secondary status accorded to women. Daughters are often considered a 'liability," who "leave" for the in-laws' home after marriage, while sons are considered an "asset" and are expected to provide for the parents in their old age. Further, many poor families in both rural and urban areas are burdened by the dowry system and other expenses at the time of marriage. Female infanticide is, therefore, a prevalent problem contributing to the adverse sex ratio.

Treating women as second grade individuals is contrary to "human welfare", which is an integral component of social development. The government must take proactive steps to curb this disturbing phenomenon. The steps taken in this regard include "care for the girl child" campaigns, legislative measures like the Dowry Prohibition Act of 1961, and the Pre-natal Diagnostics Techniques Act of 1994. The Indian Government passed the Pre-Natal Determination Test Act in 1994 to prevent the misuse of advanced scientific techniques for selective elimination of female fetuses through sex-determination tests (Indian NGOs – (a), n. d.). The State Government of Tamil Nadu initiated a unique programme called the "cradle baby scheme" to address this issue. Families were asked to leave unwanted female infants in cradles provided for that purpose in government primary health centres rather than kill them (George, n. d.).

Containing the population growth is a challenge faced by the nation's policy-makers and planners. An increasing population puts tremendous pressure on the land in terms of resource requirements and reduces the overall quality of life. The National Population Policy (NPP) of the Indian Government is one of the most recent initiatives to control population (Government of India, 2000).

Health

The World Health Organization (2003) defines health as "the state of complete physical, mental and social well-being and not merely the absence of disease or infirmity" (See the World Health Organization's *Definition of Health*, http://www.who.int/about/definition/en/). Life expectancy in India has improved from 58 years in 1991 to 65 years in 2001. The infant mortality rate fell from 80 per 100 live births in 1991to 67 in 2001. The maternal mortality rate has increased from 437 per 100,000 live births in 1991 to 530 in 2001. (Indian NGOs – (b), n. d.)

The number of registered medical practitioners in 1991-92 was 4.8 per 10,000 (Government of India, 1994). This figure has been supplemented by a manifold increase in infrastructure in terms of number of dispensaries and hospital, number of doctors (allopathic) and nursing personnel, availability of beds, and so forth. Similarly, while some diseases like small pox and guinea worm have been eradicated, the incidence of a few diseases (like malaria, polio, and leprosy) has been reduced drastically (Government of India, 2002). In addition to providing primary care for the population, the country will also have to deal with the epidemics and pandemics of the time.

Health is an indicator of social development in the sense that it is an indicator of well-being. It also determines one's productivity. Ill health not only means loss of productivity or loss of wages to the individual, but also means loss of production and increased state or governmental expenditures towards provision of medical facilities. Thus health is an important parameter not only in the interest of the individual but also in the interest of the nation.

Human Settlements

Population density is defined as the number of persons per square kilometer. The population density for India has increased from 273 persons per square kilometer in 1991 to 324 persons per square kilometer in 2001. India is primarily an agrarian economy. Consequently majority of the population lives in rural areas. According to the Census reports, the level of urbanization increased from 25.7 per cent in 1991 to 27.8 per cent in 2001 (Government of India, 2001).

An increase in the density of population is a matter of great concern as it puts immense pressure on natural resources and adversely affects the quality of life (Government of India, 2001). Concentration of population in specific areas raises issues of housing, sanitation, access to resources, quality of life, and so forth. The density of population and the level of urbanization manifest themselves in the scramble for natural resources and civic amenities. The ability of the nation to address these issues depends on the level of development.

Literacy

Article 45 of the Directive Principles of State Policy of the Indian Constitution urges the state to provide free and compulsory education for all children until they complete fourteen years of age (Government of India, 1975). The census defines a literate person as someone aged seven and above who can read and write in any language. Though "education for all" is a national goal, the literacy rate indicates a gap that is yet to be filled. The literacy rate was 65.38 per cent in 2001 compared to 52.1 per cent in 1991. The literacy rate is higher for men compared to women. In 2001, 75.85 per cent of men were literate compared to 54.16 per cent of women. The significant milestone reached in the census of 2001 was the fall in the total number of illiterates from 328,167,288 in 1991 to 296,208,952. Thus for the first time since independence, there is a decline in the absolute number of illiterates during a decade (Government of India, 2001).

Literacy and education are reasonably good indicators of development in a society. Spread and diffusion of literacy are essential for modernization, urbanization, industrialization, communication, and commerce. Literacy forms an important input in the overall development of individuals, enabling them to comprehend their social, political, and cultural environment better and respond to it appropriately. Higher levels of education and literacy lead to a greater awareness and also contribute to the improvement of economic conditions. Literacy acts as a catalyst for social upliftment by enhancing returns on investments made in almost every developmental effort, be it population control, health, hygiene, environmental degradation control, or empowerment of women and weaker sections of the society. Improved levels of literacy also are prerequisites for acquiring various skills.

Income and Economic Activity

Economic development is an integral part of social development and can be studied in terms of income levels (per capita or national). India has the twelfth largest Gross National Product (GNP) in the world. The per capita GNP in 2001 was US$ 2,840. India has the fourth largest Gross Domestic Product (GDP) based on the Purchasing Power Party (PPP), at about US$ 2.66 trillion. A majority of the population (60%) depends directly on agriculture, which contributes about 25.6 per cent of GDP. The industry and services sectors are growing in importance and account for 25 per cent and 50 per cent of GDP respectively. More than 25 per cent of the population lives below the poverty line, but a large and growing middle class of 300 million has sufficient disposable income to purchase consumer goods (Fact Index, 2004).

"Economic development is expected to achieve three things: *(i)* a rise in per capita income so that the level of living of the people improves; *(ii)* a reduction in the rate and magnitude of employment; and *(iii)* reduction of population below the poverty line" (Datt and Sundharam, 2004, p. 53). Accordingly, when the national income and the per capita income are high, the population is relatively better off compared to a population stricken by poverty and low personal disposable incomes. High personal incomes also mean more revenue for the state from personal taxes that can be used for various social welfare and social development programmes. Thus economic growth is not only a part of social development, but also paves the way for better social development.

Poverty and Employment

The Human Development Report (2003) reveals that 28.6 per cent of the Indian population lived under the poverty line in 2000. In 1999-2000, 35 per cent of the population lived on US$1 a day, while 80 per cent of the population lived on US$2 a day. The number of persons employed in the organized sector is far less than compared to those engaged in the unorganized sector in India. Agriculture remains the main source of employment in the country. The Indian work-force is characterized by a small proportion of the economically active population, a smaller ratio of females engaged in the work-force, and wide differences in work participation rates across states, and between rural and urban areas (Datt and Sundharam, 2004).

According to the Ministry of Labour's Annual Report (Government of India, 2002), only 7 per cent of the employed worked in the organized sector. In other words, the unorganized sector dominated the employment scenario. The unemployment rate in 1999-2000 was 7.3 per cent compared to 8.3 per cent in 1983 (Government of India, 2002). Significant employment generation took place in the tertiary sector, particularly in services industries. Employment opportunities in certain industries of the organized sector, like Information Technology and Information Technology Enabled Services are also on the rise. Substantial employment growth was observed in the small and unorganized sector, that is, in small enterprises. Self-employment and casual employment continued to play a pivotal role in rehabilitation of the unemployed.

Employment enhances one's personal income and consequently not only sustains an individual, but also helps in improving his/her standard of living. Full employment has always been a goal of economic planning in India. However, unemployment rates loom high and reflect the lack of adequate opportunities. As a result, in many cases, the pressure to provide for the family is high on the bread-winner families are also often forced to stop their children's education and send them for work at an early age to supplement the family income or because they cannot afford the cost of education. This affects literacy and in turn social development. Creating adequate employment opportunities and enforcing wages as per the statutory requirements are keys to social development.

Human Development

The UNDP measures human development in terms of life expectancy at birth, adult literacy rate, gross enrolment ratio for primary, secondary, and tertiary schools, and per capita income in terms of purchasing power parity. The Human Development Index (HDI) value in 1990 was 0.519. It rose to 0.553 in 1995, and in 2001 it was 0.519 (UNDP, 2003).

India ranked 127th out of 177 countries in the 2004 Human Development Report with a HDI value of 0.595. India ranked 117th in terms of GDP per capita, which was valued at US$ 2,670. The HDI value for the South Asian region was 0.584 and the GDP per capita value was US$ 2,658. Maldives, the best performer in the region, ranked 84th with a 0.752 HDI value, a GDP per capita ranking of 97, and a GDP per capita value of US$ 4,798. Pakistan, the worst performer in South Asia, was ranked 142nd with a HDI value of 0.497, a rank of 135 in terms of per capita GDP, and a GDP per capita value of US$ 1,940 (Communist Party of India, 2004). Given that the HDI value for the region is 0.584, and India's is 0.595, we can infer that India has scored slightly better than the regional average.

Indicators of Governance

The assessments of the indicators of governance according to the Human Development Report of 2002 as regards India have been presented in Table 1 and 2. The data shows that there are certain subjective indicators have favourable scores. These include law and order, political rights, and polity. However, the scores on the corruption perception index, corruption, government effectiveness, and rule of law are unfavourable. Eventually, these turn out to be impediments to effective governance. These are some of the many challenges to governance that need to be addressed to pave way for social development.

Governance and Social Development—Challenges

Governance is a critical determinant of the outcome of the social development initiatives. According to Ahuja (2001), social development involves:

"*(i)* assessing needs of people in society; *(ii)* introducing some structural changes in society which includes discarding some old institutions, creating some new institutions, or changing some existing institutions; *(iii)* making institutions responsive to people so that these really serve people; and *(iv)* associating people with decision-making processes, that is, taking planning to grassroots level" (p. 437).

The government (be it at the state or central level) has a key role to play in the social development process as it has been holistic command over the policy planning, programming, administering, and organizing aspects of social development. The government can introduce new schemes and policies that reach the broader public. It has the authority over earmarking of funds, resources to implement programmes, and so forth. However, governance is not a smooth process in a developing country like India where there are many internal and external constraints. It is at this juncture that the challenges to governance need to be studies. After more than fifty years of independence and democratic rule, growth with development is still a distant dream. Samuel (2002) remarks, "the performance of the economy, the increasing gap between the goal of macro-economic development with social development and the complete lack of political will and economic agenda for long-term social development shows how the rhetoric belies reality. Growth without development will deepen inequality and have dangerous socio-political consequences that could undermine the very essence of freedom and democracy" (p. 112). Thus, demographic, technological, political, and other factors pose challenges not only for governance, but also for social development.

According to Ahuja (2001), "the methodology involved in designing social development includes *(i) policy planning,* that is, determining goals, priorities, and strategies; *(ii) programming,* that is, allocating resources; *(iii) administering,* that is, seeking participation of individuals and groups in decision-making; *(iv) organizing,* that is, people to gain maximum benefit from services and also (preparing people) to change the system, if necessary; and *(v) evaluation,* that is, measuring gaps in goals and performance and providing feed back for further planning; (p. 438). Thus the challenges to governance may be traced from the policy planning, programming, administering, organizing, and evaluation perspectives.

Policy Planning Perspective

Government policies and programmes can be fruitful only if they are need-based. Effective economic and social planning as well as proper implementation of policies and programmes is essential for social development. Transparent systems must be developed, and institutions must be strengthened in terms of capacity and competence. A complementary relationship between state and civil society should be developed in order for civil society to participate constructively in policy formulation and implementation.

Programming Perspective

Mobilization of resources and the earmarking of adequate budgetary allocations for various programmes and expenditures require skill and experience. Further, in certain exigencies, certain "non-plan" expenditures may arise that may necessitate the reduction in planned expenditures. Earmarking adequate budgetary allocations is a challenge to governance. Having made available the resources required for various programmes, issues may arise mid-way. Civil conflict is one such issue. Civil conflicts, disputes over access/ utilization of natural resources, disputes over territory, and so forth, result in wastage of resource and are stumbling blocks to effective social development.

Administering Perspective

Government programmes are directed at the people and in the interest of the people. Consequently, it is important to elicit effective citizen participation. Citizen participation starts by electing national leaders and providing constant feedback regarding the programmes and policies of the government. Of late, India is experiencing a highly disinterested and disenchanted electorate. For example, the voter turnout for the 2004 *Lok Sabha* (Parliament) elections was 56 per cent, while the total cost for the entire exercise was about 100 million rupees (approximately US$ 223 million) (Indian Elections, 2004). Active participation of women in the affairs of society, economy, and polity is still far from encouraging. Women have to fight against various odds like male chauvinism, glass ceilings, and so forth. Ensuring effective participation of women in politics and administration is a challenge for governance. Women's participation at all levels and spheres is essential. Democracy should function not only in letter but also in spirit. It should pave the way for full citizen participation in government, ensure fair ground rules for competition and so forth. The population should not remain passive to government interventions, but be informed and participate actively. Only when the masses are informed and responsive will policies and programmes be fruitful. Further, the elected representative of the country should have the political will to bring about change and development among the masses as required. The government should also be able to successfully enlist the resources available in the civil society.

Organizing Perspective

Bad governance or poor governance not only impeded social development but also perpetuates social evils like corruption, human rights violations, and other social problems. Local, national and global institutions need be responsive, accountable and inclusive in their approach towards social development issues. In addition, the poor must be empowered and the vulnerable sections of society must also be able to participate effectively in development processes. With globalization, liberalization, and privatization, developing economies are downsizing the state, liberalizing markets, privatizing state enterprises, and reducing public spending. The state faces tasks like boosting economic growth, bridging the widening gap between the haves and the have-nots, regulating markets effectively, generating revenue, and so forth.

Evaluation Perspective

Last but not the least, ensuring effective governance is a challenge for governance. India has elaborate rules and regulations, legislations, and systems for governmental functioning. However, the governance machinery is plagued by, among other things, bureaucracy, criminalization of politics, rule of muscle power and money power, vested interests, and corruption. For example, in 2002 the Transparency International gave India a ranking of 71 based on the Corruption Perception Index of 102 countries (Transparency International, 2002). Public accountability of the institutions must be ensured. A free and independent media should provide information and news in an unbiased manner. Further, there should be adequate systems to check misuse or abuse of power by government machinery. The working of autonomous bodies of the country like the Central Bureau of Investigation (CBI), the Election Commission (EC), and so forth should not be tampered with by vested interests. Above all, the rule of law should be established and strengthened.

Dynamics of these Challenges—How they Impact Social Development

Governance is akin to tight rope walking. Inability to manage the challenges discussed earlier effectively will affect social development. For example, civil conflicts, war-like situations, and increased defense budgets result in lop-sided social development. Uniformed electorate or poor human capita result in the rule by a few. Politicians tend to capitalize on popular sentiments rather than issues of national interest. Undemocratic practices, unwillingness to share nature resources, corruption, and so forth breed injustice that sometimes result in violence from the part of those threatened or disadvantaged. These challenges if left unattended, result in "hollow citizenship", poor human development, and social injustice. Political instability and the baneful effects of the liberalization, privatization, and globalization processes result in loss of revenue for the state. Social development is thus affected either directly or indirectly. Necessary steps must be taken to minimize the plausible detrimental effects on social development.

Conclusion

India is witnessing significant changes in terms of social development indicators. While some indicators (like literacy rates) have improved, others (like employment) highlight pressing issues that need to be addressed. Governance plays a vital role in determining the social development of a nation. Governance is often not smooth sailing. Consequently, challenges to governance need to be recognized and managed.

The analysis of data on select social indicators reveals that there have been improvements in absolute terms as regards population attributes, health, literacy, and so forth. However, issues like employment and density of population need to be addressed. Similarly, the subjective indicators of governance that have favourable scores include law and order, political rights, and polity. However, the scores on the corruption perception index, corruption, government effectiveness, and rule of law are highlighted as impediments to effective governance. These are some of the many challenges to governance that need to be addressed to pave way for social development.

Table-3
RLWPR and Co-Efficient of Equalities for Rural Female: Penukonda Division (2001-02)

Sl. No.	*Name of Mandal*	*Rural Female Work Participation Rate*	*Female Co-efficient of Equality*
1.	Penukonda [R]	39.50	80.18
2.	Sommanadapalli	39.70	81.63
3.	Roddam	40.22	81.96

Contd...

Sl. No.	Name of Mandal	Rural Female Work Participation Rate	Female Co-efficient of Equality
4.	Puttaparthi	38.62	79.33
5.	Kottacharuvu	37.89	77.54
6.	Bukkapatnam	39.21	80.43
7.	Madakasira	40.12	81.87
8.	Amarapuram	38.56	78.94
9.	Gudibanda	38.97	79.85
10.	Rolla	36.96	74.37
11.	Agali	37.62	76.46
12.	Hindupur (R)	36.98	75.94
13.	Parigi	38.93	80.45
14.	Lepakshi	39.23	81.32
15.	Chilamathur	37.49	76.83
16.	Gorantla	41.52	84.99
17.	Kadiri (R)	39.18	79.64
18.	Mudigubba	40.39	83.07
19.	Nallamada	37.46	77.22
20.	N.P. Kunta	37.48	76.09
21.	Talapula	35.98	73.51
22.	Nallacheruvu	38.42	78.01
23.	O.D. Cheruvu	36.93	75.48
24.	Tanakal	37.94	77.52
25.	Amadagur	40.21	80.68
26.	Gandlapenta	39.62	79.54
	Average	**38.66**	**78.96**
	C.V.	**3.37**	**3.45**

REFERENCES

Ahuja, R. (2001). *Society in India–Concepts, Theories and Recent Trends,* Jaipur: Rawat Publications.

Asian Development Bank. (2002). *Assessing Community Perspectives on Governance in the Pacific.* Retrieved December 27, 2004, from http://www.adb.org/Documents/TARs/REG/tar_oth36192.pdf

Canadian International Development Agency. (2002). *Human Rights, Democratisation and Good Governance.* Retrieved January 24, 2003, from http://www.acdi-cida.gc.ca/cida_ind.nsf/vall/120E9700965D51CE8525691900 6BF1E5? Open Document

Communist Party of India (Marxist). (2004, July 25). India: Miles to go (UNDP Report). *People's Democracy*, XXVIII (30). Retrieved October 27, 2004 from, http://pd.cpim.org/2004/07252004.htm

Department for International Development. (2001). *Sustainable Livelihoods Guidance Sheets*. Retrieved September 7, 2004, from http://www.livellihoods..org/info/guidance_sheets_pdfs/sect8glo.pdf

Dutt, R. (2001, August 14). 2001 Census: Encouraging and discouraging factors. *Business Line*. Chennai: The Hindu, p. 5.

Datt, R., & Sundharam, K.P.M. (2004). *Indian Economy*. New Delhi: S. Chand and Company Limited.

Fact Index. (2004). *Economy of India*. Retrieved September 7, 2004, from http://www.fact-index.comm/e/ec/economy_of_india.html

George, S.M. (n.d.) *Female Infanticide in Tamil Nadu, India: From Recognition Back to Denial*? Retrieved December 27, 2004, from http://www.hsph.harvard.edu/Organizations/healthnet/SAsia/suchana/0225/george.html

Gore, M.S. (2001). *Social Development: Challenges Faced in an Unequal and Plural Society*. Jaipur: Rawat Publications.

Government of India, Ministry of Finance. (1994). *Economic Survey*, 1993-94. New Delhi: Author.

Government of India, Ministry of Health and Family Welfare. (2002). *National Health Policy*, 2002, Retrieved October 12, 2004, from http://mohfw.nic.in/np2002.htm

Government of India, Ministry of Labour. (2002). *Annual Report 2001, Ministry of Labour, Government of India – Employment Scenario*. Retrieved September 7, 2004, from http://labour.nic.in/annrep/files2k1chap-2.doc

Government of India, Ministry of Law, Justice and Company Affairs. (1975). *The Constitution of India*. New Delhi: Author.

Government of India, Ministry of Welfare. (1987). *Encyclopedia of Social Work*. New Delhi: Director Publications Division, Ministry of Information and Broadcasting: Government of India.

Government of India, National Commission on Population. (2000). *National Population Policy 2000*. Retrieved January 24, 2003, from http://populationcommission.nic.in/npp_intro.htm

Indian Elections (2004). Election *'04 facts & figures*. Retrieved October 8, 2004, from http://www.indian-elections.com/facts-figures.html Indian NGOs. (n.d). *So much for a son*. Retrieved December 27, 2004 from http: www.indianngo.com/issue/child/girl/resources/articles1.htm – (a)

Indian NGO's .(n.d.). *Statistical Profile of India*. Retrieved March 28, 2005, from http:www.indianngos,com/factfile.htm – (b)

Office of the High Commissioner of Human Rights. (1996). *Human Rights in Development-Good Governance:* Retrieved January 24, 2003, fromhttp://www.unhchr.ch/development/governance-01.html

Paiva, J.F.K. (1997). A conception of social development. *Social Science Review*, 51(2), 332-333.

Samuel, J. (2002). Growth without Development: Rhetoric and Deprivation. Retrieved October 8, 2004 from http://www.socialwatch.org/en/informesNacionales/190.html

Sharma, K. (2004, August 29). No girls please, we're Indian. *The Hindu*. Weekly Edition-2, p.1.

Statistics Division, Department of Economic and Social Affairs of the United Nations Secretariat. (2004). *Social Indicators* (2004). Retrieved September 8, 2004, from http://unstats:un.org/unsd/demographic,products/socind/

The World Bank Group. (2001). *Useful World Bank Links*. Retrieved January 28, 2003, from http://1nweb18.worldbank.org/ESSD/sdvext.nsf/64ByDovName/UsefulLinks

Transparency International. (2002). *Corruption Perceptions Index* 2002. Retrieved October 8, 2004, from http://www.transparency.org/pressreleases archive/2002/dn1d/cpi2002.pressrelease.en.doc

United Nations Development Programme (2002). *What is Governance*? Retrieved January 24, 2003, from http://magnet.undop.org/policy/glossary.htm

United Nations Development Programme. (2002). *Human Development Report*. New Delhi: Oxford University Press.

United Nations Development Programme. (2003). *Human Development Report*. New Delhi: Oxford University Press.

United Nations Economic and Social Commission for Asia and the Pacific. (2002). *What is Good Governance*? Retrieved January 24, 2003, from http://www.unescap.org/huset/gg/governance.htm

World Health Organisation. (2003). *Health*. Retrieved September 30, 2004, from http://www.who.int/about/definition/en/

26

Globalization *Versus* Polarization in India: Emerging Concerns

S.P. Gupta

> "... Globalizing influences do not work exclusively towards integration. Although there are some fundamental respects in which a planetary social order has been created, globalization also divides, marginalizes and excludes ... "
>
> —*Giddens (1992.2)*

Since last one decade the world as a whole and Indian society in particular has been marked by a rapid process of globalization. It is a fact, that this process is as old as the process of westernization, with increasing emphasis on technology communication and spread of western and modern values. In other words, this process has facilitated interaction between different socio-cultural collectivities, all over the world. It is a process emphasizing for creation of 'one world order' linking cross-national boundaries and states along with worldwide flow of capital, communication, commodities and culture from region to region. Not only this, these days even the process of militarization all over the world is linked with the process of globalization too. The global structural transformation has led the process of restructuring of economies in terms of liberalization and free-market along with accountability of authority and state, expansion of democracy to create a common international forum to fight against global terrorism. When we talk of integration of societies and homogenization aspect of globalization, one finds that it includes the components of both westernization and modernization in it.

Similarly, there has been growing consensus that the process of globalization is not providing answers only to the economic issues but also to the socio-political processes. The world seems to develop a system of governance which may gain strength from extreme interventions of other nations in the form of proposed 'New World Order'. Today, it is the utmost need of the world laying more and more emphasis on a single unified and managed world which can better serve for international security and peace as well as the settlement of disputes and conflicts both between different nations and between various groups and classes within the nations.

When we think of India, the acceptance and the rapid pace of the process of globalization has been because of growing emphasis on market principle as the consequence of the failure of the socialist pattern of development and the breakdown of the communist block during 1980's at the global level. Even prior to these events, global capitalism had already produced a whole new technology of communication, cheaper and efficient means of transportation, satellite television etc., which made India possible for a virtual leap in the field of communication and exchange. Thus, the global flows of information, money, people and culture made India to enter into the process of globalization during which 'welfare-regime' paradigm was severely put to question. Since, the 'welfare-regime' in India witnessed various shortcomings as it failed to deliver the benefits of development and could not fulfill the aspirations of masses in terms of providing jobs, technological innovation, education, health and socio-political empowerment. Consequently, liberalization of trade and investment along with globalization were initiated as a only viable alternative of development in Indian society. India had to resort to the path of such policies looking into the unsatisfactory economic record of previously closed economies such as East Germany, China, Poland and U.S.S.R. On the contrary, the open economies like Hong Kong, Singapore, Taiwan and South Korea had progressed well, thereby justifying the process of liberalization through globalization.

We should not forget here that the globalization though understood in economic terms, yet, it covers all other facets of life such as political, social and cultural. It is generally feared too, that the government would completely abandon all forms of control and place the entire economy at the mercy of the multi-nationals and likewise, it will give up its concern for equality. But officials and government say it is not so. Because the important thrust of globalization in India is to remove certain imbalances and restrictions which hamper the free of trade. It aims at the improvement of the economic performance of the nation. The government's policy is designed to generate culture of competition and to promote high efficiency in production, technology transfer, mutual sharing of benefits of research and development.

Kim and Park (1989) had established that globalization would result in better capacity utilization and economies of scale. Similarly, there has been efforts to support the hypothesis that there is positive association between degree of openness and efficiency gains. Krueger (1978) had tried to show that countries more open to global trade and competition have higher GNP growth rate.

The social aspect of globalization is that it provides an opportunity for rapid increase in knowledge as it creates an atmosphere for new potentials for developing countries to grow faster by means of global interaction and competition. It is assumed that if countries like India are attracted by western and modern life styles, will also adopt other features too such as dignity of labour, responsibility for neighbourhood or community welfare, respect for law and order and respect for knowledge and character—there would be positive advantages in terms of social change.

Thus, the process of globalization has its socio-cultural and political implications besides the economic one. It aims at the integration of Indian society with the rest of the societies of the world aspiring for homogenization that may lead to well-being of the masses.

Here in this chapter, our objective is to analyse the changing concept of nation-state and emerging processes of fragmentation in Indian society due to globalization. As it is witnessed these days that there are certain negative repercussions of this process. Having given a proper thought to the process of globalization which aims at the integration and homogenization of various nations into 'one world order', our concern here is to examine yet a very crucial aspect of this process which can be visualized in the form of cut-throat competition which is to a greater extent responsible for weakening the political, social and economic independence of the developing countries. Although, there is growing emphasis on defining the world as a global village, but on the contrary we can see increasing strength of ethnicities and pluralities of *culture consciousness that are dividing nations instead of uniting them.* The increasing dominance of superpowers of the world over rest of the world and tensions and conflicts within the nation as well as rise of fundamentalism may be treated as best examples. These experiences make us to believe that globalization has created various forms of polarization at global level. Hence, our concern as social scientists should be to probe these questions.

Let us examine first of all the polarization emerging in context of Nation-State. There is growing consensus these days more particularly in the developing societies that globalization has created an atmosphere for the marginalization of the state by growing disempowerment of the state and of the national elites, both in its power to enforce national priorities; and their control over subordinates. It is because they are being dictated either from foreign agencies or their own governments which work at the behest of foreign corporations such as I.M.F., World Bank, World Trade Organization and other such institutions in the U.S. and Western Europe. Not only this, these nations and trade institutions have been associated in one or the other way in manufacture and trade of arms to which countries like India are made hostage both due to perceived threats from abroad as well as pressures and demands from within emanating from our own people belongings to lower classes, the minorities, the revolting regions and nationalities (Kothari, 1995; 1593). Not only this, the disempowerment and marginalization of the Nation-State may be attributed to the growing evidence of individual alienation and social anomie because of the failure of the nation to provide them opportunities for their socio-economic and political empowerment. The growing disenchantment with the state because a post colonial bourgeois state has steadily lost its legitimacy largely because it followed a path of development that gave neither equality nor justice to the common person (Mahajan 1999 a: 1193-94). Consequently, the masses have begun to realize that the state is no longer available to them as the prime marker of welfare-socialist regime is on decline on the part of the state. As a result, the normative structure of society and polity are becoming weak and many institutions related to them are becoming dysfunctional. In such a situation, the masses (mostly underprivileged) have to find out some other alternatives in terms of resources, means and institutions for their empowerment and well-being. Then, why should they give weightage to nation-state? Thus, it is assumed that the process of globalization and liberalization have put the state in a situation of crisis. As the transformation initiated by these twin processes in the social structure, motivate the masses not to accept the authority of such a state which is changing its priorities just to suit the multi-nationals and developed societies (Kothari, 1991:11-12; 1994). It is derooting the masses from the social structure. The present state of disorders and maldistribution of resources at global level have initiated duality both at international and intra-national level. On the one hand, the nations of the globe are being divided into the privileged and the underprivileged. Intra-nationally, a similar form of duality can be visualized in most of the countries where a small privileged group at a centre is surrounded by a large mass of underprivileged on the periphery. It again puts a question mark at the functioning of nation-state.

The another public attribute concerning nation-state in India is the relationship between these two. We know that India as a nation consists of different identities and affiliations such as social, regional, linguistic and cultural gives a key role to the state through which the 'composite integrated nation' can be maintained. It is possible only through decentralized planning with a greater degree of participation of masses in various institutions of the state. Thus, the major dilemma in this context is intra-national centralization of governance and decentralized democratic planning. Our view is that to overcome such dilemma and to save nation-state from crisis is to maintain a proper balance between these two even in this fast track of globalization.

However, in reality the balance between these two is getting disturbed and the concept of nation-state is in turmoil as it ceased to be the central mechanism of the nation. As the nation is moving towards a state of acute fragmentation, multiple polarization and likely disintegration. Obviously centrifugal forces inherent in the form of primordial collectivities such as ethnicity, religion, culture and language are eroding the nation and retreating the state. In this process, the state is being hijacked by the global order and market (centripetal forces) and the nation is facing serious challenges from within, from the large number of peripheries as well as different regions and nationalities (Kothari, 1995: 1594). Thus, we see that along with the process of globalization, its antithesis too has emerged in the form of increasing regional chauvinism and ultra-nationalism based on primordial collectivities more importantly among these is religious fundamentalism, which seeks to suppress various pluralities. Similarly, increasing challenges to the authority and legitimacy of state by various regional movements aimed either at autonomy or separatism have weakened the state too.

The Indian state which had been making efforts for its self-reliance and autonomy since its independence, has gone to the periphery as it is being threatened and challenged by the so called super powers of the world the with the help of G-77, I.L.O., World Bank, IMF and World Trade Organization and other such agencies on economic fronts. Likewise, on the social fronts too, such polarization can be witnessed within the country with reference to providing job opportunities to the minorities, the economically backward classes, tribal communities, women and children, health, education and housing. Such dualities have been intensified with the process of democratic processes, as these have been able to create rise in mass consciousness among the vast majority of society and they feel themselves neglected and marginalized to the periphery of the society. Galtung (1971: 81) regards the centre-periphery polarization as the essence of neo-imperialism in the form of globalization which splits up collectivities. Similarly, nearly all dependentia scholars like Paul Baran, Immanuel Wallerstein, Andre Gunder Frank and Samir Amin too, conceptualise the capitalist world economy as a 'core-periphery division of labour', linked via 'external exchange relations'. They viewed core-periphery relations as one of the unequal exchange. They all agree that new form of capitalism emerging due to globalization has failed to spread economic development and socio-economic justice. The world system is constituted of core and periphery. The periphery is conditioned by the core due to its relations of dependence and in this relationship while core develops, the periphery underdevelops. There is the development of underdevelopment-a dialectical relation between the two. Frank (1969) says these days, neo-colonialism perpetuates through trade and not by the state or army etc., thus, ever-growing capitalist development will lead to ever-growing capitalist underdevelopment.

All these tendencies are examples showing erosion and retreat of the nation-state at three levels, i.e., *(a)* technology; *(b)* homogenizing mission; and *(c)* new ideology (Kothari, 1995: 2515). According to him, technology seems to be replacing politics and socio-economic factors in the functioning of the society. It may be homogenizing diverse cultures and social sectors but marginalizing the political process and weakening the nation-state. It is also true that the whole world is confronted with the situations of tension and violence due to increasing consumerism, which has tried to increase assertion of cultures, ethnicity, religion, language, nationalities and pluralism. The state is ceasing to be a protector of the minorities, the poor, the weak and the oppressed. The third challenge comes from the emergence of a new ideology or mind set. It is merely an utopia that holds of a new integration of human enterprise, of joining diverse cultures and civilizations into one single market place. In real practice, it is not an integration but a tantamount polarization with the old idea of survival of the fittest in which the poor and the dispossessed sections of population cannot be fit and dispensed with (emphasis mine) (Kothari, 1987).

Globalization which was sought for the process of social development along with the openness of economy, has left Indian society with the increasing incidence of inequality, growing injustices and inhumanities; crimes and corruption more particularly to the violations of basic human rights of the masses. It leaves us with no option but to believe that in this globalizing world fragmentation serves as the basis of integration and homogenization.

The question here is that how can one think of preserving the concept of 'Nation-State' in such a situation? The answer to this question is not so simple. It is suggested that in this dispersed and decentralized world order, it is necessary to preserve the integrity and uniqueness of each by creating a multi-cultured and plural state on federal lines so that their goals of autonomy and self-determination can better be realized instead of undermining the legitimacy and authority of the state which will contribute towards further dominance of developed nations. So, it is in the interest of the nation as well as to the people not to raise issues of legitimacy and authority of the state. But the nation-state as well as oppressed social strata, ethnic and regional groups must work towards a common goal, which will enable them both to withstand the challenge from transnational and global powers (Kothari, 1988). Our objective should be to create an atmosphere among the minds of oppressed and marginalized groups that the state is impartial and final arbiter. Their interests and well-beings is safe and secure in the proper functioning of the nation-state. Because ours is a heterogeneous, hierarchical and plural society where there is disjuncture between citizenship and nationality, the latter being defined in terms of membership in different racial, religious and language groups which is often the source of inequality. Therefore, the primordial groups of our society often purse the goal of shared sovereignty and decentralization of authority. Here the concern of nation-state should be to emphasize the issues of removal of poverty and social, economic and political disparities rather than economic and technological forces to determine the scene to acquire autonomy of its own. Similar view is expressed elsewhere too (Oommen, 1997).

In what has gone before we have seen the challenges posed by the globalization towards the weakening of 'Nation-State'. The concept of fragmentation evolved with the process of unification and integration has brought the Indian society where it has been stimulated by anti-modern and fundamentalist reactions. Here we thought it appropriate to discuss another very important aspect of globalization in context of emerging fundamentalism in our society. Pandey (1990) suggests that globalization ultimately contributes to the growth of radical cultural nationalism which is neither global nor universal nor modern but it serves as a metaphor for sub-ordination of the west.

Along the process of globalization, there have been the phenomena of increasing radical Hindu nationalism in India and Islamic radical nationalism throughout the world. During last decade, there has been an emergence of increasing Islamic revival in Iran, Pakistan and the Middle East. This revival embarked a new generation of Indian Muslims to open a discourse and strategy among the Muslim youths from the large and very poor Muslim community around distinctively religious issues and symbols. For example, the construction and renovation of large number of mosques and dargahs in western India with the help of funds generated by Indian Muslim workers in the Gulf countries. (Hansen 1996: 608). Consequently, because of growing feeling of dislocation of the Indian nation and the national identification, the Hindu nationalist movement in India grew steadily during the same period due to a highly successful strategy of cultural mobilization of Hindus against the steps taken by Muslims. These two processes are still in their crucial phases with the process of globalization.

Somewhat similar views have been expressed by Robinson (2001: 236-37) too, explaining that religion rather than caste or language alone is the main marker of Indian identities. This phenomenon, he views, has gained momentum due to managed fears of modernity resulting from globalization and the revival and recovery of spiritualism in Indian society. According to him, the rise of Hinduism is only partly linked to the suppression of it by the 'modern secular nation-state' while it must also be linked historically to the rise of identities in the colonial period when already Hinduism, Islam and Christianity were pitched against each other in the battle for soul (Ibid: 242). Saberwal (2001: 201) carries somewhat similar views when he highlights that segmentation in terms of caste and religious categories in India though has facilitated the spread of democratic process as these carry social bonds on which to build political support; but it also carries animosities and antagonism which can work for strengthening hostile feelings towards each other. He quotes the example of acute ethnic conflicts like anti-sikh riots of 1984; employment of Kashmiri Pandits from Kashmir during the 1990s; the demolition of Babri Mosque and more recently the Gujarat incident. This is all because that in this globalizing world, the search of identity is the prime factor and when it is caught in antagonistic realities may lead to the phenomena of *Jehad* and *Hindutva* in our society in terms of power and all that flows from power (Ibid: 201).

On the similar line, the ideology of Hindutva as being propagated by B.J.P. argued that true secularism is possible only through true equality, which must start from the premise that Hindus constitute the majority population, hence true secularism meant rule by the Hindu majority. Not only this, the Indian Muslims are also seen as blocking element in the process of modernity and modernization due to their cultural backwardness and excessive population growth. They also block the full realization of democracy due to their block voting. In nutshell, one can infer that according to radical Hindu nationalist, Indian Muslims are the major source of the dislocation of the Indian nation in the contemporary world. Hence, it is feared that the process of globalization will strengthen the quest for recognition for cultural purification and cultural difference in order to enter the globalized modernity as equal partners (Hansen, *op.cit:* 614). The real problem thus, is not that the nation-state is in turmoil but it is Hinduisation of the Indian nation. Chandhoke (1995: 241-45) too, is critical of the way the fundamentalist exclusivist ideology of Hindutva (that is redefining nation as the Hindu state) has been raked up by the Hindu majoritarian B.J.P. and how such ideology would eliminate any scope for contestations and dialogue. The same Indian society, which pulled between tradition and modernity has left Dalits, women, minorities and tribals in vacuum. Therefore, the real crux of problem is that of a tussle of value-system with each other and it is not an easy task to create harmony between them (Robinson, *op. cit:* 249). We should take note that to the extent cultural pluralism is perceived to be an obstacle to the realization of the political integration and economic development, our society will be in situation of national crisis. Therefore, for the Indian society, if it is to be modern, open, secular and civil must synthesize the value-system of all the communities without any bias.

From the preceding discussions, it is evident that the Indian society faces these days two major problems as a consequence of globalization, i.e., the weakening of nation-state and radical cultural nationalism. It is consequently responsible or creating cumulative disparities between various strata and groups of the society dividing them between the privileged and the deprived. Similarly, the nation-state face threats and challenges when its socio-cultural identity if linked with the ideology of 'Hindutva'. It works against the belief that India's socio-cultural identity is not a single-faceted as projected by the ideology of 'Hindutva' but by its form as a plural society (Khan, 1992: 6). Sharma (1996: 317-18) too asserts that India's spiritual-cultural identity or socio-cultural identity faces no danger of minority ethnicism, instead its current political incarnation in terms of 'Hindutva' seem to be formidable threat to ethnic minorities as well as socio-cultural identity of Indian society. He feels that Indian society, in its drive to promote modern nationalism, has attempted to suppress ethnic identities, which consequently has generated a sense of ethnic insecurity which further results in ethnic reactivity. Hence, it is not the ethnic pride but the modern nation-state that constitutes a threat to ethnic diversities and pluralist identity of Indian society (Ibid: 318). He further reveals that ninety per cent of the nations of the world are multi-ethnic rather than uni-ethnic. Therefore, ethnic unity and cultural plurality may serve as an enviable basis of nation-building and these can be achieved by maintaining pluralistic nature of society which is based on cultural rights, decentralized democracy and egalitarian development (Ibid: 319). Somewhat similar view has been expressed by Oommen (1996: 156) that homogenization part of globalization is, often oriented to establish the hegemony of the dominant collectivity, annihilation of the weak and minority collectivities which endanger the principles of maintaining diversity and developing pluralism. Not only this, most of the societies are constantly exposed to alien influences and hence characterized by frayed edges and loose textures. Our society is not an exception. Therefore, in such a situation, the only viable option is to accommodate diversity, faster pluralism and nurture inter-group equality. According to him, individual-based equality is conceptually inadequate and praxiologically untenable in heterogeneous, hierarchical and plural societies. Hence unless and until the inter-group equality is established, some of the groups would remain subjected to cumulative inequality and oppression. Therefore, inter-group equality should be our premise to establish pluralism as a value for effective functioning of society like ours (Ibid: 156).

Foregoing analysis of Indian society in the present context of globalization, changing facets of nation-state and emergence of modern radical nationalism make us to think about the future course of action for our society. Some believe that to overcome the challenges of various forms it is better to evolve the concept of civil society which is possible in a society which is liberal, pluralist and secular. They view that the core of civil societies consists of the open and secular institutions that mediate between the citizens of the state in modern democratic societies (Beteille, 2001: 287). Various institutions of civil society are able to protect individual autonomy and freedom in a non-discriminatory manner and are controlled neither by the state nor by the religion. Civil society is necessary for India as autonomy of individual, protection of individual right to equal citizenship and access to decision-making apparatus and participatory democratic process can best be attained where still Hindu caste society observes strict norms and practice of hierarchy and Hindutva, radical nationalism is in operation too (Dhanagare, 2001: 188).

Contrary to these views, Sharma holds the view that 'modern nation-state' laying emphasis on the supremacy of civil culture will render ethnic cultural diversities insignificant, promoting culture of modern nationalism, i.e., individuals will outgrow their narrow ethnic loyalties than individuate into citizens. According to him neither modernism nor nationalism has succeeded in solving ethnic identities instead these have helped in crystallization of ethnic identities (Sharma, *op. cit.* 319).

Besides these two views, there is another view which holds synthesis of the two emphasizing that modern nation-state and civil society are not in contradiction to each other. In fact, in a society like ours, democracy, state and civil society act together with the same ethos. The state formulates laws that objectively embody conditions necessary for enhancing equal citizenship. Civil society operates in accordance with the established system of laws and rights so that individuals can pursue their particular ends while simultaneously respecting claims for equal citizenships (Mahajan, 1999). Thus, civil society and citizenship are closely associated. But citizenship rights can be protected and promoted only when opportunities and privileges are more or less equally distributed. The ethos of equal citizenship requires that socially valuable assets are not the monopoly of any group or community in society (Gupta, 1998: 509-23). This could be done by deleting and overthrowing ascribed identities as the basis of distributing resources or opportunities to attain the goal of equal citizenship. In country like India which is still a soft state, rules and laws are an easily played in the hands of personal, community and other vested interests. Therefore, what is important to emphasize the primacy of rational rules and impersonal laws for cherishing the real goal of our society, i.e., to maintain the rights of all individuals as equal citizens and to strengthen such institutions that protect the rights of individuals against any sort of eventuality. We know ours is a plural society hence the rights of minorities, weaker sections, oppressed and marginalized could be protected by providing them autonomy at two lines, i.e., cultural and political instead of interference and suppression attitude by the society or the state. Unless we are cautious on these grounds, it is likely that our society may fall prey to the process of neo-colonialism in the form of globalization. It is also necessary for us to adhere to democratic decentralized planning for a self-sustained development of society. At the same time, the principle of secularism must be followed not in its current usages as envisaged by radical national fundamentalists but by the principle of plurality and co-existence. It is the strength of plural society which can protect Indian society from the war of globalization with the help of cultural rights, decentralized democracy and egalitarian development. The long-cherished values of our society have to be inculcated which are in the process of erosion by globalization. It is by process of maintaining plural society we can synthesize tradition and modernity. Different societies have territorial dimensions; in spite of globalization and emergence of 'one world', they are located in different regions. Thus, with ecological and environmental pluralism, there are differences in economy, values and institutions too. So, the society which seeks to maintain its identity and specificity should pursue the path of pluralization instead of jumping on to the bandwagon of globalization (Oommen, 1996: 158). Thus, our society should not give up its concern for equality, democratic participation and egalitarian development. Hence, there should be a proper balance between the state and the market as well as between the social responsibility and private enterprise. Similarly, by maintaining cultural plurality and their co-existence we can take our society to real secularism instead of being guided by radical modern nationalism which may prove fatal to nation-state as well as destroying the long cherished cultural identity of our society in this globalizing world.

REFERENCES

Beteille, A., 2001. 'Civil Society and the Good Society', Sociological Bulletin, Vol. 50(2): 286-307.

Dhanagare, D.N., 2001. 'Civil Society, State and Democracy: Conceptualizing a Discourse', Sociological Bulletin, Vol. 50(2), pp. 167-191.

Frank, Andre Gunder, 1969. Capitalism and Underdevelopment in Latin America: Historical Studies of Chile and Brazil. New York: Monthly Review Press.

Galtung, John, 1971. 'A Structural Theory of Imperialism', Journal of Peace Research, Vol. 8, p. 81.

Giddens, Anthony (ed.), 1992. Human Societies: An Introductory Reader in Sociology.

Cambridge: Polity Press.

Gupta, Dipankar, 1998. 'Recasting Reservations in the Language of Rights' in Gurpreet Mahajan (ed.), Democracy, Difference and Social Justice, Delhi: Oxford University Press, pp. 509-23.

Hansen, Thomas Blom, 1996. 'Globalization and Nationalist Imaginations: Hindutva Promise of Equality through Difference' Economic and Political Weekly, March 9, 603-16.

Khan, Rasheeduddin, 1992. 'Political Integration in Federal India'. The Times of India, November 19, p. 6.

Kim, K.S. and J.K. Park, 1989. 'The Utilization of Capital and Growth of output in a Developing Economy', Journal of Economic Development.

Kothari, Rajni, 1987. 'Of Human Governance', Alternatives, p. 12.

_______, 1988. State against Democracy: In Search of Human Governance, Delhi: Ajanta.

________, 1991. 'State and Statelessness in our Time', Economic and Political Weekly, Vol. 26: 11-2.

________,1994. 'Rise of the Dalits and the Renewed Debate on Caste', Economic and Political Weekly, June 25.

________, 1994. 'The Crisis of Representation', Hindu, August 31.

________, 1995. 'Under Globalization: Will Nation-Statehold?' Economic and Political Weekly, July 1: 1593-1603.

________, 1995. 'Globalization and New World Order': What Future for the United Nations? Economic and Political Weekly, October 7.

Krueger, A.O., 1978. Liberalization: Attempts and Consequences, Cambridge: Mass. Ballinger.

Mahajan, Gurpreet, 1999. 'Civil Society, State and Democracy', Economic and Political Weekly, December 4, 3471-72.

________, 1999(a). 'Civil Society and its avatars: What happened to freedom and democracy', Economic and Political Weekly, 34(20): 1188-96.

Oommen, T.K., 1996. 'Reconciling Equality and Pluralism: A New Agenda for the Developed Societies', Sociological Bulletin, Vol. 45(2): 143-160.

________, 1997. Citizenship, Nationality and Ethnicity: Reconciling Competing Identities, Cambridge: Polity Press.

Pandey, Gyanendra, 1990. The Construction of Communalism in Colonial North India, Delhi: Oxford University Press.

Robinson, Rowena, 2001. 'Religion on the Net: An Analysis of the Global Reach of Hindu Fundamentalism and its Implications for India', Sociological Bulletin, Vol. 50 (2) 2136-51.

Saberwal, Satish, 2001. 'Democracy and Civil Society in India: Integral or Accidental' Sociological Bulletin, Vol. 50(2): 192-205.

Sharma, S.L., 1996. 'Ethnic Challenge to Indian Society: Rethinking Cultural Polity Interface' in N.K. Singhi (ed.), Theory and Ideology in Indian Sociology, Jaipur: Rawat Publications.

27

Production Responses of Groundnut Crop in Andhra Pradesh

M. Usha Rani, K. Satyanarayana Reddy and K. Thulsai Naik

In a development economy the growth of agriculture products assumes a critical importance due to rising demand for them, generated by the rapidly growing population and accelerated further by rising levels of income. This problem is based on the existing possibilities of agriculture sector as well as on the increasing flow of resources into agriculture. The forces of growth build up at a slower pace than the forces of demand. With the results that the instrument of price which motivates the former to act, acquired an overriding importance provided that this instrument is effective.

Land utilization decisions of formers are motivated by a number of economic, technological and sociological factors. Out of which only a few can be quantified. They are prices, costs and yield in principle. Most of these factors govern farmer's decision to make large changes in land utilization pattern. In a subsistence economy where the production is largely for the consumption of the farmers family and only a few of the inputs are purchased. Prices have little effect on the production plan and thereby on hectareage distribution. A high price for a crop at times may not tempt a farmer to put his land under that crop, since he may be deriving a number of benefits from a diversified partner of his land utilization. If the crop production is governed by weather conditions, traditional former may not shift his land under one crop which more profitable and thereby run a risk and face uncertainty due to weather cannot be avoided at a short notice. On the other hand price is the most important factor in the change of land utilization programme of a farmer in a developed economy. In such economics an average farmer is expected to look at the future prices in order to plan the production programme and adjust the hactareage under crops in such a way to maximize his profits.

Agriculture is one of the major sector of economic development in Andhra Pradesh. Growth in area under the crops however, has not been uniform or steady. There have been year to year fluctuations in both area and production. Fluctuations in area of crops are caused by variations in prices, weather conditions, availability of irrigation facilities etc. The cultivators in poor economies are motivated by price changes. This is proved by the studies of Rajkrishna, Kamala Devi and Rajagopalan, Dharm Narain, Satyanarayana, Dayanathajha, Jhala, Kaul and Sidu, Chandresh Kumar, Rao and Jaikrishna. Andhra Pradesh is one of the important state growing groundnut crop in our country. The agro climatic conditions are different from region to region in the state. Thus the determinant of output for groundnut crop is different in its various regions.

Objectives

1. To estimate the growth and instability in area, production and yields of groundnut crop in three regions of Andhra Pradesh and Andhra Pradesh State as a whole.
2. To study the relationship between the agriculture output and prices and some important non-price variables which are having some effect on groundnut crop output.

Methodology

To fulfill the first objective of study i.e., to estimate the linear growth of groundnut crop, the linear model was adopted.

$$Y = A + B_t \qquad \text{------ (1)}$$

Where:

Y = Area, production, yield
t = Time point
A, B are the constants to be determined.

The percentage of linear growth rate is

$$\text{L.G.R.} = \frac{\hat{B}}{y} \times 100 \qquad \text{------ (2)}$$

$$\text{C.V.} = \frac{\square}{y} \times 100 \qquad \text{------ (3)}$$

To study the second objective, i.e., input output relations, the adoptive expectation model was used. Quantity produced of the groundnut crop had been offered to be a linear function of the hectarage, lagged own or lagged relative price and rainfall. The model used in the study was.

$$Y_t = a_0 + a_1 A_t + a_2 P_{t-1} + a_3 R_t + V_t \qquad \text{------ (4)}$$

Where Y_t = Quantity of Output
A_t = Area under the Crop
P_{t-1} = Lagged own price
R_t = Rainfall
V_t = Random disturbance term

Farmers faced problems in making production decisions in response to changes in price and non-price factors. The farmers are able to make adjustments while responding to various economic factors. The agricultural output might depend on the expected prices, area under the crop along with irrigation facilities etc., Hence, it suggest the necessity of adaptive expectation model in the study. Let the model be

$$Y_t = a_0 + a_1 A_t + a_2 P_t^e + a_3 R_t + V_t \qquad \text{------ (5)}$$

Where P_t^e = expected price of the crop.

The adaptive principle can be mathematically states as

$$P_t^e - P_{t-1}^e = ë\ [P_t - P^e_{t-1}] \qquad \text{------ (6)}$$

$o\ ë \leq 1$

This hypothesis was the rationalization of the Koyek's estimation of distributed lag model. Here, ë was the co-efficient of expectation. This hypothesis was known as the Adaptive expectation and it was popularized by Cagan and Friedman.

$$P^e_t = P^e_{t-1} (1 - ë) + P_t \qquad \text{-------- (7)}$$

Form (5) $P^e_t = \underline{1}\ [Y_{t-1} - a_0 - a_1 A_1 + a_2 P_{t-1} + a_3 R_{t-1} + V_t]$

$$\text{------ (8)}$$

Substituting (7) in (5) we get

$$Y_t = a_0 + a_1 A_1 + a_2 [P^e_{t-1} (1 - ë) + a_2 ë P_t + d_3 R_t + V_t \qquad \text{---- (9)}$$

Substituting (8) in (9) we get

$$Y_t = b_0 + b_1 A_1 + b_2 A_{t-1} + b_3 P_t + b_4 R_t + b_5 R_{t-1} + b_6 Y_{t-1} + U_t \qquad \text{--- (10)}$$

Where $b_0 = a_0 ë$ $b_1 = a_1$

$b_2 = a_1 (1- ë)$ $b_3 = a_2 ë$

$b_4 = a_3$ $b_5 = -a_3 (1- ë)$

$b_6 = (1- ë)$ $U_t = ë V_t$

To study the output responses of the groundnut crop in Andhra Pradesh, we had utilized the pooled data. The parameters of the equations (1), (4) and (10) were estimated by employing the "OLS" method.

Data

The time series data from 1970-71 to 2000-01 has been used in the present study. The data related to area, production, productivity, prices, rainfall were taken from various issues of "Statistical Abstract of Andhra Pradesh" and "Seasons and crop report of Andhra Pradesh, issued by the Director, Bureau of Economics and Statistics, Government of Andhra Pradesh.

Analysis

The productivity in agricultural may be increased by adapting the modern technology and also through intensive and extensive cultivation. Along with the food crops a study of commercial crops like groundnut become imperative for proper planning in agricultural development. It is important to study the growth of the commercial crops to meet the future demands of growing population. Basing the future demands and growth of crops it is useful to make policy decisions regarding the area, production and yield of commercial crops in the state. Hence it is proposed to study the growth of area, production and yield of groundnut crop in three regions of Andhra Pradesh and the state as a whole.

From the estimated linear regression equations the linear growth and the co-efficient of variation of groundnut crop in deferent regions and Andhra Pradesh State was given in the following table.

Table-1
Estimated Growth Rate and Co-efficient of Variation

Regions	*Area*		*Production*		*Yield*	
	LGR	*C.V.*	*LGR*	*C.V.*	*LGR*	*C.V.*
Rayalaseema	2.63*	23.89	2.65*	24.13	-0.07	22.89
Coastal Andhra	0.27	2.43	1.23	11.17	1.06	9.61
Telangana	0.62	5.62	1.37*	12.48	0.88	8.01
Andhra Pradesh	1.77*	16.12	2.09	19.05	0.33	2.97

* Significant at 5 per cent probability level.

The linear growth rate of area under the groundnut crop is positive and significant at 5 per cent probability level in Rayalaseema region and Andhra Pradesh State. Similarly, the growth rate of groundnut crop area was positive but not significant in Coastal Andhra and Telangana. The highest variation in ground area was recorded in Rayalaseema and the lowest variation in groundnut area was recorded in Coastal Andhra. The co-efficient of variation in Andhra Pradesh is 16.12 per cent. The linear growth rate of production is maximum in Rayalaseema region and followed by Telangana and Coastal Andhra Regions. The groundnut production growth is significant in Rayalaseema and Telangana regions. The significant positive growth in groundnut production was recorded in the entire state Andhra Pradesh. The highest co-efficient of variation was recorded in Rayalaseema followed by Telangana and Coastal Andhra. The variation in Andhra Pradesh was recorded by 19.05 per cent. A highest growth rate of groundnut yield was noticed in Coastal Andhra region. A negative growth in productivity of groundnut was recorded in Rayalaseema region. The growth in groundnut yield was positive and significant in Telangana region. The highest co-efficient of variation was record in Rayalaseema region followed by Coastal Andhra and Telangana. The groundnut yield in Andhra Pradesh State was 2.97 per cent.

The analysis of data regarding production response was estimated by using the OLS technique as method of estimation. The linear and log-linear models were fed with the data and the parameters are estimated. The results revealed the fact that the log-linear model is a better fit for the present study. Hence, the entire investigations of the study are based on log linear model. The estimated co-efficients of equations (4) and (10) are given in the Tables 2 and 3 respectively.

It is assumed that the groundnut output is a function of area (A_t) lagged own price (P_{t-1}) and Rainfall (R_t). The equation (4) reveals this general notion. The estimated co-efficients of equation (4) was given in the Table 2. The co-efficient of area under the groundnut crop was found to be positive and significant at 5 per cent probability level in three regions of Andhra Pradesh and it is positive but not significant in Andhra Pradesh State. It explained the positive relationship between crop out put and cropped area. The co-efficient of lagged price is positive and significant in Coastal Andhra and Telangana regions. The price effect is negative in Rayalaseema

Table–2
Estimated Regression Co-efficients of the Equation (4)

Regions	*Constant*	*A*	*P*	*R*	*R*	*F*
Rayalaseema	-9.3448	1.4549* (0.3123)	-0.1698 (0.1169)	0.5871* (0.2398)	0.7329*	24.71
Costal Andhra	4.6766	1.2488* (0.4082)	0.3530* (0.1443)	-0.0966 (0.6936)	0.4020*	6.0498
Telangana	1.1379	0.8849* (0.1316)	0.1282* (0.0448)	-0.0980 (0.0857)	0.7226*	23.4382
Andhra Pradesh State	7.8631	1.3886 (0.1792)	-0.0595* (0.0573)	0.3624* (0.1808)	0.8180*	40.4402

* Significant at 5 per cent probability level.
Figures in parentheses are standard errors.

Region. In Andhra Pradesh State, as a whole the lagged price effect is negative and significant. The co-efficient of rainfall is positive and significant in Rayalaseema region. But rainfall effect is only positive but not significant in Andhra Pradesh State. The rainfall is negatively influencing the crop output in Coastal Andhra and Telangana regions. The combined effect of all independent variables on groundnut crop output is expressed by the multiple correlation co-efficient (R^2). F-test was carried out to test whether the combined effect of all independent variable is significant or not. It is inferred that the combined effect is significant on groundnut out put in Rayalaseema, Coastal Andhra, Telangana and Andhra Pradesh State. Hence, it is concluded that groundnut output is responded by area and also production is responded by rainfall in Rayalaseema region and Andhra Pradesh State. Groundnut out put is responded by lagged price and area in Coastal Andhra and Telangana regions but the rainfall is negatively influencing the production.

In equation 10, the farming expectations on future prices were considered. The estimated co-efficients of the equations are given in the Table 3. Area under the crop (A_t) lagged area (A_{t-1}), own price (P_1), rainfall and lagged rainfall (R_t, R_{t-1}) and lagged output (Y_{t-1}) are independent variables. The groundnut output is the dependent variable. The co-efficient are under the groundnut crop is positive and significant at 5 per cent probability level in Rayalaseema, Telangana and Andhra Pradesh State. It is positive but not significant in Coastal Andhra region. The co-efficient lagged area is negative in Rayalaseema, Telangana regions and also Andhra Pradesh State

Table-3
Estimated Regression Co-efficients of the Equation (10)

Regions	*Constant*	*A*	*A*	*P*	*R*	*R*	*Y*	*R*	*F*
Rayalaseema	2.9242	2.1690*	-0.6541	-0.1283	0.2194	-0.5246*	-0.1212	0.8637*	25.3460
		(0.3593)	(0.4121)	(0.938)	(0.2016)	(0.2180)	(0.1453)		
Coastal Andhra	-5.9255	1.1679	0.4212	0.4709*	-0.0570	-0.2290	-0.2003	0.4820*	3.72
		(0.8282)	(0.9366)	(0.1641)	(0.7224)	(0.6639)	(1957)		
Telangana	0.8072	1.1317*	-0.4378	0.1440*	-0.0556	0.1744	0.0831	0.7560*	12.0394
		(0.2449)	(0.3048)	(0.0485)	(0.0948)	(0.0963)	(0.2002)		
Andhra Pradesh State	6.8732	2.1847*	-049	-0.03	0.23	0.0034	-0.332	0.9050*	38.095
		(0.25)	(0.35).	(0.05)	(0.14)	(0.15)	(0.15)		

* Significant at 5 per cent probability level.
Figures in parentheses are standard errors.

but it is positive in Coastal Andhra. The co-efficient of price is positive and significant in Coastal Andhra and Telangana regions. It is negative in Rayalaseema region and Andhra Pradesh State. The co-efficient of rainfall is positive in Rayalaseema region and Andhra Pradesh State. It is negative in Costal Andhra and Telangana Regions. The lagged rainfall effect is positive in Telangana region and Andhra Pradesh State. It is negative in Rayalaseema and Costal Andhra regions. The effect of lagged output on groundnut crop is positive only in Telangana region. It is negative in Rayalaseema, Costal Andhra regions and Andhra Pradesh State. The combined effect of all independent variables on groundnut crop output is expressed by multiple-co-efficient of correlation (R^2). F-test was carried out to test whether the combined effect of all independent variables on dependent variables is significant or not. The value of (R^2) indicates the groundnut output is significantly influenced by all independent factors in all regions of Andhra Pradesh State. Hence, it is concluded that groundnut out put is responded by area.

Conclusion

Observing the estimated co-efficient of (A_t), it is noticed that the area under the crop is the major factor which influencing the groundnut output in almost all the regions of the state. The Price variable influence on groundnut crop is not observed much. It is concluded that groundnut crop production is mainly area responsive, price response was observed only in Coastal and Telangana regions. It reveals the fact that the groundnut price is not encouraging the crop growers in raising the crop production. It is suggested that the government may provide the maximum supporting prices to the groundnut growers in the State. It is expressed by the negative significant price factor in Andhra Pradesh State. It is also observed that there exists some scope to raise the groundnut production by raising the output prices. This reveals that the prices are not encouraging its growers. The effect of rainfall on groundnut crop production is almost absent. This is due to lack of rainfall. It leads the negative effective on crop production. It is also suggested that by providing irrigation facilities to groundnut crop production may be increased. Finally, lagged out put variable is not influencing the current crop out put in Andhra Pradesh. The collective effect of variables in each equation is observed to be significant.

Co-efficient of Expectation

The term expectation it self relates to the future events. To some extent this expectation depends on past events. In over present study, the 'l' is the co-efficient of expectation of agricultural prices. The expectation co-efficient indicates only the psychological behaviour of producer. If the value of l > 1, over expectations takes place in future prices of the output. If l = 0, the expectation of future prices are static. If l = 0, the expectations are realized immediately and fully i.e., in the some period.

The co-efficient of expectation was calculated with the help of the estimated co-efficient of the variable lagged output in the equation (10).

Table-4
Expectation Co-efficient

Crop	*Rayalaseema*	*Coastal Andhra*	*Telangana*	*Andhra Pradesh*
Groundnut	1.12	1.20	0.92	1.32

From the above table, it is observed that the value of l > 1 in Rayalaseema, Coastal Andhra and Andhra Pradesh State. It indicates that the groundnut growers in Rayalaseema, Coastal regions and Andhra Pradesh State are in over expectations about their future prices. The groundnut growers had given importance to past year's prices for future expectations of groundnut prices and accordingly the farmers were damaging their groundnut output designs in the Rayalaseema, Coastal Andhra and Andhra Pradesh State. The co-efficient of expectation regarding groundnut crop out put was sufficiently high and less than one (l < 1) in Telangana region. It reveals the fact that the groundnut crop growers in Telangana region were influenced by every recent year's prices for their future prices expectations. Hence, it is inferred that the crop growers were taking designs on crop output considering very recent year's groundnut prices.

REFERENCES

Cagan P., 'The Monetary Dynamics of Hyper Inflation', in M. Fried man (edn.), studies in the in the Quantity Theory of Money, University of Chicago Press, Chicago 1956.

Chandresh Kumar, 'Farmers Response to Price Change, Sugarcane in Uttar Pradesh', 1951-52 to 1966-67. Economic and Political Weekly, Vol.5, Bi.18, May 2, 1970, pp. 731-741.

Dayanath Jha, 'Acreage Response of Sugarcane in Factory Areas of North

Bihar', Indian Journal of Agricultural Economics, Vol. 25, No. 1, January-March 1970, pp. 79-91.

Dharm Narain, 'The Impact of Price Movements on Areas under Selected Crops in India' 1930-39 London, Cambridge University Press 1965.

Jhala, M.L., 'Farmer's Response to Economic Incentives: An Analysis of Inter-regional Groundnut Supply Response in India', Indian Journal of Agricultural Economics, Vol. 34, No. 1, January-March 1979, pp. 55-67.

Kamaladevi, P. and R. Rajagopalan, 'Price and Acreage Response: A Study of Groundnut Crop I North Arcot District', Indian journal of Agricultural Economics, Vol. 20, No. 1, January-March 1965, pp. 31-35.

Kaul J.L. and Siddu, D.S., 'Acreage Response to Prices for Major Crops in Punjab—An Econometric Study', Indian Journal of Agricultural Economics, Vol. 26, No. 4, October-December 1977, pp. 427-434.

Rao, M.S. and Jai Krishna, 'Price Expectation and Acreage Response of Wheat in Uttar Pradesh'. Indian Journal of Agricultural Economics, Vol. 20, No.1, January-March 1955, pp. 20-25.

Satyanarayana, Y, 'Factors Affecting Acreage Under Sugarcane in India, Indian Journal of Agricultural Economics, Vol. 22, No. 2, April-June 1967, pp. 79-87.

Index